"Duriel lays out a stable foundation for transforming the 'mundane' into the magical. Drawing from various traditions and practices such as Hermeticism, Yoga, and his work as a cognitive behavioral therapist, Duriel reveals the true secrets of how to transform our inner blocks into strengths, as well as how to maintain a healthy spiritual practice even when life throws obstacles in our way. Should be required reading for anyone embarking on a magical path."

—Storm Faerywolf, author of *Forbidden Mysteries of Faery Witchcraft*

THE
LITTLE
WORK

About the Author

Durgadas Allon Duriel (San Francisco Bay Area, CA) is an occultist, Yogi, therapist, astrologer, and tarot enthusiast. He is a formal practitioner of magic with more than twenty years of experience. He has been an initiate of the Hermetic mysteries since 2005, a journey that began with two and a half years of intensive training. Durgadas is also a licensed clinical social worker and a certified holistic health practitioner, and he has studied and practiced Yoga for over fifteen years.

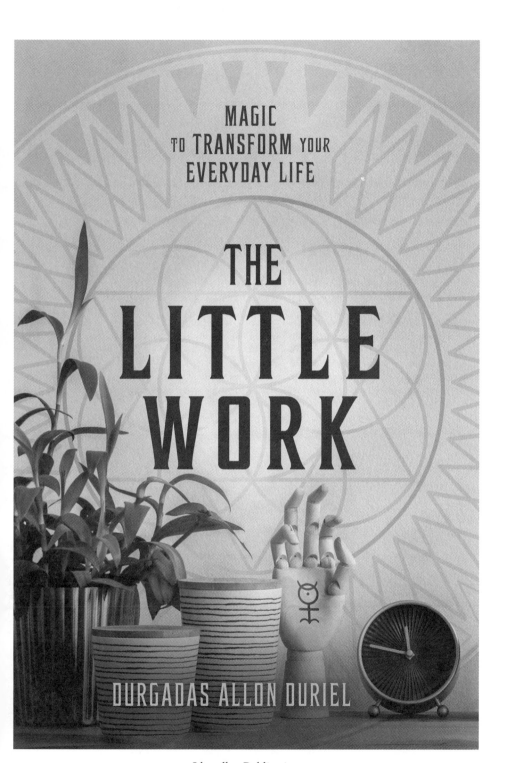

MAGIC
TO TRANSFORM YOUR
EVERYDAY LIFE

THE
LITTLE
WORK

DURGADAS ALLON DURIEL

Llewellyn Publications
Woodbury, Minnesota

First Edition
Second Printing, 2020

Cover design by Shira Atakpu
Editing by Brian R. Erdrich
Figures 2, 12, 13, and 14 by Mary Ann Zapalac; all other interior art by Llewellyn Art Department.
Tarot cards from *Pictorial Key to the Tarot*, by Arthur Edward Waite, public domain.

Llewellyn Publications is a registered trademark of Llewellyn Worldwide Ltd.

Library of Congress Cataloging-in-Publication Data (Pending)
ISBN: 978-0-7387-6147-3

Llewellyn Worldwide Ltd. does not participate in, endorse, or have any authority or responsibility concerning private business transactions between our authors and the public.

All mail addressed to the author is forwarded but the publisher cannot, unless specifically instructed by the author, give out an address or phone number.

Any internet references contained in this work are current at publication time, but the publisher cannot guarantee that a specific location will continue to be maintained. Please refer to the publisher's website for links to authors' websites and other sources.

Llewellyn Publications
A Division of Llewellyn Worldwide Ltd.
2143 Wooddale Drive
Woodbury, MN 55125-2989
www.llewellyn.com

Printed in the United States of America

DEDICATION

Thanks to:

My mother, who read voraciously throughout her life and would be thrilled to see this moment.

Prabudh Noel, for over seven years of love, support, laughter, and conversation, including while I wrote this book.

My first spiritual teacher, who taught me how to fundamentally change my life for the better in ways I wasn't sure were possible and encouraged me to write.

My three degree mentors in my occult training, who helped me learn to love and trust again.

My second spiritual teacher, who taught me through example about devotion, divine love, and how to "inflame thyself with prayer."

"*I wish I could show you, when you are lonely
or in darkness, the astonishing light of your own being.*"

—HAFIZ

Contents

PART TWO: INNER ALCHEMY

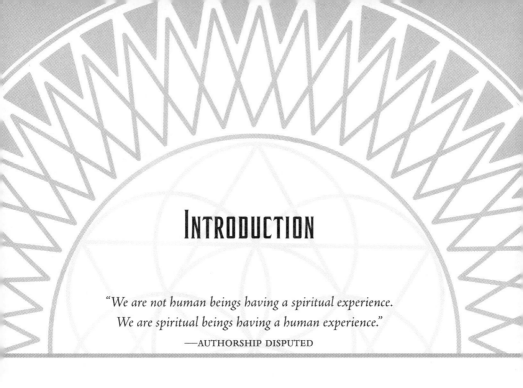

INTRODUCTION

"We are not human beings having a spiritual experience.
We are spiritual beings having a human experience."
—AUTHORSHIP DISPUTED

We live in a magical world. Many of us who are drawn to magic, mysticism, or the occult know this on some level. Perhaps we've always sensed there's more to reality than meets the eye or experienced this directly. We may not know exactly what's beyond the veil of everyday life, but we know it's not mere superstition to suspect that something's happening there. Many of us innately hunger to engage with this dimension of existence, sometimes to where disregarding the occult would feel like choosing to live blindfolded.

On the wave of this yearning, we explore disciplines like ceremonial magic, psychic development, shamanism, witchcraft, and Yoga. Many of us work with others who've walked the path before us, getting involved with groups, institutions, or spiritual teachers. We set ourselves to the task of joining the thousands of seekers throughout history who practiced magic in some form and experienced its reality and the awakening that accompanies parting the veil.

For many of us, this process is thwarted. Not because magic isn't real or because indescribably magnificent spiritual epiphanies and experiences aren't available to us. Rather, because life gets in the way, and by "life," I mean the day-to-day realities of the human experience in much of today's world—realities like developing a career, managing money, navigating interpersonal relationships, handling adversity, and establishing a healthy sense of self.

Many of us who are drawn to metaphysics are metaphysically gifted and don't feel at home in the "real world," which is unsurprising given how that world conceptualizes us (and if you're reading this of your own initiative, you're likely a metaphysically gifted person). While we may have been medicine people or seers in previous societies, we're now relegated to the cultural periphery and in some societies, what's considered sane. Consequently, we don't generally receive training in our gifts to become healthy, high-functioning metaphysical adults. This leads many of us to play to our strengths while underdeveloping our weaknesses, which can make metaphysical gifts feel more like curses. We may feel flooded by psychic sensations to where they muddy our sense of self or feel like the physical world is too insubstantial for us to be effective within it. We may unintentionally attempt to avoid life's difficulties with metaphysics, using it as an escape space, crutch, or defense.

This book answers that predicament. It's a manual for living in the "real world" in a way that facilitates metaphysical practice. It's the product of my experience as a metaphysically gifted youth who desperately needed spiritual training and then received that training and prospered. It also integrates the best of what I've gleaned from years of experience as a psychotherapist, holistic health practitioner, and Yogi. I believe you can live the magical life your heart calls for. In this book, I'll show you how.

Many of us who are drawn to metaphysics feel like running away from the world, and some of us do. But even in the remotest of ashrams, our issues follow us ("Wherever you go, there you are," as the saying goes). We must deal with these issues if we want to thrive and develop spiritually. What I've learned is that we needn't go anywhere to lead a magical, holy life. We can build one where we are by mastering what I call the "Little Work."

THE LITTLE WORK

"No one ever did great things well
who had not first done well with small things."
—PAUL FOSTER CASE

The Little Work is the development of life skills that enable us to function with increasing ease, such that we can devote ourselves to spiritual practice. It's a way of making ourselves the ashram. The name is a tongue-in-cheek reference to the

Great Work, which is the pinnacle of Hermetic magic, wherein a magician abidingly realizes their divine nature. This is the enlightenment that millions of seekers have aspired toward throughout history. Aside from the rare instances where people become spontaneously enlightened, completing the Great Work requires many qualities, not the least of which is a sturdy foundation on the physical plane. How can we seriously hope to merge with the infinite and live to tell the tale if we struggle with tasks like paying bills on time, achieving straightforward goals, and weathering relationship difficulties?

In light of this, spiritual aspirants must cultivate their minds and develop willpower. They must become emotionally fluent and proficient upon the physical plane. These tasks aren't merely supplements to the Great Work, though. They're a vital part of it, and they compose the heart of the Little Work. For healthy, deep metaphysical practice, some version of the Little Work is required, whether it occurs formally or informally. When it's absent, aspirants tend to encounter difficulties that bar them from the metaphysical experiences they seek, or they have these experiences but can't healthfully integrate them into their lives. History is littered with stories of aspirants who lacked a sturdy foundation and overexerted themselves metaphysically, leading to their ruin. Alongside this, there's the more common phenomenon of aspirants whose shaky foundations prevent them from practicing consistently, rendering them more as armchair occultists.

In Hermetic movements like the Golden Dawn and Thelema, the Little Work unfolds over a sequence of grades, wherein aspirants develop themselves to support their metaphysical practice before beginning ardent work. This development process parallels the one facilitated by the yamas and niyamas of Yoga and the Eightfold Path of Buddhism. The four Golden Dawn and Thelemic grades beyond the probationary grade each correspond with an element, and aspirants are expected to balance or "equilibrate" the forces of these elements within themselves. These elements are the classical elements, alongside their conventional Hermetic representations in the human microcosm (i.e., air/intellect, fire/will, water/emotion and intuition, earth/physicality and materiality).

Some of this equilibrating work is ethereal, but much of it is practical. In the air grade, aspirants train their intellects, refining their discernment and developing wisdom. In the fire grade, they cultivate willpower and self-discipline, learning to focus and control their actions as best they can. Emotional maturation and fluency are tasks of the water grade, as is developing psychic sensitivity. In the earth grade, aspirants pursue vitality and adeptness on the physical plane in areas like home, career, and money management. This isn't to suggest that aspirants must fully master one elemental domain before moving to another. In the original Golden Dawn, aspirants could complete the elemental grades far faster than that generally requires. The idea is to undertake a gradual, consistent process of inner alchemy and ultimately become a vessel that can complete the Great Work.

In my experience, even when working in systems that account for the Little Work, aspirants often fall short if they don't give it the attention it deserves (or, as with the rapid progress possible in the original Golden Dawn, the system doesn't require that level of proficiency). One reason this can happen is that aspirants tend to crave spiritual experiences over mundane matters, which is understandable. We don't pursue occultism to learn budgeting. One of the greatest ironies of spiritual aspiration is that we seek the Holy Mysteries only to be told to sweep the floor, and in learning to sweep the floor consciously, we begin experiencing these mysteries.

This brings up the first of many tenets for performing the Little Work: *there is no such thing as the mundane*. What appears mundane does so because of how we conceptualize it, which is a theme we'll revisit throughout this book. Everything is imbued with divinity, but discovering that is up to us. By changing our thinking about the "mundane," we can experience its spiritual dimensions. As we increasingly recognize that nothing need be mundane for us, our entire life begins to feel spiritual. It becomes apparent that much of the Great Work is in the Little Work. What we once wrote off as mundane can eventually house some of our profoundest revelations.

Another obstacle I've seen aspirants face is skimming over foundational material because it looks simple or easy and consequently not developing in the manner intended by it—for example, by completing exercises to develop willpower a few times but not enough for these exercises to significantly strengthen their will. Breezing through the basics sets aspirants up to falter as they advance, when these developments are needed to progress but are unavailable.

This raises another tenet of the Little Work: *master the basics*, which was the first commitment I made after joining a Hermetic order in my early twenties. Though I'd practiced magic as a solitary witch for over nine years and felt powerful during rituals, my life felt suffocating. I was at rock bottom, which was at least an annual occurrence for me following years of abuse, dehumanization, and illness while growing up. Consequently, I resolved to surrender as fully as I could to my order's training. What did I have to lose emotionally? Years of intense suffering made me acutely aware that I didn't know how to be sustainably happy or peaceful. I also recognized that my metaphysical foundation was shaky. I often felt like half of me was across the veil, which was tearing me apart. I needed help, and I was ready to receive it.

For the next two and a half years, I hit that training with everything I had, generally spending thirty to forty hours a week at my "magic school" or in practices from it. I did what I was told and strove to find whatever value I could in any ideas that seemed problematic. I started a daily spiritual practice that continues to this day, and my life dramatically transformed. In less time than I could've imagined, my life went from desperate to fulfilling, from a mess to an adventure. This isn't to suggest that everything was rosy after that. What kind of adventure would that be? But I became able to engage future challenges with an outlook of learning, faith, and compassion, which has helped me till even the most difficult of experiences for growth.

I went from being someone who procrastinated constantly to someone who can simultaneously balance and achieve many goals, from being someone who underperformed at work to one who speeds to promotion. I went from being a clutterbug who cleaned his bathroom semiannually to someone who enjoys housework and who transformed his home into a sanctuary. Most importantly, and much of this developed after leaving the school, I became someone who can feel the spectrum of emotions with fluency and weather depression and anxiety, someone who stopped craving relationships out of low self-esteem and who can always opt to experience the undimming love and divinity within.

We each come to metaphysics with individual hopes. I wanted to find peace, emotional and psychic stability, and enlightenment. So far, I've found the first two, and I can't convey the richness and beauty this work has brought to my life. Your reasons are whatever they are, and you may not aspire to the Great Work. That's OK. To whatever degree you practice metaphysics, the Little Work can help you become more effective in that. Relatedly, while this book is informed and inspired by my experience in a Hermetic order, it's intended for a diverse assortment of magical practitioners, from witch to ceremonial magician and beyond. It's also geared toward all levels of practice, featuring practical skills for creating a sustainable, rich magical life. What that life includes is up to you.

Before delving into the practice side of the Little Work, I lay out some metaphysical basics. This is because understanding the mechanics of magic and how the metaphysical planes function, even to a limited degree, helps us practice more effectively. Exploring the basics also illuminates some of the value of the Little Work, as does examining why magic can fail for practitioners who don't have a handle on the Little Work. Additionally, we'll review some practical magical techniques that facilitate thriving on the physical plane, which in turn facilitates inner alchemy. Experienced magical practitioners may want to skim this material. I wouldn't skip it altogether because I explore some concepts that bear on the Little Work that I don't often see in magic books, and understanding these concepts can make our magic far more effective. After that, we'll delve into ritual, meditation, and creating a daily practice. The remainder of the book features a journey of inner alchemy through the classical elements.

Part One
Foundations of Magic

Chapter One
THE BASIS OF MAGIC

"All that which is contained in the Lower World is also found in the Upper (in prototype). The Lower and Upper reciprocally act upon each other."
—THE ZOHAR

Throughout history, mystics have had visionary experiences and explored the higher planes of existence. For the betterment of humankind, some created models of reality that are like maps for guiding aspirants to these experiences. In the hands of devoted, humble aspirants, these models are up to that task. The higher planes don't follow the same operational laws as the physical plane. Some are vastly susceptible to our influence, often appearing in forms that already have meaning for us. For example, many of us have consciously shaped the dream world before, and an energy that appears to a tarot reader in tarot symbolism might manifest as a rune to a rune reader. Consequently, these models differ, sometimes significantly when filtered through religious frameworks and the imprecise mediums of language and concept. In today's world, many of these models are available for us to work with, including Jewish Kabbalah, the World Tree, the Hindu Lokas, and Tibetan Buddhist cosmology. My aim here is to present metaphysics in a barebones manner that can fit with many systems and models.

Despite their differences, these models tend to agree on certain fundamentals, which compose the basis of metaphysical work. Primary among these fundamentals is the notion that everything is made of a common substance, often called "energy." In Hermetic metaphysics, the universe is in a continuous process of becoming, which is paralleled in other metaphysical models. Energy begins in the undifferentiated unity of pure spirit and moves across a spectrum of vibrational frequencies into the apparent separateness of matter, only to return again. Along this spectrum, there are planes that exist at different rates of vibration. Because the physical plane has the lowest vibrational rate of these, the other planes are often called "higher," which isn't to suggest that they're stacked atop each other. When two things vibrate at significantly different rates, they occupy different dimensional spaces (somewhat like how radio waves can pass through walls), although all planes interconnect and some overlap.

While these concepts might seem abstract, they're actually part of our day-to-day lives. For example, our bodies and thoughts are made of energy. Because thoughts vibrate at a higher rate than matter, they lack physical form beyond neurological firing. The same is true of dreams, which occur in a higher plane of existence. The dream world doesn't cease to exist when we awaken, and the thought world doesn't cease to be when we quiet our mind. Both planes exist along the energetic spectrum, like the physical plane. There are higher planes than these too, where beings like angels and gods dwell. The Tree of Life from Kabbalah is one of the most elegant presentations of this phenomenon. I'll periodically refer to it because of its utility and central role in Hermeticism, but you needn't study Kabbalah to perform the Little Work.

———

The Tree of Life is a symbolic diagram of existence. Energy manifests along a trajectory of ten spheres, which are called "sephiroth." Each sephirah has particular qualities.

1—Kether/Crown: pure, undifferentiated energy

2—Chokmah/Wisdom: the launching of this energy as undiluted force, the celestial father

3—Binah/Understanding: the first tempering of energy into form, the divine womb, the celestial mother (Kether, Chokmah, and Binah form the Celestial/Supernal Triangle or World of Emanation, known in Hebrew as "Atziluth.")

*—Da'ath/Knowledge: a black hole–like abyss that separates the top three sephiroth from the others

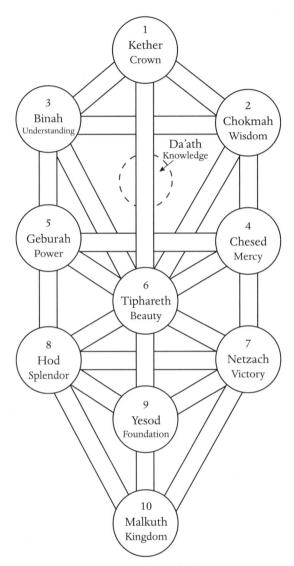

Figure 1: Tree of Life

4—Chesed/Mercy or Loving-Kindness: the matrix archetypes are built upon, the structural support of the universe

5—Geburah/Power: the disciplining force of justice that balances mercy, the purging and tempering fire

6—Tiphareth/Beauty: the apex an individual consciousness can reach, where the higher and lower selves unite; the tree's central sphere that receives most others; the reconciler and redeemer (Chesed, Geburah, and Tiphareth form the Ethical/Moral Triangle or World of Creation, known in Hebrew as "Briah.")

7—Netzach/Victory, Perpetuity, or Endurance: instincts, intuition, emotions, art, symbolism

8—Hod/Splendor, Majesty, or Glory: the rational mind, analysis, intellect

9—Yesod/Foundation: the subtle energy foundation that underlies matter, the Collective Unconscious, the subconscious mind (Netzach, Hod, and Yesod form the Astral/Magical Triangle or World of Formation, known in Hebrew as "Yetzirah.")

10—Malkuth/Kingdom: the material universe or World of Action, known in Hebrew as "Assiah"

Each sephirah, and the paths between them, corresponds with tarot cards, plants, crystals, and more. Meditating on the tree can provide insight into how spirit functions, including within the polarities in life: yin and yang, dark and light, etc. The combination of tarot with the tree offers opportunities for developing wisdom. For example, the Strength card connects Geburah and Chesed, implying that true strength is found in the balance of mercy and justice. By projecting their consciousness into the cards, aspirants can enter the sephiroth and the paths between them, which is called "pathworking."

———

Because energy manifests along a continuum of frequency from high to low, it passes through the higher planes before reaching the physical one. Consequently, whatever we create physically was first thought of, whether consciously or subconsciously, concretely or abstractly. On the surface, this is common sense, since every human-made creation began in someone's mind. Mystics discovered that there are more options when creating than simply acting on inspired thought though, including that what we think can tangibly influence what manifests in our lives. Since energy passes through the higher planes before manifesting physically and we can shift the content of some of these planes with our thoughts, our thoughts can affect physical manifestation. Amazingly, mystics around the world have demonstrated that this is true. What we create in the higher planes—usually the astral plane, which is like a blueprint for the physical one—can manifest in some fashion. Manifesting isn't as straightforward as this may read (e.g., thinking of an orange and then one materializes), but we do have tremendous power to guide and shape what comes to us.

This understanding is the basis of magic, the Law of Attraction, Yogic siddhis, etc. It's one meaning of the axiom "as above, so below." Another meaning is that the planes of existence correspond with each other. A thread of agreement exists between them, uniting reality somewhat like how instruments occupy different octaves while playing a symphony. This is apparent in astrology, which posits that the events in our lives, whether internal or external, connect with the planetary positions, relationships, and movements. Valuable information can be gleaned by recognizing the signs in the external world that correspond with our internal one. For instance, by virtue of the correspondence between planes, a tarot spread can physically reflect a query's answer.

Another meaning of "as above, so below" is that there's something of the creator in the created, the cause in the effect. Every element across the vibrational spectrum is imbued with divinity because everything emanates from an initial divine unity. *Everything is energy*, which is another tenet of the Little Work. The divine is equally present in the densest matter and the highest light of eternity. They differ in form, not substance. This is one reason why there's no such thing as the mundane. When we recognize that divinity is everywhere, we can experience it everywhere, which we'll learn how to do in part two of this book.

Where we station our awareness along the energetic spectrum dramatically influences our life experience. These stationary points are called "states of consciousness." Many of us know this to some degree, having experienced ourselves being "in our bodies," lost in thought, overcome with emotion, or in a combination of these states. There are states of consciousness beyond the standard ones in day-to-day life too, which open to us as we develop spiritually, including ones in which we perceive our energetic makeup. In addition to our physical body, we also have a form that's usually invisible called the "subtle body." The subtle body vibrates at a higher frequency than the physical plane, though it interconnects with the physical body. As with the metaphysical models, there are different models of the subtle body, and we're each free to use the ones we resonate with. In this book, I work with the chakra system from Yoga because of my experience with it and its widespread use in metaphysics. There are varying opinions about how subjective the subtle body is. In my experience, chakra work provides tangible results whether chakras are subjective or not.

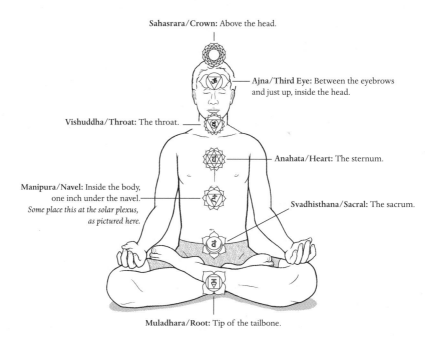

Sahasrara/Crown: Above the head.

Ajna/Third Eye: Between the eyebrows and just up, inside the head.

Vishuddha/Throat: The throat.

Anahata/Heart: The sternum.

Manipura/Navel: Inside the body, one inch under the navel. *Some place this at the solar plexus, as pictured here.*

Svadhisthana/Sacral: The sacrum.

Muladhara/Root: Tip of the tailbone.

Figure 2: The Chakras

Muladhara/Root: physical health; red

Svadhisthana/Sacral: sexuality, sensuality, creativity; orange

Manipura/Navel: the will, our individuated self, self-esteem, self-confidence; yellow

Anahata/Heart: love, relationships, community; green

Vishuddha/Throat: communication, self-expression; blue

Ajna/Third Eye: intuition, psychic vision, imagination; indigo

Sahasrara/Crown: cosmic consciousness, spiritual source; purple or white and purple

Chakras are vortexes of energy that connect the subtle and physical bodies. The major chakras are aligned along the spine, ascending in rate of vibration and corresponding with various life domains. Karma, unhealthy behavioral patterns, and psychological trauma result in blockages in these chakras, which can be cleared through meditation and ritual. Yogis seek to release these blockages and abidingly raise their consciousness to the crown chakra, resulting in an enlightened state that transcends individuality. In Hermeticism, aspirants follow a parallel trajectory by ascending the Tree of Life during meditation, called "rising on the planes."

———

Becoming aware of the subtle body and able to consciously function within it facilitates many spiritual experiences and is a core aspect of occult practice. For example, we can explore the higher planes through transferring our consciousness to the subtle body, which is called "astral projection." During magic, we work directly with the subtle body and subtle energy. Many of us who are drawn to metaphysics were born with a greater innate attunement to subtle phenomena than the status quo.

Many cultures recognize the subtle body, as well its interconnectivity with the physical body. Acupuncture, for instance, is a Chinese healing modality that involves placing needles in specific physical areas, which is believed to cause the subtle body's energy to flow in a manner that facilitates healing. This is an example of affecting the lower by influencing the higher, and acupuncture also demonstrates that we can influence the subtle via physical action. The second half of the axiom "as above, so below," is "as below, so above." By acting in particular ways on the physical plane, we can influence the higher planes, which in turn affects what manifests in our lives.

Another example of this is Hatha Yoga from India, which is the type of Yoga that looks like stretching. Hatha Yoga aligns the physical body to support the flow of energy in the subtle body, thus improving health and preparing Yogis for meditation. In light of the concept "as below, so above," how critical does taking care of our "mundane" life seem? Hence the next tenet of the Little Work: *As above, so below. As below, so above.*

By learning how to work with our subtle body and subtle energy, we can practice magic and improve our health. We can increasingly experience that we're always part of the divine unity and station our awareness higher along the energetic spectrum, which is what the expression "raising your vibration" means. This is the primary metaphysical aim of inner alchemy.

What Is Magic?

"Magick is the Science and Art of causing Change to occur in conformity with Will."
—ALEISTER CROWLEY

"Magic is the art of causing changes to occur in consciousness,
in conformity with will."
—DION FORTUNE

Now that we have a basic understanding of metaphysics, we can explore magic in greater depth. Two of the most famous definitions of magic are shared above. On the surface, many find something unsatisfying about both of them. Crowley's definition can appear mundane, given that it holds equally for both shutting a door with our hand and marshaling cosmic forces.[1] Dion Fortune's can appear too psychological. Changing consciousness sounds appealing, but how will that create the external changes we seek?

When contextualized with the information from the last section, it becomes clear that both definitions hold for more conventional notions of magic. Shutting a door involves guiding reality around intention, and any physical act utilizes the subtle body and affects the higher planes, even if we're unaware of this. Crowley wrote that "Every intentional act is a Magickal Act," and this is one reason that's true. When we intend, we rally the forces of nature around us. We can't do anything without the universe's cooperation. When we recognize this as we act, thus participating actively in the creative process of the universe, we practice magic.

Regarding Dion Fortune's definition, what happens when we change our consciousness? As above, so below. Shifting our consciousness influences the subtle body and higher planes, which in turn affects the physical plane and our life experience. By changing our consciousness, we change ourselves, and by changing ourselves, the world we experience changes. This is one of the highest forms of magic, and in fact, High Magic, by definition, is magic performed to transform our consciousness such that we experience our inherent divinity more. Low Magic, sometimes called "folk magic," is magic used for practical aims. Low Magic can overlap with High Magic if we include becoming increasingly aware of our divine nature in it (i.e., if we aim "high"). For example, if we cast a spell for a new

---

1. The "Will" Crowley refers to involves the concept that everyone has a "True Will." His definition can't be understood properly without more context. Because I'm not mirroring his definition of magic in that respect, exploring True Will felt too tangential to include here.

job with the greater intention of that job helping us evolve spiritually, the spell is both High and Low Magic.

A more conventionally palatable definition of magic could be: the science and art of causing change in conformity with will through subtle means. Though physical action may be part of magic (and it often is), what makes a process magical is the harnessing of subtle means. This clarifies that while shutting a door is magical in one respect, it isn't what most of us mean when we think of magic. In practice, magic as defined here could look like casting a career spell that brings an unsolicited invitation to apply for the kind of job we intended, which we then procure with action. Though action was involved, the subtle work was primary. Regarding High Magic, we pursue expanded consciousness through working with the subtle body (i.e., we seek change via subtle means).

Magic is a science because it follows natural law and produces replicable results when performed properly. It's an art because its involvement with the higher planes provides room for subjectivity in practice. The astral plane can be shaped in alignment with our imagination, as can the subconscious mind, which we'll see is highly involved in magic. We can also practice magic effectively across a spectrum of complexity and ornamentation in accord with our personal tastes, and the power we wield can hold different form and force based on what we believe. All of this provides room for artistry.

When studying magic, it's natural to wonder what its limits are. While I think it's important not to unnecessarily limit ourselves, I also think it's irresponsible, if not unethical, to proclaim that we have infinite creative power when, in most cases, this is patently not the case. As Dion Fortune wrote in *Applied Magic* of open-ended metaphysicians, "[They] set no limits; but if we watch the results they obtain, we can see that there are limits."[2] That said, one of the most popular metaphysical maxims is "You create your reality," which is true. Understanding what this means helps us practice magic effectively, as well as appreciate why the Little Work is so important.

---

2. Dion Fortune, *Applied Magic* (York Beach, ME: Samuel Weiser, Inc., 2000).

WE CREATE OUR REALITY—OR DO WE?

"You have projected onto yourself a world of your own imagination,
based on memories, on desires and fears, and you have imprisoned yourself in it.
Break the spell and be free."

—NISARGADATTA MAHARAJ

Every day, we bring reality into being for ourselves with our mind. In the Little Work system, it's critical to understand two dimensions of this process: the psychological and the metaphysical. Because our psychological and subtle systems are interdependent parts of a greater system, wherein each can influence the other, this distinction between dimensions is somewhat blurry. I draw it because both dimensions substantially impact our created reality, and understanding and working with one doesn't necessarily enable us to understand and work with the other. Simultaneously working with both dimensions affords us optimal magical ability. I also draw this distinction because critics of magic often point to psychological processes to explain how magic works, which we'll see is inaccurate. For these reasons, I continually differentiate between these dimensions throughout this book.

We create our reality psychologically in the sense that many elements of our lives only exist because of thoughts. From infancy, we're taught language, and with language, that certain things are real or a particular way. We're given a name, told things about ourselves that are supposed to be true, and told what's valuable, appropriate, and worthwhile. We're taught about structures like schools, governments, and religions. All of these things depend on thoughts to exist. If we collectively stopped thinking of them, they'd cease to be. To that end, anything that depends on thought to exist is an optional element of reality. Thought-dependent realities only hold sway over us because we, or others with physical power over our lives, believe they're real. In every waking moment, our subconscious mind chisels the marble of sensory input we receive, using thoughts to make reality appear a certain way to us. We know this occurs because our perceptions align with thought-dependent aspects of reality without us having to consciously think of them. Because the psychological creation of reality occurs subconsciously and automatically, we don't experience it happening, but it is.

When a critical mass of people agree that certain thoughts represent reality, they create a reality together called a "consensus reality." Nations, for example, only exist because people agree that they do. The same holds for cultural values and norms, which can wildly differ depending on where we're from. For a moment, consider your self-definitions and perspectives about the world that depend on thought to exist. What would happen if you stopped believing these thoughts? When mystics speak of the illusion of the world, this is one aspect of what they mean. Consensus realities are like group dreams. High Magic is a way of waking from them, and Yoga is another. Yoga, which means "union" in Sanskrit, is far more than the fitness option it's popularly known as. It's a science of enlightenment from Hinduism that can involve various practices to suit the individual constitutions of seekers, including meditation, chanting, devotional singing, and contemplation of truth. In the stillness of mind sought by High Magic and Yoga, thought-dependent realities vanish.

In contrast to consensus realities, there is inherent reality. Inherent reality is the reality that doesn't depend on thought to exist. It can be influenced by thoughts during the process of manifestation, but we don't think it into being. Without our thoughts, our bodies and the physical structures of the world would still exist—the moon would still orbit the earth, it would hurt if someone pinched us, we'd get hungry, etc. Inherent reality existed long before humanity. That said, our subjective experience of inherent reality is profoundly influenced by our mind. For example, children and people in vegetative mental states experience inherent reality highly differently than healthy adults. We also subjectively interpret inherent reality in that our senses register an extraordinarily limited sliver of it (and our conscious mind can only manage a fraction of that sliver).

One of the magical-feeling aspects of psychologically created reality is that we aren't beholden to our thoughts. We may have been taught, and subsequently believed, that something inherent to us was fundamentally wrong or that we have limits that have no inherent reality basis. As we dismantle these beliefs, which is often part of contemporary psychotherapy, our reality changes. This process can feel miraculous, and it'll be a primary focus of part two.

While this may sound revolutionary—and it is—many of us encounter this phenomenon in our day-to-day lives. When people sincerely convert to religions, they engage in this process. Reality literally appears differently to them as their novel religious beliefs root in their subconscious mind. For example, casual sex might've once felt fun to them, but now that they consider it immoral, they feel disgusted even seeing it on TV. This is part of how cults gain such thrall over their followers. As new cult members feel their reality shift in accord with the cult's beliefs, the magical-feeling effect of this strengthens their faith in the cult's legitimacy. This shift isn't proof that the cult's beliefs are valid, though. It's a representation of the fact that repeating and feeding beliefs makes them feel truer, which is a well-researched phenomenon called the "illusory truth effect." When we're exposed to new beliefs without much resistance to them, these shifts can happen quickly.

We also have a subconscious psychological process called "confirmation bias" wherein our mind automatically seeks evidence to affirm our preconceived notions or hypotheses while downplaying or disregarding what refutes them. The more "evidence" our mind finds that supports our beliefs, the stronger they become. As in the illusory truth effect, this has nothing to do with how accurate our beliefs are. For instance, if I believe people are greedy, consciously or subconsciously, my mind will filter my perceptions in a manner that validates this perspective. I'll be more likely to register stories about worker exploitation and write off ones about philanthropy. We tend to see what we look for, even when we don't realize we're looking for anything.

How many people cringe upon seeing a boy wearing pink? That's a conditioned reaction. Pink wasn't a "girl's color" until after World War II. Relatedly, belief is so powerful it can even overshadow biological cues. Many of us were reared to believe we should "clean our plate," yielding a drive to eat that overpowers our bodies' fullness signals. At the extreme, by virtue of the illusory truth effect, confirmation bias, and social influences, we may become willing to die for beliefs that once meant nothing to us and have no inherent reality basis. There's also the placebo effect, where people experience health benefits from taking nonmedicinal substances they believe are medicinal, which is arguably a metaphysical phenomenon. Either way, belief is extraordinarily powerful, which is part of why developing discernment is essential in inner alchemy. We must recognize that believing or feeling something strongly doesn't mean it's true. Thoughts and feelings are not facts. As our discernment sharpens, we can free ourselves from toxic beliefs and the havoc they wreak in our lives.

Realizing I could define life on my own terms was pivotal in my alchemical transformation. The concepts of success and satisfaction in my consensus reality of origin felt at odds with my spirit, and I also suffered under an antagonistic mindset that stemmed from my experiences of illness, abuse, and dehumanization. As I claimed the power of thought and started reshaping reality to honor my whole self, my life brightened, and I didn't need anyone else to validate this new reality. It was enough that it was real for me. Sit for a moment in the truth that thought-dependent aspects of reality needn't be real for you. Releasing them may not be as easy as this might read, but we can live beyond their reach. *What thought created, thought can change.* This is another tenet of the Little Work, and a core aspect of inner alchemy is transforming thinking.

The Metaphysics of How We Create Our Reality

"Why should you study and practice Magick?
Because you can't help doing it, and you had better do it well than badly."
—ALEISTER CROWLEY

Metaphysically speaking, reality creation involves the process outlined earlier of energy manifesting into matter. In each moment, our thoughts, words, emotions, and actions contribute to the universe's process of becoming. With the freedom to control or influence these things, we can participate in this continuous creative process in an intentional manner. Every intentional act is a magical act, every intentional word is a magical word, every intentional thought is a magical thought, etc., which brings us to the next tenet of the Little Work: *intention is magical.* Our subtle body, which is highly influenced by our thoughts, emotions, etc., ceaselessly generates a psychic emanation that influences the higher planes and guides a significant portion of what manifests in our lives. We can amplify this emanation with "subtle bodybuilding" via activities like rituals, spells, and meditation, which also help us refine and focus it. We either create with intent, which is magic, or unconsciously. Either way, we create. Always.

On one level, this means we manifest things that match our psychic emanation's frequency. Sometimes this is apparent, while other times it isn't. For instance, if I fixate on elephants, I'm likelier to get invited to a zoo where I then see an elephant. Conversely, if I have a cynical attitude, this could manifest in circumstances that resonate with my attitude's tone, whether I thought of them or not. For example, I could become ill, catch only red lights during my commute, have a day that seems cursed, etc. This aspect of reality creation is somewhat like being a metaphysical broadcast television, and experiences that resonate with each other share a channel. If I'm tuned to channel five, channel five experiences will come to me. Not exclusively, but there'll be a clear trend.

Confirmation bias plays into this in that we're more apt to register things in a manner that validates what's already in our mind (e.g., if I believe "everything's terrible," my mind will filter reality accordingly). We're also more likely to notice things that have significance for us, especially if we were recently thinking of them. For instance, I could walk past a triangle bumper sticker many times without noticing it, but after studying sacred geometry, it begins to catch my eye. Generally speaking, we can tell a synchronistic event doesn't solely result from psychological factors when its manifestation requires something beyond heightened awareness. Thinking about apples and then noticing an apple display that's long been in a store we frequent is more psychological than magical. But someone randomly offering us an apple shortly after we thought about one or contacting us minutes after we thought of them—that's metaphysics.

Learning about the psychology and metaphysics of reality creation is an invitation to personal power. The most powerful person in your life, in terms of potential to shape your life experience and what manifests in your reality, is you. This is true for everyone, and it's one reason we needn't feel selfish about using magic. Everyone has magic, and plenty of it. Some of us have a greater innate propensity and aptitude for it, but everyone has it. The problem is that most of us were taught otherwise and to unconsciously give our energy away. Until we learn psychic hygiene, we tend to match our society's psychic status quo and yield our power without realizing it. Unfortunately, this anchors some of us in oppressive circumstances that are extremely difficult to extricate ourselves from, even with a supportive mindset and psychic emanation. That said, I believe there's hope for anyone who reclaims their mind and psychic emanation and offers something divergent from their status quo. Doing that is difficult without training, but in today's world, training is available from many sources, including books like this. Once we own our creative power, no one but us can control it without our consent because other people can't think in our mind.

As we learn to guide our psychic emanation, we become more powerful within our lives. For now, open to the notion that how you think, speak, feel, and act affects what manifests in your reality, psychologically and metaphysically.

If we want to change our reality, the first place to start is within ourselves, with thoughts and actions that support our intentions. As above, so below; as within, so without.

Limits and Confounding Factors Regarding the Metaphysical Creation of Reality

"The occultist does not try to dominate Nature, but to bring himself into harmony with these great Cosmic Forces, and work with them."

—DION FORTUNE

Many students get carried away with the subject of the metaphysical creation of reality, often because authors make unsubstantiated claims of omnipotence, so there's value in reviewing some limits to how it operates. This can help us stay grounded, lest we fear our every distressing thought, blame ourselves when something unwanted happens to us, or think we're the Supreme Being. Worst of all, lest we join those who died of treatable illnesses that they tried to cure solely with intention, which they lacked the training to even adequately attempt. There are reasons why the metaphysical creation of reality isn't self-evident to most of us, as it will be after performing inner alchemy. Many factors bear on our metaphysical contribution to the creation of reality, and this power has limits.

One limit to this power is that we don't create reality alone. We're each a cell in the body of humanity (as above, so below). When we psychologically construct consensus realities with others, we also co-create at the subtle level accordingly, resulting in manifestations that fit with these consensus realities. This applies to every system in which we're in psychic agreement with others. We can work to shift the collective thoughts that produce these group emanations, and magical social justice work involves this, but as long as we participate in a consensus reality, we'll manifest in alignment with it.

Another limit to this power is the boundaries of natural law. There are things we can't do unless we're at the level of consciousness of a being like Buddha (and even then, who knows). For example, we can't regrow limbs. We can create a staggering amount through harnessing subtle energy, but we can't change natural law. That said, miraculous events like the spontaneous remission of illness do happen, so it's important to stay open-minded, just without sacrificing perspective. Sometimes the miracle cure we manifest for an illness we have is the one we overhear a doctor rec-ommending to someone else. Magic brought us this information, but we still must utilize it.

Beyond manifestational limits, another aspect of natural law that bears on magic is karma. Like the metaphysical models shared earlier, beliefs about karma can vary significantly between the religions that feature it, but the fundamental concept is similar. Here, I offer a barebones, practical presentation of it based on my Yogic and Hermetic studies and experience. In a nutshell, karma is the meta-physical law of cause and effect. What we do in this life and others affects what we experience, and like begets like. For example, if we harm, we bring something that matches the frequency of this harm to ourselves in this life or another. Most of us who feel metaphysically inclined do so because we pursued metaphysics in previous lives. Karma isn't an eye for an eye or a kiss for a kiss though. We could murder someone in a past life only to have our home burn down now, to die from medical malpractice, etc. Karma's impossible to understand with the intellect. We can gain insight into karma with divination and our intuition, and enlightenment brings greater understanding of it, but it boggles the rational mind.

Though karma may seem like a judge, jury, and executioner, it isn't about morality, like being punished for sin and rewarded for virtue. As with all natural laws, karma's impersonal. On one level, it's simply cause and effect. On another, all beings are in an evolutionary process back to their source, or as alchemists say, all things move toward their preordained state of perfection, toward divine union. When we reinforce our sense of separateness, we tie or tighten karmic knots within our subtle body that tether us to lower states of consciousness. Ev-eryone has these from previous lives and has likely accumulated more in this one. Because of our evolutionary drive, experiences that can help us evolve manifest for us, including ones involving these knots, since we must untie them to raise our consciousness. The most accessible way to untie these knots and prevent new ones from forming is through developing wisdom that increasingly aligns us with spirit, which is where the notion that our experiences carry inherent life les-sons can fit with this conceptualization of karma. When a knot involving hubris surfaces, for example, humbling experiences will manifest for us until we release hubris through wisdom, regardless of what we're intentionally emanating. These ex-periences tend to escalate if we resist untying the knots related to them. The Tower card from tarot represents the heaviest hand of karma. Sometimes an aspect of our reality must explode for us to evolve spiritually. When this is so, we can't prevent it.

Releasing karma is a core aspect of inner alchemy. Our evolutionary drive is like a current we can choose to swim with, swim against, or allow to carry us. By practicing inner alchemy, we swim with the current, surfacing our karma at an accelerated rate (High Magic and meditation are like karmic plungers). Through proactively working through our karma, we can quickly clear a substantial amount of it. This helps us raise our consciousness up the energetic spectrum.

In addition to karma, grace also affects what manifests in our lives. For our purposes, grace is generally two-fold. First, it's the phenomenon of beneficial manifestations coming to us regardless of our emanations (i.e., what's colloquially referred to as "divine intervention"). All signs point to doom and then we catch an unexpected break. This can be karma from previous lives, but it can also be pure grace. Like karma, grace transcends rational understanding. Sometimes we can recognize grace, but that's about it.

Otherwise, many spiritual teachers cite grace as being what catalyzes the completion of the Great Work and other spiritual transformations, which is the second aspect of it. We can devote ourselves to spiritual practice, but we can't force ourselves to awaken. We must prepare ourselves to bottle divine lightning when it strikes, but we don't make the lightning come. When people attempt to force spiritual experiences that they aren't ready for (e.g., by meditating for six hours daily without training), the results can be catastrophic.

Beyond these factors, our minds are also usually cluttered with thoughts, and a cluttered mind creates a cluttered reality. It's hard to discern the causation behind what comes to us when we emanate a jumble (especially when this jumble largely mirrors what's already there). An emanation matching the status quo brings more of the status quo, which can make us feel like we aren't creating anything, even though we are. Inner alchemy involves weeding thoughts that don't support our intentions. As we do this, our creative power becomes more apparent.

An additional factor here is that manifestation takes time, although it hastens as our magical skill increases. We may launch a calamitous emanation today, but by the time it would've manifested, others have overrun it. This has perhaps never been truer, given how much energy many of us expend with entertainment. Activities like watching TV and browsing the internet can shift our psychic emanation. A popular metaphysical saying is "energy flows where attention goes," and consequently, a key to effective magical practice is being discriminating with what we focus on and how.

Generally speaking, concentrating on something brings more of it into our experience. Thought-dependent realities grow for us relative to how much mental energy we feed them. Without our reinforcement, they fade. The major exceptions to this are thought-dependent creations with components we don't control, like laws that are enforced, and ones that connect with psychological trauma we have. Psychological trauma can indefinitely keep issues active within us subconsciously. Metaphysically speaking, attending to a subject can integrate it into our psychic emanation, tuning us to manifestations that match its frequency.

Another factor affecting our metaphysical creation of reality is that most of us can't innately concentrate strongly and consistently enough to reliably create with subtle means. Our ability to focus, visualize, sustain thought, and harness emotion directly corresponds with our ability to shape the subtle and hold an intention for energy to pass through as it manifests. Most of us need substantial practice to do this well. One-pointed concentration, which is the holy grail of High Magic and Yoga, is the key ingredient to effective manifestation. The closer we get to it, the more magically powerful we are, and the further we are from it, the less. When our thoughts lack this force, they aren't very significant metaphysically. That said, thinking many weak thoughts of a similar frequency can form a creative or destructive mass.

Hopefully this is clear, but because this topic is controversial, I want to spell it out: I'm not suggesting anything like "People give themselves cancer by thinking about cancer, and avoiding thinking about cancer will make it go away." Cancer can develop for many reasons. It could come from karma or emanations co-created with others. It could come from inherent reality factors like diet, pollution, and genetics. It could originate from a long-term toxic attitude that ravaged someone's subtle body or all of this combined and more. The big picture of reality creation is more complex than we can understand with the rational mind, and we aren't responsible for everything that comes to us—even less so when we lack metaphysical training and are largely unaware of our power. That said, as we progress in inner alchemy, our role in what manifests in our lives becomes increasingly apparent.

The Metaphysical Power of Belief

"Some things have to be believed to be seen."

—MADELEINE L'ENGLE

Aside from occasional eyebrow-raising synchronicities, like thinking about someone just before they call, most people don't consciously experience the metaphysical dimension of reality creation much. Beyond the reasons we've explored for this, another can be that they don't believe in the metaphysical creation of reality, and our strongest psychic emanations come from our beliefs. This holds for conscious and subconscious beliefs. "Belief" in this context follows the dictionary definition as "an acceptance of something as true or real." It's not what people mean when they say they have spiritual beliefs that they hope are real but feel unsure about. Many of us have subconscious beliefs that we're unaware of that manifest in our day-to-day experiences that'd become apparent through introspection (e.g., "I'm never good enough," "Most people can't be trusted"). We'll focus on this in part two.

Think about the strength a thought you firmly believe has in your mind versus one that means nothing to you, as if both are stones. Which makes a bigger splash, a boulder-like thought or a pebble-like one? So it is with magic. The conviction and emotion behind a thought determines how much energy it has.

If we believe metaphysical manifestation isn't real, we'll manifest an experience of reality that affirms this to the extent that we can individually create our reality. If we believe life is ordinary, we'll create an ordinary-feeling reality for ourselves (unless it's our karmic moment to have this notion shattered). This is why the most powerful protection against curses isn't protection spells but rather firmly believing that curses aren't real or can't affect us.

In light of this, magical practice involves learning to harness the power of belief. When harnessing belief, treading carefully is important because a deeper aim of inner alchemy is to experience the reality that's beyond the level of thought. Beliefs are tools that can help us guide our magic and move ourselves along the spiritual path, but if we lose sight of the optional nature of thought-dependent realities, beliefs can hinder us. For example, if we rigidly define magic, we can limit our ability to experience its fullness and unnecessarily restrict ourselves with superstitions. Habitually speculating or theorizing about the mysteries of reality can anchor us at the level of thought and prevent us from experiencing these mysteries firsthand, like placing a veil over our eyes. Just as a map is not the terrain it represents, the concept is not the experience, and the definition is not the defined.

Relatedly, we needn't speculate about whether or not magic is real. By practicing inner alchemy with diligence, patience, and openness, magic will become as real to us as other aspects of inherent reality. As we learn to perceive and direct subtle energy, we can have spiritual experiences we can't fathom now. While this unfolds, we start appreciating that metaphysical answers to questions about the nature of reality come through direct experience. If we get too attached to belief systems, we can keep ourselves from these experiences. So we harness the power of belief, using metaphysical models like training wheels on the bike of spiritual development, while taking care not to shackle our consciousness in rigid belief systems. The more spiritual experiences we have, the less attached to ideas about spirituality we become, particularly as we experience the parts of ourselves that are more innately us than our thoughts.

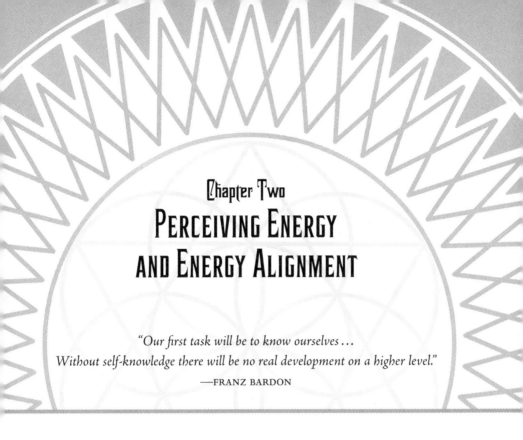

Chapter Two
PERCEIVING ENERGY
AND ENERGY ALIGNMENT

"Our first task will be to know ourselves …
Without self-knowledge there will be no real development on a higher level."
—FRANZ BARDON

To perform magic as it's been defined here, we must learn to harness subtle energy. Perceiving subtle energy helps tremendously with this, and that often takes effort because, unsurprisingly, subtle energy is subtle. Subtle things become more apparent as we pay attention to them, and in this system, perceiving subtle energy begins with cultivating awareness in general.

Building awareness is critical in inner alchemy for many reasons. As we become aware within the domains of our lives, we can act with greater intentionality within them (i.e., because of understanding how they operate and what our capacity is within them). We also get a better sense of how our behavior in these areas affects our well-being, magic, and spiritual connectedness. Consequently, a tenet of the Little Work is to *live consciously* by striving to be present in our lives.

When we bring our attention to the present moment, we become aware, which enables us to tune in to many things in beneficial ways. We can monitor our thoughts, check in with our bodies, observe what's happening around us, etc. Developing awareness begins with making a habit of becoming present and observing our levels of being: physical, emotional, mental, etc. We tune in to what's happening within ourselves, which includes observing our energy levels.

Though energy is ultimately one, it functions differently in the subtle, physical, mental, and emotional dimensions, and we have finite amounts of physical, mental, and emotional energy. For example, strenuous exercise depletes our physical energy, spending an evening studying can expend our mental energy, and a difficult emotional conversation can drain us emotionally. We can also be energized differently in these areas (e.g., nourished by food, inspired by an idea, enlivened by a heart-to-heart conversation).

Though some circumstances warrant us temporarily overstraining in one domain (e.g., cramming for exams, cathartic psychotherapy sessions), it's generally beneficial to maintain harmony across our levels of being, which promotes well-being. This doesn't mean we resist exerting ourselves. We just avoid throwing ourselves wildly out of balance. Having a consistently off-kilter mix of energy can cause us to feel unwell and even get sick. Insomnia, for example, can occur from an imbalance where our bodies are exhausted but racing thoughts keep us awake.

As we become more present and observant, we're likely to walk on an evener keel energetically. It's like we're a car that has various maintenance needs. By training ourselves to monitor our dashboard lights and act on that information, we can ensure that we run smoothly, developing a keen sense of when to course-correct, rest, and engage in self-care. When we don't regularly attend to our levels of being and energy, we may not notice something's wrong until we're stranded on the roadside. This is another reason why monitoring our energy can make us healthier (and *monitor your energy* is a tenet of the Little Work). We're more likely to recognize when something's off within ourselves and address it before it escalates into a problem. We become like a psychic chiropractor, adjusting ourselves when we come out of alignment and appreciating the benefits that accompany aligned living.

As we prioritize living consciously, we start noticing when our thoughts, words, or actions are unsupportive of our intentions or well-being and how this affects us. We feel the impact of not honoring our word, continually procrastinating on projects, and speaking ill of others (and ourselves). We perceive the difference between a state of care and harmony versus one of stagnation and overwhelm, and we begin seeing how misaligned energy affects what manifests in our reality. All of this provides motivation for aligning ourselves as often as possible and staying mindful of how we use our energy.

Techniques for Perceiving Subtle Energy

*"Imagine spirit simultaneously, within and around you,
until the entire universe spiritualizes."*
—VIGYAN BHAIRAV TANTRA

Two of the most effective techniques I know for learning to perceive subtle energy are to consistently observe how we feel and to nurture the beliefs that subtle energy is real and we can sense it with practice. Subtle energy is often perceived through feeling (and sometimes seeing). As we refine our sensitivity to what we feel, we become more able to perceive the subtleties within it. This is like training ourselves to listen for the subtle sounds in a quiet room.

Subtle energy perception can also emerge from consistent meditation practice. When we meditate, we concentrate on one thing exclusively as best we can, like a chakra. This involves becoming quiet and present, which renders the subtle more perceptible. In Yoga, there's a science of working with subtle energy via breath control called "pranayama." As is self-evident, breath is one of the primary sources of vital energy. By practicing pranayama, we can become aware of subtle energy if we witness the changes within ourselves during our practice (a simple pranayama technique is shared in part two). We can also do this during meditation, which shifts the flow of energy in the subtle body.

Another technique for coming to perceive subtle energy is to act as if our thoughts, words, emotions, and actions are directing it even when we don't sense that—for example, by performing rituals like a proficient actor, imagining the subtle energy is there and being funneled toward sought aims. With consistent practice like this, most of us will start to feel it.

Once we can sense subtle energy, we can work with it directly, still with our thoughts, words, emotions, and actions, but in a manner where we feel it flowing, which eventually enables us to guide it with finesse. We develop a growing sense of what's happening on the higher planes. This usually makes us better at magic since we can tweak what we're doing if it feels off and direct energy in a more refined manner. We also become likelier to believe in magic once we can sense subtle energy at work during magical practice, which amplifies our magical capability. This doesn't mean our rituals and spells won't work before we can perceive subtle energy, just that they strengthen after we can. Perceiving subtle energy also alerts us to how our thoughts, words, emotions, and actions affect our psychic emana-tion, making it easier to hold these in support of our intentions.

DIVINE ENERGY

"With inner peace I felt plugged into the source of universal energy,
which never runs out."
—PEACE PILGRIM

Another form of energy available to us, which subtle energy perception can help us access, is divine energy. Technically speaking, all energy is divine. This term re-fers to energy's form at divine levels of consciousness, where it vibrates at a higher frequency than what we usually experience within the subtle body. We can expe-rience divine energy to the degree that we can set our individual ego aside.

Divine energy is limitless, and humans who've tapped into it are capable of impossible-seeming acts. Mata Amritanandamayi, better known as Amma, reg-ularly demonstrates this by embracing tens of thousands of people for twelve-to twenty-three-hour stretches with little to no food or rest. Amma's done this week after week for years, like a living wonder of the world. Another example of this is Peace Pilgrim, who walked penniless and healthy across America for decades on a mission of peace, fasting until given food and sleeping outside un-less given shelter. These are miraculous acts, and miraculous things are possible through divine energy. Knowing this can help us expand our general concept of what's possible, which is profoundly magical. Relatedly, one of the greatest benefits of having a spiritual teacher is that they demonstrate to us that vistas of consciousness beyond what we've experienced exist. I don't think I would've pro-gressed like I did in magic school if I hadn't believed my teacher had experienced mysteries beyond what I had.

High Magic, prayer, and meditating on the divine can tune us to divine en-ergy, and divine energy isn't separate from us. It's our nature at a higher level along the energetic spectrum. Total alignment with this nature, and the surrendering of the individual self that such alignment demands, completes the Great Work. One way of defining inner alchemy is as the process of removing our internal barriers to this alignment.

The Guidance of Alignment

"Happiness is when what you think,
what you say, and what you do are in harmony."
—MAHATMA GANDHI

As our awareness grows and we consistently engage in spiritual practices, we won't have to wonder where to focus in inner alchemy. It'll become self-evident. We'll feel dissonance from the parts of ourselves that are misaligned. A pile of clothing on the floor will suddenly stick out to us as we perceive an opportunity for creating greater harmony in our lives through picking it up. We'll notice karmic knots and chances to untie them. We'll recognize when part of us resists the well-being of aligned living and the opportunity to heal that's inherent in addressing that. As we experience the nourishment of alignment, wanting to maintain it can motivate us to deal with these issues.

Aligning our levels of being is somewhat like cleaning a clogged pipe. When we begin inner alchemy, this pipe often has ample debris in it. As we clear this debris, the celestial waters can flow through us unrestricted, which is one reason alignment is so important in magic. When we align our levels of being, the intentions we emanate move through the planes of existence with minimal interference, and when we live in alignment in our day-to-day lives, the responses to our offerings come with minimal impediment too. This vastly increases the efficacy of our magic, and it yields a profound sense of well-being.

Alignment isn't an aggressive or draconian process where we feel guilty or ashamed, for example, for not cleaning our bathroom enough. It's like gardening within our lives. Though we do develop discipline in this system to help us follow through on our intentions, it's rooted in self-respect. We strive not to criticize ourselves as we inevitably make mistakes and to accept that inner alchemy isn't about always being comfortable or only trying to feel good. Facing ourselves and our karma, as we incrementally do during inner alchemy, can be extremely painful, but it's a pain that leads to greater alignment, freedom, and lightness of being. Magic can help us navigate this, and daily ritual is one of the best methods I know for facilitating this process. Fundamentally though, magic is a means to deepen the human experience, not avoid it.

Otherwise, alignment involves following our inner North Star, which appears brighter as we move toward it. It's about constantly listening to what our conscience tells us is helpful and healthy and heeding this as best we can. This isn't always straightforward, but it often is, and it becomes clearer as we clarify our values, which we'll do in part two.

Alignment is about living in the ecstasy of embodiment and noticing the divine and opportunities for revelation all around us. It's about recognizing that the more we approach life with awareness, intention, and a spiritual focus, the more alive and connected we feel. This produces a profound sense of serenity as it becomes our default, even amidst difficulty.

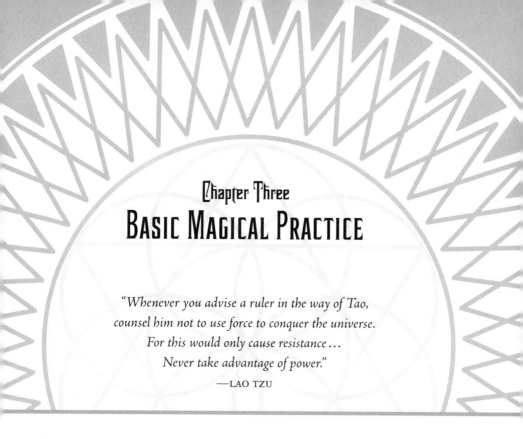

Chapter Three
BASIC MAGICAL PRACTICE

"Whenever you advise a ruler in the way of Tao,
counsel him not to use force to conquer the universe.
For this would only cause resistance...
Never take advantage of power."

—LAO TZU

Before reviewing magical techniques, it's important to consider the ethics involved in magic. Beyond the opinion of our conscience, there are karmic repercussions to magical work: it can reduce our karma, increase our karma, or have a somewhat neutral effect. This is important to understand because resolving our karma as best we can is a primary aim in inner alchemy.

Historically, many magical practitioners have labeled magic "white," "black," and "gray" to differentiate its uses and their karmic outcomes (e.g., magic can be used to heal, harm). Many today find these labels deeply problematic given the history of assigning the terms "white" and "black" values that are rooted in racism (i.e., whiteness being "good" and blackness being "bad"). Also, these labels can foster an unhealthy psychological schism between light and dark, which we'll explore in part two. These labels misrepresent magic as well, which isn't actually white, black, or gray. Magic is an aspect of nature, like the laws of physics, and like the laws of physics, we can harness it for good or ill.

In this system, we perform High Magic rituals to facilitate inner alchemy and increase our sense of union with the divine. Magic like this aims to reduce our karma, and there's no ethical concern with practicing it. In fact, practicing magic like this tends to make people more ethical in general.

If we aim lower, performing magic to practically benefit ourselves or others without intending to harm or manipulate anyone, we may or may not increase our karma. Examples of this type of magic include manifesting items, like money and inexpensive flights, and protection spells. Whether these spells increase our karma usually depends on how attached we feel to the results we seek. If we preface magic like this with an intention like "If this aligns with the highest good, let it happen; if not, let it not and help me develop wisdom from either outcome," it can facilitate inner alchemy or at least stay more karmically neutral. Also, with this caveat, we needn't worry about how our magic might inadvertently affect others. The highest good is good for all. It's the evolutionary current. It may not always give everyone what they want (e.g., sometimes disappointment is what's in our highest good), but it aligns with the flow of karma.

Lastly, performing magic to harm others or otherwise subjugate their will increases our karma, as comparable physical action would. Curses, love spells directed at specific people, and aggressive binding spells (e.g., keeping a coworker from receiving a promotion we seek) are examples of magic like this. Unless we're in a caretaker role, forcing others to bend to our will is a severe karmic violation.

In the Dhammapada, the teachings of the Buddha, there's a saying that "Whatever you do, you do to yourself," and a classic metaphysical adage is "Like attracts like." When we fixate on hate, vengefulness, greed, etc., we amplify these qualities within ourselves. The same is true for qualities like compassion, kindness, and reverence. This is metaphysics, but it's also psychology. What we water in the garden of our mind grows.

To harm someone with magic, we must place ourselves in an antagonizing state, matching the frequency of the effects we seek to induce. Recall a time you felt consumed with hatred. Did that feel healthy? Working magic like this harms us psychologically and warps our psychic emanation to support our antagonistic intentions, which affects the manifestations that come to us. Lashing out with magic may feel emotionally satisfying, but it can cause us serious harm. We may also feel unexpectedly guilty or remorseful about it later, and accordingly, many people have a much harder time resolving karma that involves having hurt others than they do with karma that doesn't. If emotional satisfaction is primarily what we seek, better to write a journal entry instead and leave things there.

Regarding manipulating others with magic, that only seems justifiable to me in response to danger. The frequencies of spells for defensive binding and justice are also unlike those described above, unless they're fueled by hatred or other comparable emotions more than a desire for protection or justice. Their karmic repercussions would logically differ too. This raises an important point about karma, which is that generally speaking, the karmic effects of an action have more to do with how we think and feel about it than the action itself (hence the earlier point about attachment to outcomes). That's what forms the knots in our consciousness, and that's part of why we can release them internally. This is a primary lesson of the *Bhagavad Gita*, a classic treatise on Yoga, wherein Krishna, a divine incarnation, encourages Arjuna—a hesitating warrior who faces the unthinkable task of battling kinsmen, friends, and teachers—to fight because that is Arjuna's sacred duty (what Thelemites would call his True Will). Krishna instructs Arjuna to anchor his mind in the divine, release his thoughts of self, surrender his attachment to his actions' outcomes, and fight because that is necessary for the defense of himself and others, doing so without malice. If he can do this, his fighting will help purify him spiritually. Critically, Arjuna fights to protect, not to harm. Even though he must kill to win the battle, he has no desire to hurt anyone.

Returning to defensive magic, we can also always pray that people develop compassion and awaken spiritually, and if we really want justice, there is no greater reckoning than that. Otherwise, when people seek to harm or manipulate with magic, there's often an alternative approach that can achieve a satisfying, if not equivalent, end without incurring the same karmic or psychological impact. For example, in a contest, there'll be at least one winner and loser, and we can use magic to help the winner win or the loser lose. Using magic to aid someone in achieving something they want has a vastly different effect on the magical practitioner than tearing someone down, yet both can yield the same outcome in the contest.

Additionally, when working magic involving other people, it's important to consider where we have the strongest influence. For instance, we have far greater magical power over ourselves than others. If someone's antagonizing me, it's often more effective to tune myself to the frequency of peace or shield myself, which will sidestep most antagonistic forces, than bind that person, whose disbelief in magic, passionate thoughts, etc., could subvert the binding. I also have more power to manifest my best-fitting lover through becoming resonant with that general intention than I do to ensnare a specific person (and I'll probably be happier with the outcome).

Further, when we work magic directly on other things, we establish a metaphysical connection between them and us, and concentrating on something anchors and amplifies it in our experience. Consider just the psychological effect of working magic on a specific person. Whenever we think of the spell, that person comes to our mind, which weaves them into our present mental experience. Conversely, when we seek the same outcome without including them in the spell, they can filter out of our experience, sometimes entirely. For example, a protection spell needn't be framed as "I'm protected from [specific person]." It can be equally effective, if not more so, as "I'm protected." Per the earlier example about shielding versus binding, we can frequently add energy to a protection or peace-promoting spell without even thinking of the other person. For a binding to be as powerful, we'd need to give it comparable attention, which would greatly amplify the presence of the other in our consciousness. That said, if a person or organization is harming a number of people and we feel we must address the matter with magic, a binding spell might be more effective than a protection spell (i.e., binding one person takes less energy than protecting a thousand). Magical ethics, like life, isn't black and white.

Before performing magic, it's responsible to consider our motivation behind a working, how the working aligns with our ethics and greater life intentions, and whether we're willing to accept the potential karma of the working. We can also ask ourselves if what we intend to do is likely to foster our awareness of the divine, which is a helpful general practice for inner alchemy. Otherwise, since we don't all share Arjuna's good fortune of having a deity literally telling us what's beneficial for our spiritual growth, I recommend using divination to gain insight into a working's potential impact—for example, by using tarot to get a feel for how what we seek relates to our life paths. Maybe what we want isn't in our best interest, which divination helps us realize, and why. With this clarity, we might decide to abandon a working or consider it in greater depth.

Magical Technology

"Magic evolves, just as does every art and science…
as our understanding changes, our technology and practice changes and evolves."
—CARL LLEWELLYN WESCHCKE

The fundamental act of magic is the spell. A spell is traditionally defined as being a word or combination of words or other formulas that are believed to have magical power. A more accurate and expansive definition is "an act intended to cause change via subtle means." There are many magical systems and methods for casting spells, and we're each free to explore to find ones that suit us. For example, let's say we want to manifest a job. A ceremonial magician may draw a traditionally derived sigil for this and summon the expansive energy of Jupiter. A witch may burn a green candle for abundance placed upon the Ace of Pentacles from tarot while incanting words that express this intention. A New Thought practitioner might recite an affirmative prayer to this end. A Conjure doctor may dress candles and create a mojo bag of roots, coins, and other elements that they then dedicate to this aim. A Hindu might pay a priest to perform a puja (ritual) to Lakshmi, the goddess of abundance.

If we consider the basic metaphysical principles we explored earlier, each example involves influencing the higher planes through aligning subtle energy with intent. Even though the way the higher planes are affected differs, the results need not. Competently performing each method mentioned above can lead to the desired outcome. These approaches have different internal effects though, which is important to consider when opting to work with a magical system. On the psychological level, practicing witchcraft can deepen our sense of being a witch, working with Laskhmi can cultivate devotion to her, etc. Some approaches will also likely resonate more with us than others, which is helpful to appreciate because well-fitting approaches generally yield better results.

Otherwise, it's beneficial to remain cognizant that magical technologies and systems are thought dependent. While they can have accumulated power and other benefits due to multiple practitioners working with them, like a fire that's been fed by many sources or a trail that's been paved, they were initially invented. Fallible human beings formulated and developed them with factors like reasoning, intuition, experimentation, and the occult knowledge of their time (there are rare exceptions to this, like rituals received in dreams). Even the storied Golden Dawn system was woven from preexisting elements that were created at some point, representing forces that transcend their symbolic depictions, like the metaphysical models shared earlier do. Along these lines, my experience is that there's ample room for innovation, creativity, and flexibility in manifestational magic. I've effectively combined ceremonial, New Thought, and witchcraft elements, and I see no reason not to experiment once we're magically proficient. Importantly, this recommendation holds less for the mystical practices we'll explore later, where persisting with set practices is critical for achieving necessary depth.

If you feel wedded to orthodoxy in magical work, I encourage you to research the traditions you're drawn to. For example, rather than just taking tarot symbolism as immutable, explore where contemporary tarot symbolism originated. Pulling back the curtain like this can liberate us from falling into unnecessary, unwarranted occult dogmatism, and it can also acquaint us with the richness of the elements we engage with that have deep roots. For instance, Sanskrit mantras are said to have a powerful effect on the subtle body, which was discovered (alongside many mantras themselves) by mystics over three thousand years ago who practiced at a level that's rarely seen today. Though these mantras are thought dependent in an ultimate sense, it's also possible that the vibrations produced by chanting them have an inherent reality effect. Declaring that mantras only work because we believe in them or others have funneled energy into them is irresponsible without investigating how they function at the subtle level. In other cases, something may be in use that someone essentially just thought up, and there's little reason not to tinker with it. Like with other technologies, as we understand how magical systems work, which comes with learning and experience, we can develop them further or use this knowledge to create something new. We'll explore many of the basics of this learning in the following sections (beyond the basics we've already covered).

When discussing magical systems, it's important to address the topic of cultural appropriation. Cultural appropriation occurs when a person from one culture adopts a custom, practice, or concept from another in an offensive or otherwise disrespectful manner. Usually, this definition includes that the person appropriating is from a more dominant or oppressing culture. For example, a white American fashion designer who creates a clothing line featuring kente cloth, a traditional fabric from Ghana, is likely culturally appropriating. Whether the use of something constitutes appropriation can only be decided by people whose culture it comes from.

In the 1990s, when I was a young witch, cultural appropriation wasn't a widespread concern in occultism. Many of us leaned more toward postmodern concepts of culture, with some of us practicing chaos magic, which centers upon the premise "Nothing is true, everything is permissible." This concept means, in essence, that magical and religious systems are largely mental constructs that lack inherent reality, so why not do what we want with them? If I feel like performing a Hermetic ritual with the I Ching, who cares? Aren't occultists supposed to move beyond cultural conventions, borders, dogmas, and traditions? The times were so different then that many of us actually saw incorporating elements and deities from diverse cultures into Pagan ritual as inclusive and welcoming.

While these questions were valid to ask, there was more to the picture than this. Traditions and systems can have value beyond what meets the eye of a philosophizing intellect, and magical elements can too, as in the example above about Sanskrit mantras. Additionally, some people did care, a lot. Many people cherish their cultures, and it can be belittling, offensive, and oppressive to take what's sacred to someone and use it in a manner that they deem inappropriate. For many, contemporary cultural appropriation continues a long history of having their cultural elements taken while they suffer under the weight of oppression. This oppression is often unacknowledged or unaddressed by the appropriating group, which can make the appropriation like salting a wound. The postmodern notion that culture is more art than identity has also lost much of whatever popularity it held. That said, many people find a gray area within this topic when it comes to metaphysical matters. For example, if a Wiccan falls in love with Kali, who's to say that Kali didn't inspire that or minds being addressed via Wiccan ritual? Can anything metaphysical belong to one group of people? Since most people agree that religious conversion is not appropriative, where do we draw the line? As a Jew, I've felt uncomfortable at times with the Kabbalah boom among non-Jews, but I also respect and appreciate those of them who are sincere.

Where I've landed with this is that there's a critical distinction between public and private practice. What I believe and do in my home is my business, but what I practice publicly and spend money on involves others. Because I believe people deserve to have what's sacred to them honored (assuming those things aren't harming others) and I don't want to foster oppression, I strive not to culturally appropriate. If I feel drawn to another culture's metaphysical systems or elements, I may study and work with them privately, but that will usually be it unless there's a public context I'm welcome to participate in that honors their origin. That said, most explorations I've seen of this topic affirm that there's a difference between cultural appropriation and reverentially sharing something we learned that comes from another culture, provided we don't speak over or exploit people of that culture and ideally, learn it from them. This is my intention with Yoga, which appears at various moments in this book. I studied Yoga with an Indian spiritual teacher and in the order I trained with (where it's traditionally integrated with Hermeticism). It's been part of my daily life for over fifteen years and is sacred to me, and I share it accordingly. Ultimately, there isn't always a clear right and wrong in this area, and staying mindful of it is crucial if we want to practice magic in a way that honors others.

FUNDAMENTALS OF RITUAL

*"When we [perform ritual], consciousness, subconsciousness,
and superconsciousness are brought into alignment,
and there is a straight run through of cosmic force."*
—DION FORTUNE

In this system, we make magic part of our day-to-day life through performing High Magic rituals each day. We also approach rituals and spells in essentially the same manner, so even though we won't explore ritual practice until part two, it's important to review the aspects of ritual practice that apply to spellwork now.

A ritual is a ceremony in which a set of words and actions are performed in a given order. Common rituals include weddings, funerals, and graduations. Rituals like these connect us with the tides and themes of life. They bring us to a different vantage point than our status quo, which can help us gain insights into our lives that are difficult to realize otherwise.

Ritual is defined differently in magic, though magical rituals also provide the benefits listed above. Although they may be improvised, magical rituals generally involve performing words and actions in a given order with specific intent, which includes mental and emotional components (from here on, when I use the word "ritual," I mean magical ritual). When we perform rituals and spells, we become as present as we can and align our levels of being toward particular aims through attentively executing the designated thoughts, words, actions, etc. This orients our psychic emanation to these intentions, and the harmony between our levels of being amplifies it.

To unite our levels of being toward particular aims, we must concentrate, which we do by harnessing emotion. In *The One Year Manual: Twelve Steps to Spiritual Enlightenment*, Israel Regardie wrote that "emotion induces concentration." We all know this to some degree from our day-to-day lives. For example, when we're passionate about something or freshly in love, we can't help but focus on the subject in question. Conversely, when we have no emotional investment in something, it may as well not exist for us. Our degree of concentration and emotion hugely affects the flow of energy in our subtle body, as well as the amount of it (many people conceptualize emotion as "e-motion," energy in motion). Most of us have experienced the psychological dimensions of this when feeling like we could level a building while angry or ecstatically fantasizing about sex. Consequently, learning how to raise energy and induce concentration through emotion is critical to effective magical practice.

To do this, we emotionally connect with the purpose, significance, and content of a ritual or spell, like how we would with a compelling song, poem, or theatrical piece. As we summon this emotion, we practice experiencing it in a refined, focused manner, like what a champion athlete does during competition. Though we may involve grand swells of passion and ecstasy in magic, which some traditions emphasize, that is subsequent to this development, which helps us become skilled at concentrating and steadily guiding energy. When we combine this type of concentrating emotion with a firm belief in magic and sustained thought connected with what we intend, our magic soars.

Practicing magic yields many benefits beyond manifesting intentions. On the psychological level, unless we were raised with magic, practicing it is countercultural and represents a huge break from our status quo. Who stops what they're doing to banish negative astral influences and hold court with occult forces? Consequently, ritual and spellwork can help liberate us from unhealthy cultural conditioning by challenging some of the thought-dependent realities we grew up with. Rituals and spells seeming unusual, odd, or even ridiculous to us is part of what makes them powerful, psychologically speaking. They help us weaken the notion that we must exist within certain socially sanctioned parameters because we're repeatedly diverging from those parameters. They also help us experience firsthand that we can shift our perception of reality through altering our thoughts, words, and actions (because as we practice magic consistently, our reality shifts). Daily High Magic practice in particular provides us with a vantage point for experiencing that much of our reality is socially constructed.

Because rituals and spells diverge from our status quo, they stick out in our mind as contrasted with our day-to-day activities. This augments their psychic power, and the sense of occasion and import in spellwork is one reason spells are more effective in manifesting than casually thinking about intentions. Carving out special time to directly ask for something we want, often with vivid implements and ornaments, yields a greater energetic heft than our day-to-day thoughts have. The heightened concentration we use during spells, as contrasted with our standard thought processes, further increases this potency.

In my experience, little can teach us how to perceive and harness subtle energy faster than rituals and spells, provided we perform them attentively while paying attention to how we feel and imagining the energy is there. With dutiful practice, our subtle senses will develop over time. Once we can perceive subtle energy, we're more effective not only in our magic, but also in meditation because, for example, it's easier to meditate on a chakra when we can feel it. Ritual and spellwork creates a bridge space between the physical and higher planes, which can be felt as our ability to perceive energy grows.

FOUNDATIONAL SUPPORTS FOR PERFORMING EFFECTIVE MAGIC

"Be humble for you are made of earth. Be noble for you are made of stars."
—SERBIAN PROVERB

To perform magic effectively, there are some additional techniques and concepts I know that are helpful to learn and bear in mind. The first is to practice with as much sincerity as possible. By practicing magic, you've chosen to run your fingers through the river of creation and connect with the universal life force, which is a remarkable, magnificent undertaking! Feel the profundity of this, reverence for the divine, and awe as best you can, without forcefulness. Doing that automatically fosters sincerity. As our practice deepens, these feelings do too.

Relatedly, another critical piece is to always *try your best*, which is a tenet of the Little Work. This applies in and out of magical practice. When we try our best, we can rest with the peace of knowing we did all we could in a given situation. In magic, this means giving our all to our rituals and spells in the moment. Since rituals and spells are often under ten minutes long, this is a reasonable amount of time for us to strengthen the muscles of attentiveness and presence (and generally speaking, being attentive with what we're doing and present is what trying our best means). The ability we develop in magic to flip a mental switch and give our all will benefit us in many life areas, including work and relationships. Doing our best also feels good and increases the likelihood that our undertakings will succeed, magically and otherwise, and when they don't, it isn't for want of trying.

As we practice trying our best, it's important not to criticize ourselves when we don't perform optimally. Our best is relative to where we are in a given moment, which can fluctuate. One part of the Little Work system is training ourselves to perform at our optimal level, and another is developing the compassion for ourselves to accept whatever that is in the moment. It's OK if our magical work isn't always at our peak levels of focus or enthusiasm. The important thing is that we tried our best, and when we make a habit of doing that, the best we can bring to each moment increases over time.

Another important matter for performing effective magic is establishing a supportive ritual attitude. Though rituals and spells can feature diverse words, visualizations, gestures, etc., the baseline ritual attitude we cultivate for them in this system is the same. This is an attitude of assurance in our ability and power, coupled with reverence and humility, alongside some detachment from the results of our magic. Clinging to results often has fear in it that can sabotage our outcomes by warping our psychic emanation. Fixating too much on results also takes us out of the present moment, which is where our magic is the strongest. The aim with this ritual attitude is to become like a surgeon who keeps concerns about the results they seek out of their mind to facilitate focusing entirely on what they're doing.

We also enter a semi-trance state during magical work, which is another facet of this ritual attitude. Focusing on the present moment, quieting our mind, and relaxing naturally evokes this state. There's a slightly hypnotic quality to it, which makes us abler to influence our subconscious mind. This state parallels the one we enter during meditation, and studies on meditation have demonstrated that our brain waves shift during it, particularly with experienced practitioners, which likely also happens here.[3] The more we practice magic, the more readily we can enter this state at will and the more alert we become within it. This state is higher in vibration than our day-to-day mental state, and thus closer to the subtle levels. Consequently, it's often where we begin perceiving subtle energy.

3. Cahn, Rael B., and John Polich. "Meditation States and Traits: EEG, ERP, and Neuroimaging Studies." *Psychological Bulletin*, Volume 132 (2006).

Figure 3: Magician and High Priestess Cards from the Rider-Waite-Smith Tarot

This ritual attitude is embodied in the Magician and High Priestess from tarot, which are archetypes, and ritual and spellwork is often archetypal. In Jungian psychology, archetypes are universal, essential elements of the human experience that appear throughout the world in various forms. They can be events (e.g., birth, death, initiation, marriage), motifs (the creation, the apocalypse), figures (the Mother as Gaia and Parvati, the Hero as Hercules, Hanuman, and Superman), and beyond. The archetypal dimension is where myth touches our lives. When we enter archetypal consciousness during magic, we're no longer simply individuals. We assume the mantle of the Magician and High Priestess too. In High Magic, setting aside thoughts about ourselves to focus on the visualizations and additional elements of a ritual fosters our ability to enter archetypal consciousness. As our consciousness raises, it becomes increasingly archetypal in general, making our alchemical journey and life feel accordingly profound.

Assuming the role of the Magician and High Priestess day after day makes these archetypes more pronounced in our psyche, which yields practical benefits. For example, we become able to embody the Magician's self-assurance on command, which can aid us in doing inner or outer work that scares us, like starting a new business or exploring our shadow. The shadow is the internal region where things about ourselves or our lives that we generally avoid or deny often dwell, like shame, guilt, and trauma.

When assuming this ritual attitude, it's essential to appreciate the Magician and High Priestess's humility and mirror it. If we consider how the tarot is usually situated upon the Tree of Life, this humility becomes apparent. Aside from the Fool, which represents the divine innocence evident in children (in this context), the Magician and High Priestess are the only major cards that touch the highest manifestation of Godhead, Kether. Both exist above the abyss, which is the break in consciousness between our individual ego and what lies beyond it. We can only cross the abyss by surrendering our ego. The Magician and High Priestess, having done this to reach Kether, are archetypal enlightened beings. They're models of the accomplished Great Work and guides on the path to enlightenment, demonstrating how to be utterly powerful, humble, and of service while living in harmony with natural law.

Understanding this at the beginning of magical work helps us sidestep the pitfalls of hubris and becoming drunk with power that many of our forebears have fallen into. We must become as strong as possible during inner alchemy, but this might is contextualized within humility. Performing magic with this understanding gradually raises our resting vibration, opening us to new spiritual vistas. In the Great Work, this marriage of strength and surrender, at the moment grace descends, moves us across the threshold of revelation.

The foil to the Magician and High Priestess in tarot is the Devil, which represents these pitfalls. Many have reclaimed the Devil archetype in accord with Pagan mythology, which isn't what's addressed here. This Devil is the part of us that lustfully disregards the deeper spiritual dimensions of the material and seeks to dominate whatever it can. Superficially, the Devil may seem more powerful than the Magician and High Priestess since he's adorned with baubles that represent success in many societies. The chains he uses to bind others also bind him, though, and when we operate as the Devil, we lock ourselves in lower states of consciousness. As we accumulate magical power and our desires begin manifesting, it's easy to lose our way in the consciousness of the Devil, even to a subtle degree. Consequently, knowing about this potential pitfall and that we can sidestep it by cultivating a healthy ritual attitude is critical when beginning magical practice.

Figure 4: The Devil Card from the Rider-Waite-Smith Tarot

Another helpful technique for trying to avoid this trap is bowing at the beginning and end of magical practice. This gesture symbolizes reverence for the higher, recognizing that even if we're a grand magus, we're still just a proton in the body of creation. It helps us accept our place in the natural order and greater whole and open to the part of us that's beyond the ego, which makes us powerful in a way we couldn't have imagined before.

Fundamentals of Spellcraft

"Magic is a convenient word for a whole collection of techniques,
all of which involve the mind."

—MARGOT ADLER

In the next few sections, we'll review the basics of creating effective spells. Earlier, I defined a spell as "an act intended to cause change via subtle means." All spells have intention behind them. We cast them because there's something we want to create or change. During a spell, we utilize intention to influence the higher planes and orient our psychic emanation with what we seek. The clarity of intention we bring to spells facilitates this and amplifies their psychic power.

Clarity of intention in spellwork is also powerful psychologically, and some of the greatest benefits of spellwork are psychological. When we declare that we want something, our mind takes note. We become more apt to notice things that relate to our intention. For example, after casting a financial prosperity spell, we're more likely to notice financial opportunities because our mind is primed to register them. We're also more apt to avail ourselves of these opportunities since we already determined that we want what they provide. A spell can increase our confidence in taking opportunities too. For instance, applying for a job feels easier if we believe it came to us because of a spell we cast. After casting a spell to bring us new love, we can become likelier to ask people out and recognize when others seem interested in us. Generally speaking, setting clear, attainable intentions and acting and thinking in support of them aligns psychological and metaphysical forces to facilitate their manifestation.

To rally subtle energy behind an intention during spellwork, we utilize tools like visualization and speech, though many others can be used too. A barebones spell is one where we: formulate an intention, quiet our mind, become present, visualize things related to this intention manifesting and/or speak affirmative words regarding it, align our feelings with this intention, and imagine that energy is flowing toward it. For instance, to manifest financial prosperity, we could imagine ourselves comfortably paying bills while saying, "I have the money I need," and feeling like that's true. If we feel sincere while doing that, this can be an effective spell.

When we visualize, we mold the clay of the astral plane, establishing thought forms that are invigorated by the energy of our sustained focus and strong emotion toward an intention. These thought forms can be images, abstract symbols, words, mini "movies" like the one mentioned above, etc. They become blueprints or guides for incoming manifestations, whether these manifestations are physical or solely in our consciousness. Repeated visualization of a thought form further energizes it, which can accelerate any manifestations it's tied to.

We can also create structures on the higher planes out of thought forms for purposes other than physical or psychological manifestation, like a temple we use during astral travel. We can fashion tools and conduits of subtle energy to use in our magic too. The Tree of Life is an example of this. As we build its image in our mind through visualization, study, and ritual, we gain access to a host of dimensions of consciousness and magical resources by virtue of it. Adepts who worked with it before us established many of these on the higher planes, and all thought forms become part of the Collective Unconscious, which is a psychic storehouse we can access. Much of this may sound abstract, and that's OK. It'll become more concrete while working with visualization consistently.

When using a direct approach in magic, like in the financial example above, it helps to imagine how we'd feel having attained the sought result—for instance, feeling the relief and security of financial prosperity. It's like if we can sincerely feel that the reality we envision already exists, it'll eventually manifest, provided it's attainable for us.

In addition to visualization, words are another key part of magical work. Words are so powerful that it's daunting to even attempt to explain why. Many of us have heard of "magic words," which is something of a misrepresentation. It's not so much that particular words are magical, although some may be, like Hebrew divine names and Sanskrit mantras, where a word's vibration is believed to have specific subtle effects. Rather, it's more that words are magical in general. We each live in a reality that's loaded with elements that only exist because they're consistently thought into being. Words are the atoms that form these elements, making and unmaking perception based on how they're assembled and projected onto inherent reality. Whenever we use words, there's always a thought-dependent reality we reinforce, reduce, develop, or create. We can dramatically influence our perception of reality through using language, creating something from nothing or fundamentally altering our experience of what's there. What's more magical than that?

Additionally, words are one of the primary tools we can use to focus and direct energy because of how they enable us to guide our thoughts and emotions. Most of us have experienced this with poems that take us to a certain place emotionally and mentally or with an idea we got excited about and then made happen. When assembled as thoughts, words can help us clarify, set, and sustain intentions. In spellcraft, we harness words by choosing ones that validate the changes in reality we seek. By speaking these words while feeling that they're true, which becomes easier with practice, our psychic emanation orients in support of the intentions they connect with. As thought forms, we can also use words to influence the higher planes and create there. Words symbolically connect with what they represent too, which we'll cover in the section on symbols.

When exploring the power of words, it's also important to consider the medium of sound. When we speak, we physically vibrate, and many spiritual traditions affirm that vibrating words in a manner that resonates within the physical body can affect our subtle body and the higher planes. For example, vibrating deity names, which is common in ceremonial magic, is said to tune our subtle body and consciousness to the frequency of these deities, which reverberates across the higher planes.

Everything in the universe vibrates, and vibration has powerful effects even at the physical level, given how singing can shatter glass or connect us with others. When we harness vibration with our voice, we interact with the constellations of vibrations around us and can powerfully affect our subtle body. My first experience with consistently vibrating words of power came during magic school. I was amazed by how doing this cleared and strengthened my aura and increased my sense of spiritual connectedness. When vibrating words in magic, experiment to find a resonant tone within you, which should feel somewhat tingly or rumbly in your body.

For magic to work, it's critical to believe we can manifest what we seek. Emanations of doubt or worry can overpower our emanations in support of an intention. If we feel doubtful about our ability to manifest something, it's important to work in a manner that sidesteps or mitigates this doubt. For example, if we feel anxious visualizing ourselves as financially comfortable, that's not a strong approach for us for manifesting financial prosperity. That direct type of magic is best used when we lack significant emotional resistance to manifesting something (e.g., a parking space). For matters where we feel considerable resistance, supports like symbols, candles, crystals, etc., can increase our confidence in our magic, helping us release or sidestep our resistance. The more confident we feel in our magic, the likelier it is to pan out. Our strongest spells will always be the ones we believe will work.

On Metaphysical Law

*"Electricity was a reality ... when Moses led
the children of Israel out of the land of Egypt.
This is true of all natural laws; they have always existed
but only when understood may they be used."*

—ERNEST HOLMES

To choose supports for our spells, it's beneficial to review metaphysical laws, which helps us understand how these supports work. Once we have a sense of the mechanics behind spellcraft, we can design effective spells. Throughout history, mystics have posited many metaphysical laws. The following laws, which are the Laws of Correspondence, Similarity, and Contact/Contagion, are widely used. My aim here remains to provide information that can apply in many magical settings without being unnecessarily complicated or prescriptive.

The Law of Correspondence refers to the interconnection between the planes of existence (i.e., "as above, so below"). This is where we find the concept we've already explored that energy moves up and down the planes in a manifestational cycle, as well as that the macrocosm is reflected in the microcosm (and vice versa). For example, planetary positions and relationships (above) play out in some manner at the societal level (below) and in our internal experience (below). The planets themselves are the "below" of another "above" too. Understanding how the planes interact and reflect each other, to whatever degree we can, can help us create effective spells. For example, if we want to manifest something that resonates with an astrological event, we can ride that wave. The energy of Venus conjunct Mars, for instance, can be used to start a new relationship cycle (a conjunction occurs when planets appear close to each other in the sky, which fuses their energy). Without our spell, this energy would still manifest in our lives (because below remains as above), but possibly in a very different manner, like feeling driven (Mars) to redecorate (Venus).

The next law is the Law of Similarity, which posits that when things resemble or relate to each other, they can affect each other. This law holds the concepts that like attracts (or begets) like and that an effect resembles its cause in some way. In herbal medicine, similarity historically appears in the notion that a plant that resembles an organ has healing properties related to that organ. The theory is that the harmony of nature (and between the planes of existence) will yield these types of relationships.

In spellcraft, many, if not most, conventional correspondences are based on similarity. For example, if we seek financial abundance, we might design a spell with:

+ A green candle, since green, as the most prevalent color in plant life, represents growth, fertility, etc. (Also, for Americans, money is green.)

+ The Empress card from tarot, which represents abundance by design.

+ A packet of grass seeds, since grass grows abundantly.

+ Honey that's the color of gold, "rich" in taste, and sticky, as if to adhere wealth to us.

Similarity indicates a resonance of frequency between things, like two different instruments playing the same note. Consequently, if we seek to shape subtle forces to manifest an intention (e.g., creating an astral "like" to beget a physical "like"), items that resonate with the intention's frequency can support this process. For example, since green and the Empress match the frequency of abundance, tuning in to them can orient our psychic emanation to match it too, which is like replicating a musical tone we hear others singing.

When we can find a literal or figurative connection between two things, the Law of Similarity links them, and we can then use this link in magic. Some of these connections, like an herb resembling the lungs, may have an inherent reality basis. Others are thought-dependent and can vary between cultures (e.g., in countries where money isn't green, another color may be used to represent it). Because of the subjective nature of the astral plane, similarities exist even when we alone believe they're there. The moment we draw a similarity, it's metaphysically legitimized. Consequently, there's ample room for creativity in magic. If we can find a way for something to resonate with our intentions, literally or figuratively, we can use it in magic, provided we feel the similarity is legitimate (e.g., a song that evokes a response in us that we believe will support a spell). We can also symbolically represent actions we want a spell to take, like tying a cord around a box to seal a matter shut or planting a seed so a spell will unfold organically. Working with something via the Law of Similarity is somewhat like featuring it in a poem. If it fits the metaphor, it fits the magic.

The last law is the Law of Contact or Contagion. This law posits that physical contact between things forges an abiding connection that can be used for metaphysical ends. For example, when someone owns a ring or even uses a fork once, these items become connected to that person. Any part of their body (e.g., a lock of hair) is connected to them too. Dirt from a business's location is connected to that business, etc. We can use these items in many metaphysical ways. For instance, someone might ask us to help them manifest a new relationship, and their personal item can help us root them within the spell. Many also find that an object a person contacted holds information about that person, which can be received psychically.

All magical practitioners don't necessarily believe in these laws or believe in them the same way. This is an area where we can defer to personal experience. For example, some people believe the depth of contact between a person and an object affects the strength of its connection to that person, while others don't. There's also no universal agreement on whether these connections can be severed or how long they last for. In my experience, while having a personal item may make connecting with an individual easier, it's not necessary. A photo of a person or anything that enables us to tune to their frequency can connect us with them. The Law of Contact was formulated well before the invention of the personal camera, much less social media.

Magic and the Subconscious Mind

"The subconscious is our direct link to the Astral Plane."
—DONALD MICHAEL KRAIG

On the psychological and metaphysical levels, magic involves working with the subconscious mind. Consequently, learning about the subconscious mind and how it functions is helpful for effectively practicing magic. There are many models of how the subconscious operates that we can pursue if interested (e.g., Freudian, the triune brain, Kabbalistic, etc.). Here, I present the barebones of what I think is essential for effective alchemical practice.

The subconscious is the part of our mind that operates outside of our conscious awareness. While our conscious mind is home to our will, decision-making, and conscious thought processes, our subconscious manages the rest of our lives. This includes our bodily and psychological processes that occur without us thinking of them, like digestion. The subconscious is also the storehouse of our routines, behavioral patterns, and long-term memories (even ones we don't consciously remember). It performs the unseen work of living.

Earlier, we explored some other aspects of the subconscious mind, including the notion that it projects thought-dependent realities onto inherent reality for us. Our subconscious constantly interprets the stimuli around us, fitting it into preexisting frameworks to help us live without having to stop and think about everything we do. Too much sensory information comes at us in any moment for us to process it all, so our subconscious filters in what it thinks is relevant to us and instantly interprets that. An upside of this system is that we can readily function in complex situations, like driving. A downside is that it inclines us toward bias, like when our subconscious latches onto a belief like "Men are scary" and shapes our perceptions accordingly.

The subconscious holds our core beliefs about ourselves and life. As we explored earlier, we may be unaware of some of these if they're not mirrored in our conscious mind, yet they profoundly impact our perceptions and experiences. These are beliefs like "Nothing ever works out for me," "People are usually trustworthy," and "I'll never measure up." They're like lenses we see reality through that frame it in a certain light, likely sitting at the root of thousands of our thoughts, beliefs, and choices. On an emotional level, they're what we "really" believe is true, and they guide many of our emotional reactions accordingly. For example, if I subconsciously believe men are scary, yet I consciously believe that's an unfair stereotype, my subconscious belief will steer my perceptions more when I meet a man (i.e., by manifesting a feeling of fear). Given how powerful these core beliefs are, they compose a substantial part of our psychic emanation.

When we have psychological trauma, it burrows into our subconscious and can generate pessimistic subconscious beliefs, sometimes ones we're oblivious to. After a wounding event passes, this trauma may only enter our awareness when circumstances evoke it, yet it can still influence our day-to-day perceptions. By confirmation bias, for example, someone who was constantly told they'll "never amount to anything" can subconsciously find evidence that validates this sentiment while rejecting what doesn't, thereby deepening in this belief over time. As this belief strengthens, they'll increasingly manifest evidence of it too. It becomes a self-fulfilling prophecy. Consequently, we seek to reach the subconscious during magical work because if we can shift its beliefs about reality, our experience of reality and the manifestations that come from those beliefs will change accordingly (e.g., by moving from "Nothing ever works out for me" to "Some things work out for me"). This can be like a house of cards tumbling down within our reality for the better.

To alter the content of our subconscious, we feed it thoughts we want our reality to mirror, which we'll focus on more in part two. The subconscious always listens to us and absorbs information from our environment, and it doesn't think independently or discriminate with what it's told. Consequently, a key part of magical work is to think and speak with language that supports our intentions and to surround ourselves with influences that do too. This is another reason why the words we choose in magic are critical. The subconscious hears us in a literal manner. If we say one thing and mean something else, it'll absorb what we said. For example, if we want to manifest new love and say, "I'm ready for love," our subconscious hears that we're ready for love, not that love is imminent, which is what it and our emanation then match. We could be ready for love yet remain single for the next fifty years! "I'm ready for a healthy romantic relationship and ask that it begin soon" actually captures our intention.

States of trance and deep relaxation, like the semi-trance state we use during rituals and spells, are like bridges between the conscious and subconscious that enable us to reach the subconscious more easily. In a trance state, our subconscious absorbs what we think about more deeply than it does with our day-to-day thoughts, if for no reason other than that we're quiet and listening to ourselves attentively. Recording ourselves reciting specific intentions and playing that while falling asleep or in a state of deep relaxation can powerfully aid in transforming our subconscious beliefs. We can also shift the subconscious through working with symbols, which we'll explore in the next section.

Some life functions, like breathing, can be performed consciously or unconsciously. Our psychic emanation is one of these. Until we learn to direct subtle energy, our psychic emanation is curated solely by our subconscious mind, and even once we can, it, like breathing, remains mostly under the subconscious's governance. This is another reason the subconscious is so integral in magic. Though our conscious mind sets intentions, our subconscious does much of the heavy lifting of seeing them through, and the subconscious, like our psychic emanation, is always functioning.

When we set our psychic emanation a particular way during a spell, that configuration can hold for a significant period of time, especially if we reinforce it with supportive thoughts and actions. These thoughts needn't be about the spell or our intentions, just supportive of them. For example, thoughts like "I welcome opportunities," "I'm grateful for what I have," "Things generally work out for me," and "I rise to challenges" create a supportive psychic environment for love and prosperity spells. We needn't even consciously think thoughts like these as long as our general attitude reflects them, which we'll learn how to do in part two. Once we can feel our psychic emanation and how it's influenced by magical practice, thoughts, emotions, etc., and align our levels of being, we can keep it in a supportive state, which tremendously amplifies our magic. Doing this consistently establishes a psychological and metaphysical inertia that fosters our intentions, which our subconscious maintains when we're not focused on alignment. This holds unless we expose ourselves to a nullifying influence (e.g., a song that plummets us into feeling hopeless).

During inner alchemy, many of us discover that our subconscious is littered with beliefs that don't support our well-being or intentions. This is normal. We've likely heard unsupportive statements about ourselves, life, or the world since childhood. When we're young, it's difficult not to internalize these (a common conditioned belief that's relevant to this book is the notion that magic isn't real). Even as our brains mature and we start thinking more independently, our newfound independence resides in the consensus realities we were reared in. Thinking outside the box is normal for young people, but throwing it away? That's extraordinarily rare.

Thankfully, we can use magic, meditation, and other alchemical practices to liberate ourselves from the thought-dependent realities of others. There's a grand frontier within each individual consciousness upon which to paint reality. Through practicing inner alchemy, we can clear external influences off of ours and paint what we want on it.

On Symbols

"By names and images are all powers awakened and reawakened."
—FROM THE GOLDEN DAWN NEOPHYTE RITUAL

Symbols are one of the most common and effective implements in magic. Conventionally, a symbol is defined as being something that represents or suggests something else. For example, a plus sign represents addition, the word "fear" represents fear, a company's logo represents it in sum, etc. Symbols help us communicate, literally and figuratively. They can span a spectrum from being concrete and straightforward, like the word "chair," to complex and abstract, representing many things and with levels of meaning. For instance, the pentagram symbolizes a variety of concepts and functions (e.g., protection, strength, the macrocosm represented in the microcosm, the harmony between the four elements and spirit). A symbol can evoke its complex significance in an instant.

Figure 5: Pentagram

The pentagram is also a good example of how a symbol's meaning can vary and how what we believe about symbols can profoundly influence the way they affect us. In magic, the pentagram is a holy, powerful symbol. Outside of magic, many people believe it's evil and even experience distress upon seeing one.

Per the Law of Similarity, what we can represent, we can connect and work with. When we suggest something with a symbol, it links us to that thing. This is highly useful in magic, as is the ability of symbols to encapsulate complexity within a simple form. A single symbol can represent multiple intentions and magical forces (like the pentagram does), and using it focuses and funnels subtle energy toward these intentions while building them in our psyche. We don't even have to think about these intentions when we see the symbol for this to happen. Knowing they're there is enough, and as with other thought forms, focusing on the symbol will increase its power.

Pictorial symbols that are imbued with magical power are called "sigils." There are involved systems for creating sigils, but sigils can also be simply made—for example, by dedicating an astrological symbol to an intention that we feel it supports or even creating an original figure that we feel resonates with an intention.

A powerful aspect of symbols is that we can use them to represent and connect with abstract, archetypal, and religious things that may be difficult to reach otherwise. For example, a deity name or image can help us connect with the divine. Visualizing the astrological symbol for Neptune can evoke the planet's visionary qualities within us or link us with the deity Neptune. Assuming the god form of Isis, which is a symbolic act, connects us with Isis on the higher planes and the part of our psyche that corresponds to Isis.

When we use symbols that others have worked with, we access some of the power they poured into them. This is part of the value of using traditional symbols, rituals, and spells. For example, if we perform the Lesser Banishing Ritual of the Pentagram (LBRP), a Golden Dawn ritual that's widespread in occultism, we gain a boost from the practitioners who performed it before us, like catching a wind with our sails. Additionally, whatever personal meaning we have about a shared symbol further shapes its power for us. We can also isolate ourselves from a symbol's power if we believe it's powerless over us, regardless of how charged it is. A shared symbol doesn't only have power because we believe it does, but by not believing in it, we can evict its power from our lives.

A downside of working with symbols and rituals that others have used is that we can become linked to these practitioners' issues. This effect isn't usually that significant if we utilize a stray symbol or so, but when we use a critical mass of symbols or rituals from a system, we join that system's energetic current and group consciousness, which is called an "egregore." This can bring its own particular set of challenges, benefits, and experiences.

Symbols enable us to work with our psyche in a different manner than day-to-day thoughts do. For example, if we have psychological trauma that we've addressed in psychotherapy yet are struggling to heal, we can incorporate symbols into our healing process. We could visualize ourselves within a golden lotus daily, paint the astrological glyph of Cancer on our bathroom mirror, or imagine offering our painful memories to the alchemist's forge. The subconscious is fluent in the language of symbols, as many of us know from dreams, and since trauma gets stored in the subconscious, communicating with it via visualization and symbols can be quite powerful. Sometimes we're unable to find a route to the healing or changes we seek, but our subconscious can (or our psychic emanation can draw one to us). Symbols can help us enlist our subconscious's assistance with these intentions.

One of the greatest benefits I've found in using symbols is that they give us a way to support an intention without evoking the story we have attached to it. For example, let's say we want to banish a condition from our lives. By speaking and thinking about this condition while casting banishing spells and worrying afterward about it not leaving us, we can feed it energy. Not to mention that if we get worked up about it, we'll contort our psychic emanation into an unsupportive state. In contrast, by visualizing a banishing pentagram whenever the subject crosses our mind, we can banish it without wading into the mud of our story about it. Consequently, symbols can be extremely useful in magic when we have a significant emotional investment in an outcome. They don't tend to evoke doubt or fear the way an affirmation like "I'm safe from harm" might, yet they can be equally effective in creating change.

Additional Considerations for Creating Effective Spells

"Prepare your mind to receive the best that life has to offer."
—ERNEST HOLMES

Before getting to the nitty-gritty of spell design, it's useful to review some additional considerations for creating effective spells. One is to mind what we've already learned and use language that precisely articulates any changes we seek (e.g., affirming "I am healed" rather than "I will be healed"). The tricky piece here is if we don't believe we're healed, our contrary emotional reaction to our voiced intention can derail the spell.

The internal conflict that arises when we don't believe what we affirm is called "cognitive dissonance," which is the psychological discomfort of holding contradictory beliefs. When we experience cognitive dissonance in magic, the stronger belief will usually win out, as it's the one our subconscious mind currently aligns with. We can generally tell what side our subconscious is on by how we feel as we approach a working. We may not even know we hold an unsupportive subconscious belief until we try to affirm something like "I'm open to love" and feel a knot of "yeah, right" in our stomach. A workaround for this is to incorporate time into a spell to make the result feel more realistic to us. This way, we account for the subconscious's literality and the need to believe in our magic. For instance, in a spell to mend a broken heart, we can incant something like:

May I experience what I must to heal my heart.
I submit myself to this willingly,
trusting that if this spell aligns with the highest good,
my heart will be healed by autumn.

We can also affirm that we trust in divine timing (e.g., "my heart will heal when the time is right").

If we feel unsure about an outcome but confident in our magic's speed, a workaround could be:

The path before me is uncertain.
With this spell, I pull the curtain.
It will soon place the way before me,
to heal my heart and reassure me.

Many magical practitioners seal their workings with the phrase "so mote it be" or "and so it is" to validate that the manifestational course is set. We can also opt not to use words in spells, focusing purely on visualization, symbols, etc. As a reminder, when practicing Low Magic, including a recognition that we only want manifestations to come if they align with the highest good is critical because of our aim of inner alchemy. Working otherwise runs counter to the alchemical process.

Many people believe that spells should always rhyme. I've experienced solid results with and without rhyme, though there are some potential benefits to using rhyme. One is that by sticking out from day-to-day speech, rhyming adds to a spell's sense of occasion. The rhythm of rhyme can also help evoke the semi-trance state we've explored. Otherwise, poetic language, whether rhyming or not, can arouse a spell's emotional component. Poetry also speaks to the head and heart, and poetic language can aid us in uniting them toward an objective. All of this helps a spell reverberate within our being and tune our psychic emanation to the spell's aims.

Additionally, many practitioners believe that all magical work should begin with alignment with the divine. A popular maxim in ceremonial magic is "the highest is always invoked first." In practice, this can mean starting magical work with prayer, vibrating deity names, etc. Affirmative prayer, which is the equivalent to spells in the New Thought movement, begins with aligning with the divine through affirming something like:

All That Is manifests from a Divine Unity, which is whole and perfect.
This Source operates by Love, and its power is infinite and eternal.

I am a part of this Source, which always supports me with its creative powers.
By virtue of this truth, miraculous manifestations are available to me.

After this, practitioners tie in specifics about what they want to manifest, like:

I know a magnificent job has manifested for me.
I trust that it will become visible to me soon.

Whether or not this type of aesthetic appeals to us, there's palpable benefit in aligning with the divine during magical work, and we can do that in a form that suits our tastes. The LBRP, for example, achieves a similar alignment. My experience is that consistently tuning to the divine increases our general sense of connectedness with it, which is an aim of inner alchemy.

When we set intentions in magic, it's important to specify what form we want them to manifest in. This helps us tune our psychic emanation precisely, increasing the likelihood that manifestations will match our intentions. It's common, for example, to intend for something like a new job and then manifest job ads, so if we want to manifest an actual job, specifying that helps. This doesn't mean we must overtly say something like "I want to manifest a job, not a spam email offering me one," but it does mean holding a clear vision of what we seek.

That said, it's also beneficial to let higher forces deliver us the best match to our desire (e.g., "I want a new job, and I'm somewhat flexible regarding what it is"). There are options available to us that we don't know about or may have misunderstood or underestimated. These can be far better for us than what we specify from our limited perspective. As we allow our energy to follow the path of least resistance, which is what energy does when left to its own devices, we may find ourselves pleasantly surprised by the outcome.

Additionally, identifying any result we explicitly don't want from a spell is also helpful so that our magic doesn't manifest it. For instance, we may want a better-paying job but not one in the corporate world. If we don't specify this, we could manifest a corporate job because that's where the path of least resistance led.

Another important consideration when designing spells is personal growth and psychological healing. Aside from the fact that inner alchemy generally requires both of these things, when we seek something we aren't ready to have, we can manifest it and then lose it. Many lottery winners lose their winnings within a few years because they didn't develop the financial management skills to stay wealthy. Many dieters lose large amounts of weight and gain it back because they didn't work through the issues that contributed to them being overweight.

Consequently, it can be helpful to overtly weave personal growth and healing into spells. If we go to cast a love spell and notice that part of us is terrified, we've identified an area within ourselves that needs care and possibly healing, which we'll learn to address in part two. If we subsequently realize our fear relates to lacking healthy relationship skills, we can place an intention to develop them into our spell. This will prime us to notice opportunities for developing these skills and make us likelier to seize those opportunities. It may also bring more of these opportunities to us (e.g., we might "randomly" encounter a self-help book about the skills we seek).

One of the main reasons for undertaking the Little Work is that our personal issues, developmental problems, and psychological trauma can derail what we seek for ourselves. We can learn how to deal with this though and clear a path for manifesting our intentions, provided they're attainable for us. When we turn to magic for aid in becoming healthier, it's a powerful and willing ally. To that end, the most satisfying changes in my life that have come from magic are the alchemical ones within myself. Physical plane manifestations pale in comparison for me with healing from psychological trauma and the serenity of experiencing that we're irrevocably divine.

The What, Why, How, Who, Where, and When of Spellcraft

"Proper preparation is the basic rule for every phase of the magical arts."
—ISRAEL REGARDIE

Having explored the basics of magical practice, we can now move on to spell creation. When designing a spell, it's useful to consider the what, why, how, who, where, and when of it. The "what" is the intention behind a spell. What outcome do we seek? The "why" is our motivation for casting a spell. To facilitate inner alchemy, we dig deep with our whys. Saying "I want this to change because I don't like it" is insufficient. What about it don't we like? Why is that important to us? How does this connect with our alchemical process? Another why question is "Why am I using magic rather than just action?"

Next, we consider the "how." In light of our answers to "why," how do we want to do this? Does it make sense to use a direct approach or a more symbolic one? A combination of these? Will we cast a spell once or over a period of time, thus funneling more energy to it? Will we use implements? Prewritten language? Particular gestures? If so, why? In magic, every word, thought, movement, and implement should contribute something to the working. This helps us align our levels of being with a spell's intention and tune our psychic emanation to the frequency of the sought change.

In terms of "who," we consider if we'll partner with others for a spell, like other practitioners, spirits, angels, deities, etc. If we opt to collaborate, how and to what end? Partnering with others isn't required in magic, but it can significantly augment a working. One reason for this is that sharing magical work can help us feel capable of manifesting changes we doubt we could manifest alone. For example, believing that working with a spirit guide can make a manifestation happen will mitigate any vibrations of doubt in our psychic emanation about the manifestation (not to mention the aid that can actually come from the guide).

Finally, we consider where and when. "Where" is usually straightforward: where's a safe, private place to perform a given spell? We can also consider if performing a spell in a particular setting would be beneficial (e.g., in nature). If a spell involves using symbols outside of the formal casting, where will we place them? Do we intend to leave any supplies out (e.g., a candle that we light for some time each day)? If so, where can we safely put them?

For "when," we address practicalities, like "When do I have time to do this?" We can also ask if this is more of a day or night spell. When considering that, remember how figurative the Law of Similarity can be. For example, a spell to illuminate something or that requires a vast amount of energy (like what the sun provides) makes sense to perform during the day.

Many practitioners also consider astrological factors when designing spells. Transits, which are the movements of the planets and their resulting astrological effects, always occur and can be beneficially incorporated into magic. For instance, the sun boosts magic related to pragmatic goals when it's in Capricorn. It spends about a month in each sign and its position in the zodiac is worth minding. Additionally, the moon is said to have the strongest astrological impact on subtle energies, and we can time our magic to benefit from its zodiacal positions too—for example, by casting a healing spell when the moon is in Cancer. The moon moves through the zodiac every twenty-eight days, spending about two-and-a-half days in a sign.

When working with the moon, we can also utilize the Law of Similarity. For instance, the waxing/increasing moon traditionally suits spells related to growing, building, connecting, etc. The waning/decreasing moon fits spells to diminish, undo, release, etc. Full moons suit magic related to culmination, completion, reaping results, etc., as well as illumination and revelation. New moons fit rebirth, new beginnings, initiating projects, catalyzing change, etc., as well as journeying into the shadow. There are also greater degrees to which we can work with the moon in magic, which I encourage you to research if you're interested (e.g., first quarter, third quarter, dark moon, etc.).

Beyond the sun and moon's zodiacal positions, considering additional astrological events can also be helpful, which we explored some earlier with the example of Venus conjunct Mars. Many of us have likely heard of Mercury retrograde, a transit that often results in effects like disrupted communications and computer malfunctions. Magic to launch a new business is best not performed during Mercury retrograde. Additionally, some ceremonial magicians work with the specific hours of the day that are associated with particular planets when seeking to harness those planets' energies. The days of the week are traditionally associated with planets too (e.g., Monday was once "Moon Day"). Some practitioners go as far as to generate astrology charts for discerning the most harmonious times for casting particular spells.

"When" can become an extremely complex consideration in magic. I think this is an area where using our judgement is best. I've worked effective magic with little concern for timing as well as with substantial attention to it. My experience is that most things we can create can be created at most times, but the degree of difficulty and support in this varies based on timing. For example, I can launch a business during Mercury retrograde, but that may be like building a house in a thunderstorm. Conversely, working with the astrology can be like placing a boat in a fast-moving river that does much of the work of ferrying it to a desired destination. One way to navigate astrology that's unsupportive of our intentions is to aim to work higher than the planetary level through aligning with the divine source, like what New Thought practitioners aspire to (e.g., "I'm an extension of the Divine Unity, the supreme power that transcends conditions…" etc.). This is like trying to fly above the clouds during a storm, though it must feel sincere to work and be supported by our general mindset. We can also usually modify spells to align with what's happening astrologically. For instance, if the moon is waxing and we're struggling with relationship toxicity, instead of banishing the toxicity, we can augment our boundaries.

CORRESPONDENCES AND ELEMENTS

"Theoretical perfection is not necessary for successful magickal work.
All you need to do is your best."

—DONALD MICHAEL KRAIG

This section contains correspondences we can utilize in magic. Many of the popular correspondences in contemporary magical literature stem from the Kabbalah of the original Golden Dawn and Thelema. In these systems and their immediate forebears, correspondences were often drawn via the Law of Similarity or meditative work. This includes the attributions of tarot cards and astrological figures to the Tree of Life. Other correspondences are more traditional, but all traditions began at some point and were invented or received by someone, so please don't take these correspondences as sacrosanct.

Relatedly, rather than just memorizing these lists, try to understand the correspondences. For instance, by design, the Empress from tarot corresponds with fertility and therefore the planet Venus. Venus also corresponds with beauty because Venus was the Roman goddess of beauty, so the astrological signs ruled by Venus, which are Taurus and Libra, correspond with beauty too, albeit in different ways.

Some of these correspondences predominantly make sense with an understanding of Hermetic Kabbalah. For example, Mars is linked with the number five (and consequently, the pentagram) because it's associated with the fifth sphere on the Tree of Life, Geburah, which is the sphere of severity. The pentagram's association with martial power may have originated with this correspondence (and the pentagram has signified various things in throughout history). Consequently, studying basic Hermetic Kabbalah could prove useful if you want to understand the correspondences that seem puzzling, but also bear in mind that many of these correspondences weren't set in stone. In *777*, Crowley's seminal work of Kabbalistic correspondences that's often referenced, he acknowledged that some of his correspondences didn't fit perfectly where he placed them. We're free to tweak correspondences when we can make a solid case for amending them.

Beyond using preestablished correspondences, it's also beneficial to discover our own. When you hold an amethyst, for example, what do you feel? When you look at the High Priestess from tarot, what arises in you? This is valuable information. Though some things have conventional and relatively set meanings, this doesn't necessarily invalidate our subjective interpretations. Many of the metaphysical properties of herbs and crystals that aren't evident given the Law of Similarity came from people's intuitions. In most cases, the strongest magical correspondences for us will be the ones we believe are there.

I designed the following lists for facility of use in creating spells. This is to get you started. I encourage you to research correspondences and add to these. The most efficient way I know to arrange this material is by element, since the classical elements and their astrological associations encapsulate the human experience. Where applicable, I've included the symbols that represent an item. Also, feel free to utilize relationships you see that aren't listed. For example, the Moon from tarot links Kabbalistically with Pisces in the Golden Dawn system, which is where it's placed in the following section, but clearly also with the moon itself and the sign it rules, Cancer.

Furthermore, even though a correspondence exists between two entities, we may not want to use one because of other meanings it has. Correspondence indicates similarity, not equality. For instance, the Tower corresponds with Mars, but if we're utilizing Mars for its assertiveness, better to pick a different symbol and avoid the Tower's potentially cataclysmic influence.

Additionally, crystals and plants have their own unique character and correspondences and uses beyond those listed below. When working with crystals and plants, I find benefit in developing an intimate relationship with them. We can do this by tuning in to their subtle energy, researching their uses, and interacting with them on the higher planes via trance work.

To use these lists to create spells, consider what you seek and how it fits with the elemental categories. Next, find the aim you intend within the lists (either with the raw element, its manifestation in a sign or planet, or involving a combination of these). Then select a correspondence within that domain. For example, a spell to locate something involves information, which is the province of air. In the air list, we see that Mercury is associated with information. Therefore, we can use the invoking hexagram of Mercury (shared below) and other Mercurial correspondences to help manifest this information.

Otherwise, here are some additional considerations to mind while using these lists: All signs correspond with their element's color in addition to their individual color. Planets aren't elemental since they can manifest in each sign, but they're linked with the signs they rule here for simplicity's sake. When signs share a planetary ruler, the planetary energy manifests differently based on each sign. For example, Venus gives Taurus an appreciation of creature comforts and sensuality while infusing Libra with an inclination toward relationships and refinement. Also, Pluto wasn't discovered until after the first wave of Hermetic Kabbalistic correspondences were created (and Uranus and Neptune weren't included in them). Many of Uranus, Neptune, and Pluto's correspondences are new or based on their retroactively assigned positions on the Tree of Life and in tarot (e.g., the Fool with Uranus). Because of conflicting attributions of these planets on the tree, I didn't include numbers for them. Also, in much of Western astrology, Pluto's still considered a planet. Additionally, all traditions don't agree on the attributions of magical tools, and there are many more tools than the four listed here (e.g., the bell, censer, cord, etc.).

ELEMENTAL CORRESPONDENCES
Air △

The intellect, the breath of life, the winds of change, the rational mind, discernment, inspiration, innovation, communication, genius

Alchemical Properties: Hot and moist/wet

Color: Yellow

Magical Tool: The dagger or sword

Tarot Card: Ace of Swords

Libra ♎

Air in its cardinal/raw and initiating state; artistic, balanced, considerate, creative, diplomatic, harmonious relationships, inspiration (artistic, intellectual), justice, peacemaking, refined, seeing all sides of an issue, social skills

Colors: Emerald green, yellow
Plant: Aloe
Crystals: Emerald, malachite, opal
Tarot Card: Justice
Ruling Planet: Venus

Aquarius ♒

Air in its fixed/stable state; creative problem-solving, genius, innovation, individualism, rebelliousness, revolution, unconventionality
Colors: Violet, yellow
Plant: Coconut
Crystals: Amethyst, aquamarine, moldavite
Tarot Card: The Star
Ruling Planet: Uranus

Gemini ♊

Air in its mutable/adaptable and flexible state; analysis, communication, curiosity, inquisitiveness, multitasking, quickness, versatility
Colors: Orange, yellow
Plant: Orchid
Crystals: Agate, alexandrite, pearl
Tarot Card: The Lovers
Ruling Planet: Mercury

Venus (Ruler of Libra and Taurus) ♀

Abundance, affection, art, beauty, fertility, friendship, harmony, love, luxury, relationships, sensuality, values
Colors: Green, pink
Number: Seven
Plants: Clover, elder, geranium, lilac, myrtle, rose
Polygon: Heptagram
Crystals: Emerald, jade, malachite, turquoise
Tarot Card: The Empress

Uranus ♅ or ⛢

Discoveries, genius, progress, reform, revolution, science, societal advancement, sudden changes, uniqueness

Colors: Violet, pale yellow

Plant: Aspen

Crystals: Aventurine, blue topaz, labradorite, quartz

Tarot Card: The Fool

Mercury (Ruler of Gemini and Virgo) ☿

Analysis, communication, computers, decision-making, knowledge, information, information processing, learning, local or short trips, mental strength, rationality, self-improvement

Colors: Orange, yellow

Number: Eight

Plants: Lavender, lemongrass, mint, vervain

Polygon: Octagram

Crystals: Agate, fire opal, opal, serpentine

Tarot Card: The Magician

Fire △

The will, the spark of life, that which beats the heart, the alchemist's forge, courage, instinct, passion, sex, strength, survival

Alchemical Properties: Hot and dry

Color: Red

Magical Tool: The wand

Tarot Card: Ace of Wands

Aries ♈

Cardinal fire; adventure, assertion, courage, new beginnings, pioneering, self-focused, strength, warrior

Colors: Red, scarlet red

Plants: Geranium, tiger lily

Crystals: Diamond, garnet, red jasper

Tarot Card: The Emperor
Ruling Planet: Mars

Leo ♌

Fixed fire; ambition, assertiveness, fun-loving, leadership, optimism, performing, playfulness, self-expression, regality, theatricality
Colors: Greenish yellow, red
Plant: Sunflower
Crystals: Cat's eye, chrysolite, sardonyx
Tarot Card: Strength
Ruling Planet: The sun

Sagittarius ♐

Mutable fire; benevolence, exploration, generosity, idealism, inspiring (like how a leader or philosophy inspires), justice, optimism, righteousness, wanderlust, zeal
Colors: Blue, red
Plant: Rush
Crystals: Blue zircon, turquoise
Tarot Card: Temperance
Ruling Planet: Jupiter

Mars ♂

Aggression, assertion, conflict, energy, initiative, passion, sex, victory, willpower
Colors: Red, scarlet red
Number: Five
Plants: Blood root, dragon's blood, galangal, rue, thistle, wormwood
Polygon: Pentagram
Crystals: Bloodstone, garnet, lava rock, ruby
Tarot Card: The Tower

Sun ☉

Authority, birth, fulfillment, health, identity, individuality, integrity, purpose, willpower, vitality

Colors: Gold, orange, yellow

Number: Six

Plants: Cedar, ginseng, heliotrope, juniper, laurel, sandalwood, sunflower

Polygon: Hexagram

Crystals: Carnelian, chrysolite, heliodor, topaz, zircon

Tarot Card: The Sun

Jupiter ♃

Abundance, expansiveness, growth, higher education, honor, lengthy or distant trips, luck, morality, philanthropy, philosophy, prosperity

Colors: Blue, purple, violet

Number: Four

Plants: Bodhi, clove, dandelion, oak, hyssop, meadowsweet, poplar, star anise

Polygon: Square

Crystals: Amethyst, lapis lazuli, lepidolite, sapphire

Tarot Card: Wheel of Fortune

Water ▽

The emotions, the river of life, the mirror, the subconscious and unconscious, the subtle, dreams and visions, adaptive, fluid, healing, love, wisdom

Alchemical Properties: Cold and moist/wet

Color: Blue

Magical Tool: The chalice

Tarot Card: Ace of Cups

Cancer ♋

Cardinal water; compassion, domesticity, empathy, healing, imagination, intuition, maternal instincts, memory, nurturance, privacy, protection (emotional), psychology, sensitivity, the womb; the archetypal mother

Colors: Amber, blue

Plant: Lotus

Crystals: Amber, ruby, moonstone

Tarot Card: The Chariot

Ruling Planet: The moon

Scorpio ♏

Fixed water; depth, discovery, intensity, manipulation, perception of the hidden, secretive, shedding the skin, speaking what usually goes unsaid, spiritual union through sex, transformation, willpower

Colors: Blue, green blue

Plant: Cactus

Crystals: Bloodstone, topaz, obsidian

Tarot Card: Death

Ruling Planet: Pluto

Pisces ♓

Mutable water; art, compassion, dreams, escapism, immersing oneself in the divine, intuition, malleability, open-mindedness, psychic sensitivity, spiritual devotion, vision

Colors: Blue, ultra violet

Plant: Algae

Crystals: Bloodstone, pearl

Tarot Card: The Moon

Ruling Planet: Neptune

Moon ☽

Dreams, emotions, empathy, habits, imagination, intuition, psychic ability, the subconscious, visions

Colors: Blue, lavender, silver, white

Number: Nine

Plants: Algae, calamus, lotus, passionflower, moonwort, myrrh, poppy, sandalwood, wintergreen

Polygon: Enneagram

Crystals: Fluorite, moonstone, pearl, quartz

Tarot Card: The High Priestess

Pluto ♇ *or* ♀

Alchemy, death, energy healing, exposing that which is hidden, intensity, occultism, regeneration, shadow work, transformation, truth at any cost, the Underworld, unrelenting

Color: Glowing orange scarlet

Plants: Hibiscus, red poppy

Crystals: Kunzite, spinel, quartz

Tarot Card: Judgement

Neptune ♆

Astral travel, clairvoyance, the Collective Unconscious, confusion, illusions, the intangible, psychic phenomenon, the subtle, visions

Color: Deep blue

Plant: Lotus

Crystals: Amethyst, celestite, lepidolite, mother-of-pearl

Tarot Card: The Hanged Man

Earth ▽

The body, the manifested world, fertility, physicality, physical health, rootedness, manifestation, material things, nourishment, reliability, solidity, structure, vocation

Alchemical Properties: Cold and dry

Colors: Green, brown, black

Magical Tool: The pentacle

Number: Ten

Tarot Card: Ace of Pentacles

Capricorn ♑

Cardinal earth; ambition, career-orientation, determination, discipline, down-to-earth, economical, efficiency, goal-orientation, hard-working, managerial, persistent, practical, prudent, responsible; the archetypal father

Colors: Brown, indigo

Plants: Hemp, orchis root, thistle
Crystals: Garnet, jet, onyx
Tarot Card: The Devil
Ruling Planet: Saturn

Taurus ♉

Fixed earth; dependable, earthly, hard-working, loyal, luxury, patient, pleasure-seeking, protection (physical), sensual, sexual, stable, stubborn, strong-willed
Colors: Brown, red orange
Plant: Mallow
Crystals: Emerald, lapis lazuli, red coral
Tarot Card: The Hierophant
Ruling Planet: Taurus shares Venus with Libra

Virgo ♍

Mutable earth; analytical, conservative, critical, detail-oriented, devotion to an ideal or cause, discriminating, efficient, neat, perfectionistic, picky, practical, service
Colors: Brown, yellowish green
Plants: Lily, narcissus, snowdrop
Crystals: Peridot, sapphire
Tarot Card: The Hermit
Ruling Planet: Virgo shares Mercury with Gemini; in Virgo, Mercury is more analytical and precise than it is in Gemini

Saturn ♄

Authority, awareness of time passing/time-related, awareness of limits, constriction, definition, discipline, instructive, organization, orthodoxy, limiting, maturation, patience, planning, protection, responsibility, rigidity, stability, structure, a taskmaster, tradition, wisdom; the archetypal teacher
Colors: Black, brown, gray, indigo
Number: Three

Plants: Ash, belladonna, buckthorn, cypress, elm, hemp, mullein, skullcap, slippery elm, wolf's bane, yew

Polygon: Triangle

Crystals: Anthracite, black tourmaline, hematite, jet, obsidian, onyx, salt

Tarot Card: The World

Astrological energies can be combined in magic. For example, if we want to perform a healing spell for increased energy after illness, we can unite the healing power of Cancer with the vitality of the sun by combining some of their correspondences or drawing their symbols together: ☉ ♋. We can further add the intensity of Mars (or other planets) by incorporating Mars correspondences or including Mars in the sigil with the symbol for conjunction: ♂. Sun conjunct Mars in Cancer can be represented like this:

☉ ♂ ♂ ♋

In Western astrology, we traditionally draw the sun or the planet that's closest to it first. We can also create a sigil that merges the astrological symbols together or otherwise represents them, like:

Figure 6: Sigil for Sun Conjunct Mars in Cancer

Many magical practitioners find benefit in integrating chakras with magic. Since the major chakras connect with the domains of the human experience, they can be woven into spells and rituals for healing, transforming, activating, and harnessing these domains. The major chakras and some of their correspondences are shared on page 14.

Crystals are often part of magical practitioners' toolkits today. The following crystals are widely available and most can be affordably purchased in their tumbled state. Though I recommend buying crystals in part based on what we feel drawn to, these compose a solid starter set. Many people believe crystals should be cleansed before use, excluding the few crystals that are considered to be self-cleaning. There are numerous ways to cleanse crystals, including running them under water, placing them in the light of the sun or moon for several hours, encasing them in soil, or visualizing them being filled with purifying light. Not all crystals are waterproof and some fade in sunlight, so be sure to check before cleansing a crystal in those ways.

When working with crystals, we can charge them with intent, which is often called "programming." I prefer to use the term "charging" instead because programming can make it sound like crystals are inert pieces of technology rather than imbued with consciousness. To charge a crystal, we hold it, visualize an intention, and direct our energy into it. If we're working with a sigil, we can visualize it during this process being inside the crystal and fed by the crystal's energy. This is believed to enlist the crystal's aid in manifesting that intention. Initially, we can do this for thirty seconds to a minute. With practice, most people develop a feel for when crystals are charged. Any item can be charged with our intention and energy as part of a spell, but with crystals, the notion is that they assist with the magic. We can also avail ourselves of a crystal's innate properties in a more general way by holding it, tuning in to it, or placing it near us. Here are some correspondences for crystals in addition to those mentioned above:

Amethyst: alleviating fear, amplifying psychic ability, attuning to higher frequencies, calming, cleansing, focusing the mind, mitigating addictions or compulsions, promoting peaceful sleep, protection, spiritual awakening

Black Tourmaline: absorbing negativity energy, grounding, increasing vitality, protection, transmuting negative energy, scrying, supporting shadow work

Carnelian: building courage, dispelling doubt, increasing vitality, raising energy, stimulating sexual energy

Citrine: absorbing negative energy, abundance, alleviating fear, cleansing (citrine needn't be cleansed), increasing energy, increasing self-confidence, increasing vitality (citrine's said to hold the power of the sun), promoting peace, promoting sound sleep, regenerating, transmuting negative energy, warming

Fluorite: absorbing negative energy, amplifying psychic ability (when purple), cleansing, focusing the mind, grounding spiritual energies, heart-opening/ healing (when green), promoting openness, protection, stabilizing

Hematite: absorbing negative energy, centering, concentrating, confidence-boosting, grounding, protecting, stabilizing

Lapis Lazuli: amplifying psychic ability, aligning the levels of being, healing, promoting communication/self-expression, promoting peace, protection, soothing, uplifting

Obsidian: absorbing negative energy, amplifying psychic ability, centering, clearing energy blockages, grounding, promoting clarity, promoting emotional healing, protection, scrying, supporting shadow work

Quartz: amplifying energy, amplifying psychic ability, conducting energy, facilitating karmic resolution, healing (sometimes called "The Master Healer"), scrying, spiritual awakening

Rose Quartz: encouraging empathy, healing trauma, heart-opening, increasing self-esteem, love-attracting, processing grief, promoting compassion, promoting peace, promoting unconditional love

Selenite: amplifying psychic energy, attuning to higher frequencies, aura cleansing, calming, promoting clarity, promoting peace

Many practitioners work extensively with color (e.g., colored candles, symbols, etc.). Here are some additional correspondences for colors:

Black: absorbing/neutralizing negativity (or other things), authority, mourning, self-control, the shadow, the unseen

Blue: communication, healing, self-expression

Light Blue: serenity, spiritual awareness, understanding

Brown: domestic matters

Green: abundance, fertility, healing, heart-opening, love, luck

Indigo: spiritual vision

Orange: creativity, encouragement, sensuality

Pink: harmonious relationships, honor, love, success

Purple: power, royalty, spiritual attunement

Red: courage, lust, passion, physical vitality, strength

White: faith, peace, protection, purity, spirituality, truth

Yellow: attraction, confidence, mental ability, persuasiveness, will-power, wisdom

Please note that while these color correspondences are traditional in much of Western magic, they are not universal. In China, for example, white is associated with mourning.

The Law of Similarity connects things that share a similar color. For example, red and reddish crystals generally correspond to the root chakra and are helpful for root chakra issues, as are red candles. Also by similarity, a geometric figure can represent anything it agrees with in number. For instance, a triangle can signify any triad (e.g., maiden, mother, crone; mother, father, child; etc.). Two of the most common geometric symbols in magic are the pentagram and hexagram. Both have an assortment of meanings spanning diverse cultures throughout history. Today, the pentagram is commonly used for protection and to represent the synthesis and balance of power between the four elements and spirit. It's called the "Sign of the Microcosm," corresponding to a person with their arms and legs spread. With the spirit point upward, it represents the harmony of matter under the governance of spirit. As a symbol of Mars, it has potent energy.

Figure 7: Pentagram

Each point of the pentagram corresponds to an element, as pictured in figure 7. The easiest way I know to memorize the elemental symbols is that "air" looks like an A, "earth" like an E, fires rise up, and water rains down. Regarding memorizing the elemental placements, the elements move clockwise in astrological order (i.e., fire/Aries, earth/Taurus, air/Gemini, water/Cancer).

Pentagrams can be used to invoke or banish elemental energy. Invocation typically indicates summoning things into ourselves, so the invoking pentagram of air, for example, brings air energy into us. We can also use the invoking pentagrams to bring elemental energy into our environment or an item. Our intention when casting the pentagram will guide whether the elemental energy enters us or something external. For invoking pentagrams, we draw the first line of the pentagram toward the angle of the element we want to invoke, beginning from the highest angle possible. For earth and fire, we start from spirit and move down. For air and water, we begin from one and move toward the other. To banish, we go backward, starting at the element's angle and moving toward its invoking pentagram's starting point. A simple way to remember this is if we want to invoke something, we move toward it, and if we want to banish it, we move away from it. Pentagrams are traditionally visualized in blue flame, like that of a gas stove. For help visualizing this, draw a pentagram in neon orange highlighter on white paper and stare at it for about thirty seconds. Then close your eyes and look at the pentagram that appears.

We can also work with spirit using the pentagram, but the spirit pentagram method is somewhat cumbersome and, in my experience, unnecessary outside of Golden Dawn work (where it originated). In the LBRP, the banishing earth pentagram is utilized to clear elemental, day-to-day, and astral influences from our outer and inner space, affording maximum banishing efficacy at the earthly level.

Figure 8: Leo Pentagram

If we want to work with an astrological sign's energy, we can draw it within its element's invoking or banishing pentagram (as pictured in figure 8) in its elemental color. These symbols are drawn from left to right (clockwise, following the sun's course) when invoking a sign's energy and conversely when banishing it. In ceremonial magic, the fixed signs are often used because they're stable. They "fix" energy in place (for Scorpio, ceremonialists traditionally draw an eagle's head, which signifies the mature version of the sign). Additionally, there are Hebrew divine names associated with the pentagrams and hexagrams, which I encourage you to research if you connect with Hebrew. In my experience, intoning these can add substantial power to a working, but they aren't required. Many magical practitioners have fruitfully used pentagrams and hexagrams without Hebrew for over fifty years.

To limit or contain a pentagram or hexagram's magic, we can draw a clockwise circle around it beginning at its highest point. Circles also symbolize infinity, equanimity, wholeness, balance, cycles, and equality and can be used to these ends in magic.

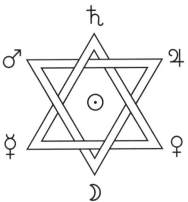

Figure 9: Hexagram

Where the pentagram symbolizes the microcosm, the hexagram is the "Sign of the Macrocosm." It's also tremendously powerful, corresponding to the vitalizing sun and representing the harmonious synthesis of the seven classical planets (the sun is positioned in the middle of the hexagram). As a combination of two triangles, it represents the merging of heaven and earth, positive and negative, etc., thus symbolizing the Great Work.

The hexagram's points correspond to the classical planets. A way to remember their order is that they follow the planetary placements on the Tree of Life. If you're unfamiliar with these, you can imagine a lightning bolt on the hexagram that zigzags twice, starting at the top and moving down right, with the planets ordered by distance from the sun, followed by the moon.

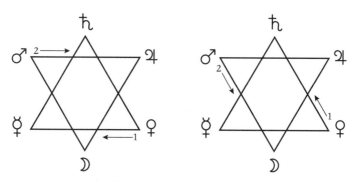

Figure 10: Invoking and Banishing Hexagrams of Venus

Hexagrams can be used to invoke or banish planetary energy. A simple way to remember how to draw them is that invoking hexagrams are drawn clockwise/sunwise (left to right), and banishing hexagrams are drawn counterclockwise (right to left). Whether invoking or banishing, we begin in the angle that corresponds to the planet we're working with and draw the first triangle. Then we go to the opposite angle and draw the next triangle. Traditionally, these hexagrams are visualized in golden light. We can draw the planetary symbol we're working with in their center in golden or white light or the planet's corresponding color. The moon is traditionally drawn based on the phase it's in, with a crescent pointing left for waxing, right for waning, an empty circle for full, and a dark circle for new.

Otherwise, the Golden Dawn's sun hexagrams are even more cumbersome than its spirit pentagrams, and in my experience, we can work with any of these energies by drawing their symbols alone. There are also many other effective approaches for harnessing these energies, well beyond what's been shared here. These energies are more fundamental than any symbolic system. This doesn't mean there's no added value from using the pentagrams and hexagrams, though, especially given the rich significance of these symbols.

My main sources for these correspondences were:
777 by Aleister Crowley

Cunningham's Encyclopedia of Crystal, Gem, and Metal Magic by
   Scott Cunningham
Cunningham's Encyclopedia of Magical Herbs by Scott Cunningham
The Crystal Bible by Judy Hall
The Golden Dawn by Israel Regardie
Modern Magick by Donald Michael Kraig
Self-Initiation in the Golden Dawn Tradition by Chic and Sandra Tabatha Cicero

Designing Spells

"If opportunity doesn't knock, build a door."
—MILTON BERLE

Now that we've explored spellcraft, we can put the pieces together and create spells. As a reminder, a barebones spell generally involves the following:

+ A clear intention of change
+ Cleansing ourselves and the space, or at minimum, becoming present and quieting our mind
+ Utilizing symbols or other supports aligned with our aim
+ Visualization and/or speaking affirmative words about the intention
+ Aligning our feelings with these visualizations and/or words
+ Imagining that energy is summoned and moving toward our aim
+ Sealing the working with a phrase like "so mote it be" or "and so it is," or simply feeling clearly that the spell is set

To design a spell, we can answer the six questions shared earlier and utilize the correspondences from the previous section. Below is an example of a spell created this way. I overcomplicated it to demonstrate how to work with the correspondence lists. Regarding how many supportive elements to incorporate into a spell, I recommend deferring to what feels appropriate to you and tweaking things in subsequent magic in light of your results.

A Spell for Professional Improvement

+ What? To manifest a new job or an improvement in my current one.
+ Why? I'm bored at work and not earning enough money to be financially secure. I want to harness my skills and grow more.

- How? By working with the energy of Jupiter (creating opportunities) in Capricorn (career): (1) with the symbol of Jupiter in Capricorn, drawn on a brown candle, (2) by tracing the invoking pentagram of Capricorn and invoking hexagram of Jupiter over the candle, (3) by burning thistle during the spell, (4) by charging a piece of lapis lazuli with this intention, (5) by placing this crystal atop a piece of paper with a sigil composed of a square with the symbol of Jupiter in Capricorn inside it, (6) by placing the Ace of Pentacles behind the candle, (7) with affirmative words and visualization.
- Who? Alone, but with the highest good invoked.
- Where? The altar in my house (altars will be covered in part two).
- When? Since Jupiter corresponds with the number four, I'll work this for four days. Because the spell seeks improvement and not necessarily something new, I'll perform it during the waxing moon or the new moon. Ideally, I'll start or end on a Thursday (which corresponds with Jupiter).

Here's the finished spell:

Stand before your altar. Carve the candle ahead of time (because there could be hiccups in that process) while holding the spell's intention in your mind. Place the candle in the center of the altar. Cleanse and become present. Bow your head and align yourself with the divine. Light the candle. Place the thistle on a piece of burning incense charcoal and put the Ace of Pentacles behind the candle. Visualize and feel the supportive energy of Jupiter in Capricorn for a few moments and then draw the square in purple ink and the symbols for Jupiter and Capricorn within it (in purple and brown ink, respectively). Place the square under the candle and the crystal in front of the candle, such that the crystal is inside the square. Raise your wand with your right hand (or extend your joined index and middle fingers, with the others in a fist) and draw the invoking pentagram of Capricorn and the invoking hexagram of Jupiter on a horizontal plane over the square. Imagine their energy as vividly as possible, radiating and charging the items below. Next, hold the crystal in your closed right hand at the level of your navel chakra. Imagine yourself radiating golden energy and feeling strong as you say:

The moon is waxing. I summon to me improved professional conditions. I'm willing to do the work necessary to sustain this sought change. May the next steps in this process become clear to me soon. May any necessary support for

this process appear as it is needed. This crystal and sigil will maintain the en-
ergy of this spell until this intention manifests. If this aligns with my highest
good, it will happen. So mote it be.

Place the crystal back on the square. Bow reverentially. Snuff out the candle
and leave the altar. Perform this spell for the next three nights. On the fourth
night, let the candle burn itself out. Place the crystal and sigil where you'll see
them daily or more. While falling asleep, visualize the sigil for at least thirty seconds. Let concerns about the results of the spell fade and patiently wait for the
manifestation to appear in whatever form it takes.

There are myriad ways to craft spells. Even the brief lists in this chapter could
be used to create millions of unique spells, and this is just one approach. We can
embrace a variety of new or old techniques and even combine them. For example,
we can make vision boards, where we create collages of our intentions on poster
board, alongside talismans we charge with energy, like pouches filled with items
that resonate with our intentions. We can also simply center ourselves and ask for
what we want. Magic is a force of nature involving innate powers that predate every magical system. Systems can help us access, develop, and direct these powers,
but these powers always transcend those systems. Like other natural forces, magic
can be harnessed by technology, but that technology doesn't govern or limit it.

Exercise
Practice creating spells by designing three using the process demonstrated above.
They can be about anything you want, and you needn't cast them. Try involving a
variety of correspondences to help you become comfortable using the lists.

WHY DOES MAGIC FAIL?
"See that you are in harmony with the effect you wish to produce."
—S. L. MACGREGOR MATHERS

Having explored the basics of spellwork, it may seem like smooth sailing from here,
and yet, it's not that simple. Even the most impeccably designed spell can flop. Understanding why magic fails and how to decrease the likelihood of our magic failing
can make us stronger practitioners. This also provides us with motivation for undertaking the Little Work because it addresses most of these issues.

We've already covered some reasons magic can fail—for example, if we're trying to violate natural law or are running into karmic resistance. The latter is one reason including intentions for inner alchemy is beneficial in spells. This way, if there's a karmic obstacle to a spell, we proactively facilitate releasing it. Other reasons from earlier, which we'll also address with inner alchemy, include our mind being cluttered with thoughts that overwhelm our spells and us offering emanations that contradict our intentions. We might need additional practice with the skills involved in magic too, like concentrating, visualizing, and raising and directing energy. We might also not believe in magic or our ability to perform it effectively yet, leading our doubt to torpedo our spells. We'll tackle this in an upcoming section. Additionally, we explored how we can manifest what we seek yet be unprepared to sustain it (e.g., the terrific-fitting lover comes, but our lack of relationship skills and intimacy issues sink the relationship).

Otherwise, we can also be too impatient or attached to what we seek. Though excitedly believing a manifestation is imminent can facilitate it, an inexperienced practitioner is more apt to have thoughts like, "Why hasn't this manifested yet?" and "I feel like this isn't working." Thoughts like these can warp our psychic emanation to block an intended manifestation. When we're highly attached to a result, we usually have some concern about it not manifesting, which can also subvert our magic. For example, if I desperately want something, part of me feels desperate. The frequency of desperation doesn't resonate with something like prosperity or well-being (though it can lead to miraculous magic via one-pointed concentration, like a mother who lifts a car to save her child). Along these lines, worry, fear, frustration, etc., can all tank manifestations.

Many people have anxiety disorders today, including me. One way to keep anxiety disorders from sabotaging our magic is to cultivate the belief that excessive anxiety is a symptom of the disorder and nothing more. When feeling anxious, we can practice thinking, "This feeling is a symptom, not a fact. It doesn't make a concern legitimate." This thought is far less disruptive to our magic than validating whatever the anxiety's story is (it's also greatly helped me mitigate my anxiety, along with other practices we'll explore in part two).

We eventually reach a state of finesse in magic, usually after significant alchemical work, where we can strongly intend for something without feeling too attached to it manifesting, which greatly facilitates its manifestation. One way to develop this detachment is by making peace with a working's outcome in advance through believing that if it aligns with the highest good, it'll manifest, and if not, it won't. This type of attitude helps us stay open to whatever results come. That said, this also assumes that the working in question was performed and designed well, in accord with the points made in this section, which are worth reflecting on if a spell flops.

Another reason magic can fail is if we intend for something that's unattainable (yet within the bounds of natural law). For example, if I recently started college, I can't earn a legitimate PhD next week. When we seek something that's part of a consensus reality, it's subject to that consensus reality's conditions. We can still use magic to aid us in getting a PhD though; the route to it will just have to somewhat fit with convention, even if that route's littered with astonishing synchronicities—for example, "randomly" meeting the professor we want to research under and connecting vibrantly, which helps us get into our dream program. This concept generally applies to inner work too. For instance, if I want to establish a healthy relationship with food overnight after decades of disordered eating and I've done no inner work around this issue, that's unlikely to happen. Though healing miracles do occur, in most cases, deep conditioning and psychological trauma require a lengthier process.

Generally speaking, the more probable or feasible it is that something could happen, the easier it is to manifest. One reason for this is we inevitably have less doubt about manifesting something that seems probable, and a manifestation feeling probable often indicates that it's within our current capacity. Importantly, our magical capacity grows over time with practice. If we can make peace with what's within our reach and build from there, astonishing creations will progressively come our way. Better to cast a spell to find a part-time job to earn an extra $1,000, which we believe can work, than ask for the $1,000 to spontaneously manifest and sabotage our spell with doubt. When the job comes, our faith in our magic, and therefore our magical capacity, will grow accordingly.

Another reason magic can fail is unintentional self-sabotage from unsupportive personal narratives, like feeling we don't deserve a manifestation. For example, traumatic experiences may have convinced us we're unworthy of realizing our dreams or that "nothing works out for me." External forces may also have told us we can't realize our dreams because "things like that don't happen for people like us." Additionally, we may have absorbed notions about life that tell us it's selfish to ask for certain changes, even healthy ones. As we think these types of thoughts, our energy shifts away from manifesting what we intend.

Earlier, we explored fears related to manifestations not happening, but we can also fear them happening. We may worry about how a manifestation could alter our lives, and this worry can block our spell. Fearing what we want when it involves the unknown is normal, and this is a place where the emotional dimension of inner alchemy comes in. We can learn to face fear and release unsupportive narratives, leading to sustainable healing and transformation, either completely or enough to turn our magical tide.

Meeting the Ego

"The ego is like a cloud. The Sun cannot be seen
on account of a thin patch of cloud; when that disappears one sees the Sun."
—RAMAKRISHNA PARAMAHANSA

In the fear of the unknown, we come to the next type of self-sabotage, unconscious self-sabotage, and we meet a part of ourselves that'll be a focus of inner alchemy: the ego. In a nutshell, the ego is the individuating principle within us, the internal agent that distinguishes us from the divine unity and seeks to reinforce this separateness. The ego resides in the navel chakra, which is home to self-assertion and will. Conventionally, when someone's aptly accused of having a "big ego," they have an overactive navel chakra. This could appear as a superiority complex, savior complex, narcissism, or another form of self-aggrandizement.

The ego wants to know "What's in it for me?" When we live with our resting awareness at this level of consciousness, we're at our most selfish. People who trample others at a Black Friday sale or cut their workers' benefits to make an extra million dollars are operating at the ego level. When people say, "It's human nature to be selfish," they're right in the sense that the ego is fundamentally selfish.

The ego is defined differently in various spiritual traditions and psychology. In my experience, the best way to understand and work with the ego depends on what we're trying to do. For performing inner alchemy, the ego has three key facets. I differentiate between these facets below to describe them, but after this, I'll generally refer to them collectively as "the ego."

First, the ego is an outgrowth of our biological survival system that seeks to keep us safe by maintaining our status quo. In prehistoric times, when danger lurked around many unknown corners, maintaining our status quo was a matter of survival. Having an aspect of ourselves that inclined us to stay with what we knew was safe protected us. Importantly, "safe" here means "not life-threatening." It doesn't mean "free from harm." The ego can strive to keep us in an extremely painful, uncomfortable, or unhealthy "comfort zone" because it knows what to expect there. Even though most people no longer live under the types of threats that prehistoric humans faced, this part of ourselves still operates within us. It perceives the world as being rife with danger, and in its aim of self-protection, it can exert immense power over how we feel and think.

This aspect of ego commonly manifests in today's world to maintain the inertia of our status quo, especially when we seek something that involves fear of the unknown, whether that fear is large or small, rational or irrational. It can also try to keep us from reexperiencing known pain, like by making us feel anxious at the thought of dating after being in a difficult breakup. If we don't challenge ourselves often, we won't encounter this dimension of ego much, but when we make a habit of stretching outside of our comfort zone, we get to know it well. Many call it the "inner saboteur" because when we seek to change our status quo, even in healthy ways, it generally resists those changes. The inner saboteur can wear an unlimited assortment of masks in its aim of derailing our intentions of change. For instance, it's the deflated feeling that keeps us home after two weeks of wonderful-feeling workouts following getting a gym membership after New Year's (and New Year's resolutions flopping may be the most common experience people have with the inner saboteur). If we push through this resistance, we may think something like "I feel awesome! How could I have felt so unmotivated to work out?" The short answer is: because the inner saboteur didn't want us to.

The inner saboteur is also the voice in our head that insists, "Why would you think you can do that?" It's what makes us forget to work on a goal one day and then lose track of that goal for months. We can intend to start a creative project and then fall down a procrastination spiral because of the inner saboteur until the impetus behind the project dries up. It's the primary part of us that keeps us in relationships we know are unhealthy, second-guesses our big dreams, depletes our motivation to challenge ourselves, etc. A critical point to understand here is that we can have a huge desire we're working to realize that the inner saboteur's terrified of, and if we don't know how the inner saboteur operates, it can blow us off course without us even recognizing what's happening.

There can be other reasons than subconscious fear of the unknown that keep us from following through on healthy, bold, or revolutionary life changes too. Some resistance can arise because we have established habits, and changing any habit will evoke resistance. For instance, we might feel gross if we don't brush our teeth for a couple days if we have a habit of brushing them daily. That'll be the extent of our discomfort if the ego isn't involved though, as opposed to something like panicking about not brushing our teeth. Resistance can come from other fears besides fear of the unknown too. For example, part of what keeps us from initiating a creative project could be a subconscious fear that people will criticize it, which makes us hesitate starting it. This hesitation then manifests as procrastination.

The inner saboteur exploits these fears too. They're more fuel for the fire of keeping us within specified parameters. One way of defining the inner saboteur could be as the part of us that uses our conscious and subconscious fears to maintain our status quo. If we seek a healthy life change and continually feel blocked or sabotaged, that's the inner saboteur. "I'm afraid of getting hurt again." "I'm scared of failing." "I'm worried I can't handle that." "I'm terrified I'll disappoint you." These may be reasonable fears given our lived experience and circumstances, but the part of us that's convinced the worst will happen and therefore dead set against changing despite any evidence to the contrary? That's the inner saboteur, and fear of the unknown is still present in these examples, alongside the extra layers of resistance. The ego would rather stay with the pain we know than risk the pain we don't. One reason we face our fears and heal from psychological trauma as best we can during inner alchemy is to take these footholds away from the ego.

When we begin magical practice, the ego often kicks up dust because magic is an unknown. Those of us who are metaphysically gifted usually have an advantage here because we've long felt drawn to the occult. Even if we've never cast a spell, there's something familiar enough about all of this for us to do something unorthodox like try out magic or contact a coven. Once we become comfortable with magic, the ego shifts to mostly fearing magic when what we intend is outside of our comfort zone. It has no qualms about manifesting parking spaces or concert tickets. The ego may even revel in manifestations like these, feeling more assured than ever that it can protect and please itself. But with something that demands significant change? That's when the inner saboteur reemerges. The spell goes unwritten or unperformed, or it conveniently doesn't even occur to us that we could use magic in this situation. We may also cast the spell only to fall into conscious self-sabotage inspired by impulses from the ego.

With regard to High Magic, the inner saboteur generally offers creative and persistent disruptions, especially if we try to practice daily. Studying occultism is one thing, but the unknowns involved in consistently practicing it terrify the ego. This is especially true if we seek to complete the Great Work because the ego knows it can't cross the abyss. It manifests as excuses not to practice, the imaginary bug we feel crawling on us during meditation, or the amazing insight we "must" break our practice to write down. It can even make us feel ill and masquerade as our intuition (e.g., "My guides told me to stop meditating because I'm the reincarnation of Buddha"). This may all sound overwhelming, but don't worry. There's plenty we can do about this. The upcoming elemental sections feature many time-tested techniques for dealing with the inner saboteur.

Otherwise, it's important to understand that despite its sabotaging, the ego isn't a villain. It's trying to protect us, and like anything else, how we think of it will affect how we perceive it. Many people frame ego work in the language of battle and war, which brings unnecessary internal violence into the alchemical process. That said, the ego isn't an ally either, and though it calms down some as we demonstrate that we'll proceed with our intentions despite its eruptions, staying mindful of it is critical. This brings us to another tenet of the Little Work: *keep an eye on the ego*, which is especially true if we don't have a spiritual teacher pointing ours out to us.

The second aspect of ego that pertains to the Little Work is that it's the part of us that's thought-dependent. Anything within us that exists by virtue of thought alone that we define ourselves by is a component of our ego. As we grew up, external forces (and how we responded to those forces) spun thought-dependent realities within us. Now, we find ourselves identified with labels, stories, and concepts about ourselves, the world, etc., that have little to no inherent reality yet feel as if they do. In the moment, it usually seems like these thought-dependent realities are just how things are, and it's normal to feel like our thoughts and emotions just happen to us as we go through life, but that's frequently not the case. Often, they result from our experiences and societal conditioning, and they're the children of this aspect of ego, which ceaselessly coalesces as it integrates our novel experiences into itself. This is the part of us that would be profoundly different if we grew up in another country. Though certain heritable dimensions of our personality would persist (as would our astrological makeup), much of how we think, feel, and perceive would differ.

This aspect of ego is interwoven with the thought-dependent realities our subconscious mind projects onto inherent reality. It's what tells us we are our thoughts and emotions, when really, we're neither of these things at a deeper level. Beyond the exceptions we reviewed earlier, we could forget a thought-dependent reality issue and our lives would continue as if it never existed. That's the beauty and difficulty of thought-dependent realities: they're only real when we believe in them, but while we do, they feel as real to us as anything else, and our psychic emanation manifests in resonance with them. The ego clings to these realities, recognizing that at the prospect of their change, we face great unknowns, including what lies beyond the foundations of our reality itself.

Inner alchemy at this level of ego involves claiming our ability to shape our thought-dependent realities with intention. We explore our thoughts and perceptions to understand what makes us tick, alongside establishing healthy mental habits that support our intentions. This generally includes aligning our thoughts more with accuracy, wisdom, and inherent reality and deconditioning ourselves from harmful beliefs that resulted from external influences. Doing this usually takes consistent practice (and time for our novel thoughts to reprogram our subconscious), but the results can seem revolutionary and miraculous. By working with a basic understanding of how our subconscious operates and processes like the illusory truth effect and confirmation bias, we can boldly reshape our experience of reality.

The third aspect of ego, which mostly pertains to the Great Work, is our total sense of separation from the divine. Work with this aspect of ego is Yoga, which involves moving beyond our likes and dislikes and sense of "I" and "mine" to cross the abyss and complete the Great Work. Our likes and dislikes are like hands at the surface of our being that grasp for our attention. As we release our attachment to them and our strong beliefs about ourselves, we can move deeper within, toward the stillness that exists beneath our mental chatter and the weather of our emotions. This doesn't mean we stop enjoying our experiences or become a robot. It's about releasing our attachment to being comfortable and feeling good enough to engage with ourselves at a deeper level.

A child may believe a wooden horse is a real animal, but fundamentally, the horse is a piece of wood. The ego is like the horse in this scenario, and our perception of it is like the child's perception of the horse. Work with the third aspect of ego is about awakening from this illusion. We realize the horse is a block of wood and set it aside.

Work with this aspect of ego appears superficially in the Little Work system in learning how to make ourselves do things we don't feel like doing. Without this ability, the inner saboteur has a surefire way of sabotaging our intentions. We also learn not to identify as strongly with what we think or feel. This aids us in healthfully processing difficult emotions (a difficult emotion is any emotion that feels difficult to you) and perceiving inherent reality more clearly. Additionally, inner alchemy involves opening our hearts and raising our resting awareness above the navel. This automatically loosens our attachment to our likes and dislikes and sense of "I" and "mine" a bit.

Overcoming Doubt in Magic

"Magick is not something you do. Magick is something you are."
—DONALD MICHAEL KRAIG

Having doubts about magic or experiencing the other issues mentioned earlier doesn't guarantee that a spell will fail. This just means it's more of a dice roll. As we learn to navigate these issues and hold our psychic emanation in a supportive state, the likelihood that our spells will work increases considerably.

In my experience, there are two primary steps to overcoming doubt in magic. The first is to believe that magic is real, and the second is to believe we can use it effectively. Daily High Magic practice builds both of these beliefs. Since High Magic rituals generally have abstract rather than concrete aims (e.g., connecting with the divine versus manifesting an object), they help us practice aligning with an intention with less worry or urgency about its manifestation. They also aid us in developing skills used in magic like concentration, energy raising, visualization, etc. Consequently, as we become proficient in High Magic, we naturally become more proficient in spellwork, and as we start feeling like something's happening during High Magic rituals, our faith in magic's reality increases. Along these lines, we can also undertake practices to increase the skills used in magic, like energy work and visualization exercises.

To foster the belief that we can manifest physically, it helps to develop an open-minded attitude, which holds for whatever psychological changes we seek too. For example, rather than "I can manifest that" (or on the psychological level, "I can heal from that"), which we may struggle to believe, we strive to just stay open. The pivot from "I can't do that" to "Maybe I can do that" is tremendous. It unlocks a door within us for the magic to pass through. We don't know whom we're going to meet or what we're going to experience that dramatically changes our lives, and we can't know what experiences will be like until we have them. But we can sabotage opportunities with pessimism, psychologically and metaphysically. We needn't be falsely hopeful though, just open.

Another helpful way to build confidence in our ability to physically manifest is to start with things that don't summon much emotional resistance in us (e.g., a pen). Then we build from there. For example, after manifesting a pen, we can move to something like seeing a pink car, which is further outside our status quo. From there, we can try for something more significant, like manifesting a magical altar. We may spend money on this, and buying a manifestation doesn't invalidate our magic unless we set out not to spend money. The important piece is that the altar appears and we can tell that it's ours. As these things come, our faith in magic grows.

Eventually, magic becomes such a facet of our day-to-day lives that we don't doubt its reality. Then the journey becomes more about doing what we must to support the lives we seek, which is the focus of the Little Work.

Exercises

1. Manifest a pen. Close your eyes, get present in your body, and take some deep breaths. Next, visualize a pen as vividly as you can. Feel that this pen is real and coming to you soon. After about thirty seconds, return your focus to your body and open your eyes. Repeat this daily until the pen manifests. Try not to think about this manifestation outside of the visualizations. The only stipulation in this working is that you mustn't buy the pen. It may take a while for the pen to manifest if you're new to magic. Please don't worry if it does.

2. Create a manifestation journal. For thirty days, document any synchro-
nicity that appears in your life. For example, thinking about a rarely heard
word and then encountering it, thinking of mermaids and then seeing a
book about them, driving by a sign that says "You are magical" (which happened to me minutes after writing this paragraph), etc. Amazing results can
come from this exercise. If you don't experience compelling results, try this
again after a few months of inner alchemy.

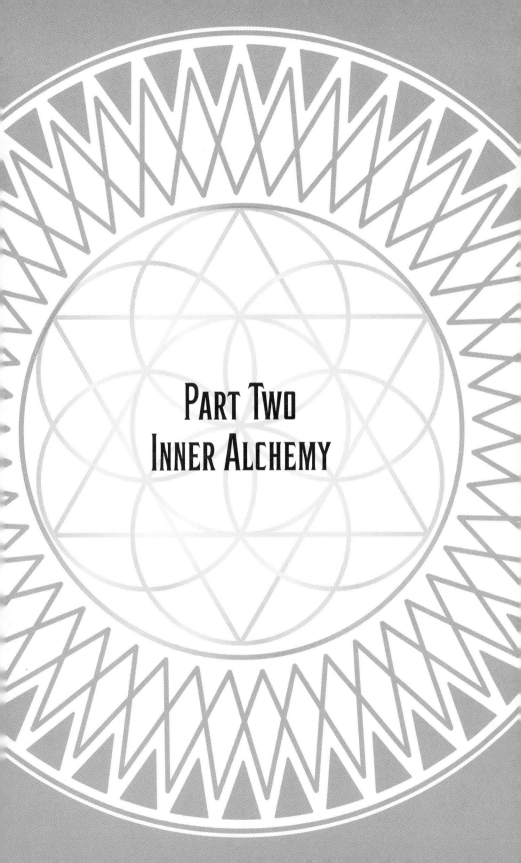

PART TWO
INNER ALCHEMY

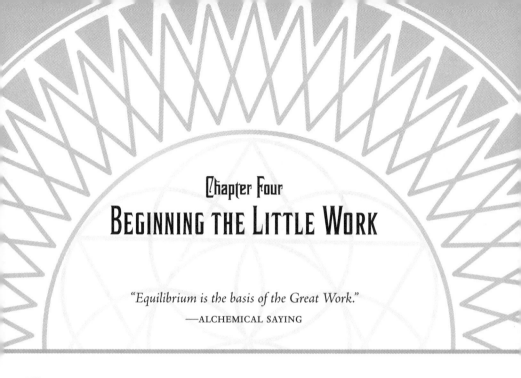

Chapter Four

BEGINNING THE LITTLE WORK

"Equilibrium is the basis of the Great Work."
—ALCHEMICAL SAYING

Having covered the foundational material of the Little Work, we can turn our focus to practice. We'll begin by exploring inner alchemy and some keys to effective metaphysical practice as well as developing a balanced daily practice. After that, we'll journey through the classical elements. First, I want to clarify that this inner alchemy isn't modeled after classical alchemy. Though many basic tenets of alchemy align with the Little Work, the term "alchemy" is used here to signify that this is a personal development process of profound, fundamental transformation. There's no reference to things like calcination, fermentation, the squared circle, etc.

To set the stage for our elemental work, it's beneficial to delve into what elements are, alongside reviewing how they're involved with inner alchemy. Before the advent of modern science, an element was considered to be one of the four substances that composed the physical universe: air, fire, water, and earth. This phenomenon was seen in many cultures, and it continues, albeit with slight variation, in Ayurveda—the traditional medicine of India—and traditional Chinese medicine. Each of these systems includes spirit in some manner, which is sometimes considered to be a fifth element, although it isn't really an element like the others are. Spirit is their underlying essence and the animating force of the whole. Aristotle gave the classical elements their alchemical properties: hot and dry, cold and moist, etc. Additionally, the elements correspond with the four directions, with spirit at the center providing height and depth. In Hermeticism, the elements are traditionally assigned to the four directions as follows: east/air, south/fire, west/water, north/earth.

Although we now know the physical world is composed of more than four elements, there's still benefit to using an elemental model when symbolizing our interior universe. By equating the intellect with air, feelings with water, will with fire, and physicality with earth, we can facilitate working on these areas and find innovative ways to develop ourselves. For example, Yogis have taught for millennia that we can mirror the qualities of whatever we meditate upon, and meditating on elements can help us develop qualities within ourselves that could be elusive otherwise. For instance, we may not know how to become more grounded, but we know what solid ground is, and meditating on its image (or the alchemical symbol for earth) can help us learn to ground. We can also work like this with elements in combination (e.g., meditating on lava for fire and earth). Additionally, we can invoke and banish elements as we learned earlier (e.g., by drawing a banishing air pentagram while struggling to stop ruminating).

By recognizing the elemental processes within ourselves and equilibrating them, our lives dramatically improve. We gain a discerning mind, ironclad will, liberated heart, and stable physical experience, all while increasingly living from our spiritual center. This dagger-like mind can cut through the machinations of the inner saboteur with objectivity and wisdom. This indomitable will can set an intention and see it through in most circumstances, burning through fear and doubt. This open, healed heart can meet all beings with compassion, including ourselves. Throughout this alchemical process, we become better able to navigate life in the world, making each step we take increasingly contribute to our alchemical work.

Inner alchemy enables us to withdraw energy from the day-to-day aspects of life, like paying bills and working, while showing up more attentively in these areas than we did before. We learn to healthfully maximize our potential and resources. This provides us with more freedom to devote our energy to deeper spiritual practice, creation on the physical plane, or both, and inner alchemy gives us the capability to see these through too. The healing, spiritual connectivity, and depth of living that accompanies a path like this is impossible to adequately describe. It's utterly worthwhile, even when it's difficult.

As touched upon earlier, part of inner alchemy is doing things we don't feel like doing in service of a higher aim. Without stretching outside our comfort zone, our lives won't change much, and alchemy is about fundamental change. Also, facing our shadow, which is highly uncomfortable for most of us at first, is part of inner alchemy. We approach the alchemist's forge with everything we believe we are and incrementally offer these beliefs with love and trust, a love and trust that strengthens as we experience alchemical results and root in spirit.

Some people feel intimidated by the prospect of inner alchemy, which is unsurprising. Doing things we don't want to isn't fun and the unknown can be so scary that part of us specifically exists to keep us from it. Many people leave this work before beginning it, worried about how difficult it'll be or that it'll remove fundamental parts of themselves. In my experience, we don't miss what burns off in the alchemical process. These are qualities like jealousy, resentment, pettiness, laziness, superficiality, immaturity, codependency, hubris, insecurity, hatred, bitterness, narcissism, fundamentalism, impatience, dogmatism, harshness, cruelty, and malice. I'm not saying these necessarily leave our lives completely, though that can happen. In most cases, they become an echo of what they were, which is worth striving for too. By practicing inner alchemy, we also lose unhealthy habits like treating people poorly, judging ourselves and others unfairly, and taking what we have for granted. As these qualities and habits erode, it becomes clear that they weren't authentic parts of ourselves, especially as our consciousness rises above the navel chakra. The authentic parts of ourselves actually become enhanced by this work, as they're liberated from the influence of these unsupportive qualities and habits.

Sometimes people also worry that a system that emphasizes humility and compassion will turn them into weaklings or doormats. In my experience, this work makes us stronger and surer, able to give when it's appropriate and maintain healthy boundaries when it isn't. From the vantage point of our individual ego, there's only so much we can be or do, and there's a veil between us and the divine. When we part this veil even an inch, we connect with an unconditional strength, love, and serenity that we couldn't have understood before. Even if we only touch this for a second, we know it's there. It becomes the biggest secret we can never tell but hope everyone gets let in on. Connecting with this part of ourselves leads to a fulfilling life experience, and it gives us the wherewithal to weather the storms of karma and thrive.

THE BASICS OF COGNITIVE THEORY

*"Not until the mind and the emotional system have been cleansed
and unified by the cathartic process of psychotherapy
can the full spiritual benefits of magical work be reflected."*
—ISRAEL REGARDIE

On the psychological level, inner alchemy is about maturing and living in a manner that supports our well-being, which we accomplish in this system through utilizing psychotherapeutic techniques. Marrying psychotherapeutic techniques with occultism isn't new. Dion Fortune and Israel Regardie, leading occult voices of the twentieth century, encouraged budding occultists to engage in psychotherapy. Though psychotherapy was different then, the notion of equilibrating ourselves with psychotherapeutic processes remains valuable and relevant. My experience as a clinician and practitioner has repeatedly validated how effective psychotherapeutic techniques can be for inner alchemy, particularly when married with metaphysical practice. Consequently, I've incorporated a manual's worth of psychotherapeutic material into this book. This includes a system of seven pillars of psychological healing I developed years ago. These pillars are: allowing emotion, mindfulness, a learning outlook, heart meditation, a compassionate mindset, affirmation, and intentional action. We'll explore each of these in depth.

Many of us come from cultures that lack a healthy relationship with emotion, thought, action, body, or environment. In a setting like that, we almost inevitably develop dysfunctional behavioral patterns, and there's usually little guidance for how to fix them. Fixing some of them may even misalign us with our society's expectations (e.g., turning down a lucrative job because of extreme work hours). Dysfunctional behavioral patterns are also likely to develop if we experience psychologically traumatizing situations. This trauma can come from forces that antagonized us individually, and it can also derive from observation or be passed down intergenerationally. For example, witnessing an assault can traumatize us, and my anxiety disorder may have partially resulted from growing up around my mother's anxiety, which stemmed from her experiences as a Jew just after the Holocaust. Inner alchemy helps us heal from our psychological trauma and amend these patterns over time as best we can.

In contemporary psychology, cognitive behavioral therapy (CBT) has addressed these difficulties with great success. In my experience, this is particularly true when CBT is married with the best of psychodynamic therapy. Psychodynamic therapy is how therapy is conventionally known, where we explore our past experiences with the notion that they shape our thoughts, feelings, and actions. For example, if I excessively fear intimacy, that's likely because something in my past scared me off of it. If I can determine what that was and process my emotions about it, my excessive fear of intimacy will resolve.

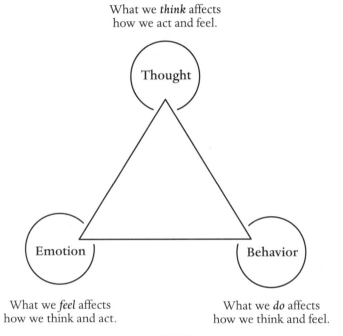

What we *think* affects
how we act and feel.

Thought

Emotion

Behavior

What we *feel* affects
how we think and act.

What we *do* affects
how we think and feel.

Figure 11: CBT Triangle

CBT, in a nutshell, rests on the notion that how we think and act affects how we feel, and vice versa, as expressed in the image above. For example, if I think of myself as useless, I'll feel bad about myself. If I think my job is a waste of my time, I'll dislike it. Feeling bad about myself makes me less likely to act on behalf of my well-being, and disliking my job makes me less likely to perform well at work. As I increasingly stop acting on behalf of my well-being, I feel worse about myself, which exacerbates my self-disparaging thoughts. As I perform poorly at work, I resent being there even more. The consequences? In the first example, I fall into a vicious cycle of harmful thinking, acting, and feeling that can lead to depression. In the second, I can end up stuck in a job I loathe. In both situations, the illusory truth effect and confirmation bias will rally behind my unsupportive thoughts until I struggle to see reality any other way. This is where CBT comes in to snap us out of our distorted perspectives through challenging our thoughts and shifting our behavior.

Another way of expressing the CBT framework is through the ABC model. In ABC, there's an activating event (A) that we have a belief about (B), which results in an outcome or consequence (C) that is usually an emotion and/or action. For example, if my coworker gets a promotion (A) that I believe I deserved (B), I'll feel wronged (C). If I believe instead that my coworker also deserved the promotion, I won't feel wronged. The beliefs we hold about situations affect how we feel about them, and if we change these beliefs, we'll feel differently. Emotional reactions aren't always this simple, particularly when they emerge from subconscious beliefs, psychological trauma, or mental illness, but enough of them are that this is worth understanding.

During CBT, we consider the following areas, which are all part of inner alchemy:

Thoughts: Are our thoughts fact-oriented, accurate, and wise? Do they support our well-being? When we feel insecure, worthless, inept, etc., it's often because we hold distorted beliefs about ourselves, consciously or subconsciously. These beliefs usually stem from factors like how people treated us while growing up, societal messaging, etc. If we can shift these beliefs in a fact-oriented, accurate, wise, and compassionate manner, our mood will improve. Importantly, this doesn't mean forcing ourselves to think "positively." Removing the distortion and bias from our current thinking is usually enough to significantly lift our mood.

Actions: Do our actions support our well-being? If we don't properly care for ourselves, and many of us were conditioned not to, how are we supposed to feel? At minimum, we need the human equivalent of what a dog or cat does to feel physically and emotionally well. This means at least sufficient healthy food, water, rest, exercise, socialization, affection, stimulation, and recreation, relative to our individual preferences. When we don't care for ourselves adequately, we can develop a host of problems, including feeling depleted, stressed, anxious, and resentful in our relationships. Caring for ourselves sufficiently hearkens to airplane safety videos that insist we "place the oxygen mask on yourself first before helping others." In this area, we also identify any unhealthy actions we take (e.g., smoking cigarettes), recognizing that we can only feel so well while consistently engaging in unhealthy behavior.

Emotions: Many of our emotions result from how we think, consciously and subconsciously. When we believe thoughts that are distorted and extreme, we feel parallel emotions to them. As we bring our thinking to a more fact-oriented, accurate, and wise place, most of these emotions will shift accordingly, with the ones that don't weakening considerably. Additionally, we must learn to healthfully process difficult emotions to be well. When difficult emotions aren't healthfully processed, people tend to suppress them or express them harmfully, which can cause physical and mental health problems and lead to issues in relationships, at work, etc. As we learn to healthfully process difficult emotions and the psychological trauma from our past, our mood improves.

Situations: Are the circumstances in our lives healthy? It's hard to feel well when we're immersed in circumstances that impede our sense of well-being. Sometimes this warrants making changes, like switching jobs or setting healthier boundaries in relationships. Other times, particularly in circumstances we can't influence much or leave, we learn to make peace with them as best we can so they don't constantly derail our mood. This doesn't mean trying to force ourselves to like something we don't or anything comparable. This is about self-care and mitigating harm. In either case, doing this tends to improve our mood.

Authenticity: Are we connected with our sense of purpose and deepest desires? How are we supposed to feel if our lives are full of moments where we feel inauthentic and disconnected from our hopes and dreams? Authenticity and passion elevate our mood. On another level, if we don't prioritize engaging in behaviors we enjoy, we're less likely to feel good.

In looking at these areas in alchemical terms, we can see the elements at play. When they're healthfully and harmoniously expressed, we feel well, and when they aren't, we don't. This doesn't mean we're only supposed to feel good and balanced. There are plenty of healthy emotional experiences that don't feel good, and many difficult experiences we must have to evolve. Instead, it means that by minding these areas and nurturing ourselves within them, our overall sense of well-being will improve. We'll also become better able to manage future difficulties. Tough times are easier to weather when we don't blow them out of proportion with distorted thoughts, suffer from extreme emotions that stem from those thoughts, and then flee from this intensity by engaging in unhealthy behaviors.

For instance, let's say we have a difficult breakup from a relationship that lasted several years. At the dysfunctional extreme, we think thoughts like "I knew this would fail, like everything in my life," "I just made the biggest mistake of my life," and "I'll never fall in love again." Thoughts like these aren't justified by the facts of the situation, despite how we feel. The only way to know we'll never fall in love again is if we know the future, which we don't. It's also almost never true that someone's life has only failures, but when we attend to our failures more than our successes (and discount our successes), we can readily feel like this. The tag team of confirmation bias and the illusory truth effect can rally behind this belief until it feels like a truth of our existence. Lastly, there's no way to know if something is the biggest mistake of our lives until our lives are over. Further, what if this doesn't prove to be a mistake? Maybe breaking up was the healthiest next step for us, which we'll recognize one day. As always, it's critical to understand that feeling something strongly doesn't make it true. If we validate these thoughts, we'll feel worse, and then likely think even worse things, making us feel more upset, and so on. This is critical for those of us with mental illnesses like depression or anxiety to understand since both can make us feel and think things that are patently false.

To continue with the example of the breakup, on the wave of these distorted thoughts, we feel hopeless and worthless. We're too caught in our intense thoughts and feelings to work through our grief, so we don't. To escape these feelings, we get blackout drunk for a few days and have sex with a stranger, which makes us feel worse yet distracts us from our grief. Eventually, new problems numb us some to our grief, but the pain abides. It filters into our subconscious, reemerging as debilitating anxiety the next time someone tries to get intimate with us. Even years later, we can barely bring ourselves to think of our ex because the pain is still raw. We cast a love spell because we feel lonely and it explodes, wrecked by our contrary emanations.

Alternatively, we think fact-supported thoughts like "I'm devastated by this breakup," "I believed we were soul mates," and, "I wish we could've made it work, but I don't see how." We feel grief and regret, allowing ourselves to cry and cry. We talk our feelings out with friends, binge-watch our favorite movies, and eat comfort food. We sleep more than usual. We accept that this grief may be with us for a while, and we don't judge ourselves for how we feel. We remind ourselves that we've survived every disappointment in our lives until now, so we can probably survive this too. We play the relationship out in our mind, reflecting on what we can learn from it while continuing to be with our pain. When we feel ready, we allow ourselves to begin letting go. Eventually, we start dating again. Because we healthfully processed this loss, we don't have a new complex to reckon with as we date potential partners. What we learned from our breakup makes us a better partner in the next relationship we land in too.

Pivoting from the former approach to the latter may seem impossible, but having crossed this chasm myself and guided clients accordingly, I know it can be done. In my experience, this often just takes consistent practice with tools like those provided in this book.

As a disclaimer, the Little Work system isn't synonymous with psychotherapy or intended to be a substitute for psychotherapy. I encourage anyone experiencing psychological symptoms to seek appropriate care.

Keys to Effective Alchemical Practice

"All things human change."
—ALFRED LORD TENNYSON

In this section, we'll explore some attitudes and concepts that can help facilitate effective alchemical practice. These come from my experience with inner alchemy, work as a psychotherapist, and relationships with hundreds of spiritual seekers. They address common pitfalls I've fallen into or seen others fall into. After this, we'll delve into the topic of creating a daily practice.

The tenets of the Little Work show up frequently in this section because they support effective practice. Staying mindful of them can stabilize us when we feel shaky or guide us when we feel unsure of where to turn.

As a reminder, the tenets thus far are:

+ Master the basics.
+ Everything is energy.
+ There is no such thing as the mundane.
+ As above, so below. As below, so above.

108 | CHAPTER FOUR

- What thought created, thought can change.
- Harness the power of belief.
- Intention is magical.
- Monitor your energy.
- Live consciously.
- Try your best.
- Keep an eye on the ego.

As we continue, I'll add more tenets.

One key to effective alchemical practice is to *accept change* as best we can, which is another tenet of the Little Work. Change is inevitable in life. We can try to fight it, but the reality is that most things change. In magical practice, we don't just allow change to happen though. We seek it out. After all, change is in the definition of magic. At the same time, change involving the unknown is what the ego fears most, so emotionally preparing ourselves for change is beneficial. One of the best ways I know to do this is to contemplate the fact that if we're serious about inner alchemy, our lives will change.

It may sound obvious, but to really change your life, you have to really change your life. Our status quo thoughts and actions that brought us where we are won't take us from there. There's also no pill that transforms our circumstances overnight to match our dreams. As we explored earlier, even winning the lottery can end in disappointment if we don't ready ourselves for it, as the inertia of our status quo returns us to where we were. To support our intentions, we must develop new ways of thinking and behaving, sometimes simultaneously. These may be minor if a change is minor. Other times, changes require fundamental shifts in our consciousness and actions. Thankfully, changing consciousness is another part of magic, which rituals and spells can greatly aid us with. We must develop a willingness to change too, though, alongside being open to doing things that don't necessarily feel comfortable in support of our intentions. Once we start getting beneficial results from inner alchemy, our fear of change diminishes as we begin trusting that what awaits us in the unknown is worth striving for. Also, despite being highly resistant to change on one level, humans are extraordinarily adaptable on another.[4] As we increasingly accept change, our alchemical process and magical workings accelerate accordingly.

Another matter to accept in inner alchemy is sacrifice, which can be part of change efforts. For example, if we enjoy going to happy hour, but that's the only time we can meditate and we want to perform inner alchemy, we must set aside the smaller desire in favor of the larger one. Choices like this demand that we evaluate how serious we are about the changes we seek. Sometimes what we desire is so inconsistent with where we are that we must leave something behind altogether. If we want to be healthy and are lactose intolerant, for example, we must stop eating dairy, but perhaps that feels like extreme deprivation to us. This type of sacrifice can be difficult, particularly if it involves relationships, but it's ultimately about accepting and honoring what's in our best interest. Eventually, we'll discover that we're better off (i.e., happier, healthier, etc.) without what we left behind.

Additionally, there are ways to change that evoke huge ego resistance and others that don't. Generally speaking, the further something is from our status quo, the greater the ego's resistance to it will be. For example, trying to climb Mount Everest tomorrow without preparation will make our ego revolt, but if we train in climbing for years, it won't give us as much grief. Many bold changes can be approached this way and also be broken into smaller pieces that don't feel as psychologically overwhelming, which is called "partializing." This reduces the resistance they evoke within us. For instance, if I need to lose fifty pounds for medical reasons, the thought "One pound to go this week" is less intimidating than "Fifty pounds to go." Once we have momentum toward a goal, flipping this strategy around may be helpful (i.e., "Ten pounds to go" may feel energizing if we've already lost forty.).

How we prefer to navigate all of this can vary based on constitution. An Aries, for example, might want an inner alchemy process that feels like cliff jumping, while a Libra may prefer something more even keel. There's room for these differences. The salient point is that relative to our constitution, we work sustainably. Inner alchemy takes time. Our psyche needs to process and adjust to the changes we make, and it will, provided we give it room to. This brings us to another tenet of the Little Work: *seek moderation, even with moderation.* Once in a while, it's

---

4. DeMichele, Thomas. "Humans are Quick to Adapt to Change." Fact or Myth. March, 2016. http://factmyth.com/factoids/humans-are-quick-to-adapt-to-change/.

beneficial to go wild, but most days, moving in a steady, sustainable manner is best.

Another aspect of accepting change, and an additional tenet of the Little Work, is to *release your attachment to control*. Many of us feel a strong urge to control our environment, ourselves, and even other people. Some of this is just part of having an ego, though an extreme attachment to control is usually caused by other factors, like a history of volatile relationships, frequent childhood moves, etc. If we don't work to release our attachment to control, which mainly involves opening to things not going our way, occult practice can turn into a self-made prison where we isolate ourselves from what we can't control. The point of inner alchemy isn't to use magic to build a kingdom of what we can control at the expense of taking risks. The ego may love that, but our lives become like a windowless tower, and we can become highly anxious about things not going our way.

As we deepen in magical practice, we experience that while we're far more powerful than we realized, this power has limits, and much of what manifests is out of our hands. If we want to find peace, we must accept that. This acceptance is a karmic knot we all have, and framing what comes to us as karma can also help us release our attachment to control. Taking what manifests for us as being for our evolution, which is a traditional practice in Hermeticism and Yoga, helps us bear it, look for opportunities in it, and develop wisdom. This no light undertaking when what comes to us is painful, and doing this doesn't involve minimizing our difficult emotions or shunning them with notions like "I shouldn't be upset because this is God's plan." Releasing karma isn't about denial or pretending like a silver lining takes the gray out of every cloud, and we also needn't focus on finding opportunities or developing wisdom until we've sufficiently honored our pain. Also, recall that karma can't be understood rationally, and it's not a cosmic Santa Claus. The wisdom we develop here comes less from figuring out why things happened and more from choosing to use our experiences for alchemy. When we're dedicated to developing wisdom and evolving, these experiences eventually become alchemical.

Consequently, another tenet of the Little Work is to *embrace your karma*. The legendary dark night of the soul, when we reach the lowest of lows, is part of approaching the Great Work. We may face many such nights. Magic can fortify us to pass through them, but it doesn't take them away. When we allow ourselves to be transformed by these experiences, we open more to the divine. Generally speaking, as we release our attachment to control and embrace our karma, attachment-based tension leaves our magic. We come into greater alignment and our psychic emanation evens and expands.

Another way to help ourselves accept change and release attachment to control is to root within what doesn't change. As we connect with the divine through High Magic and meditation, we increasingly feel its presence in our lives, eventually catching a glimpse of the divine unity that exists between all things. Experiencing our innate divinity gives us a more profound fulfillment than manifestations can, and since this part of us doesn't change, that naturally makes us less attached to external conditions remaining the same in our lives. This is pivotal in inner alchemy because if we get too fixated on manifesting, we can create a state of constantly grasping for what we don't have that steers us from the serenity of the present moment. Instead, the aim is to increasingly manifest less because we're unsatisfied with our lives and more because we feel we could enrich them or better serve others—for example, by thinking it would be amazing to live in a forest or beneficial to start a retirement home for aging occultists.

Reaching this internal oasis is one of the biggest breakthroughs in our alchemical journey, and its nourishment supports and empowers us. Experiencing our inherent divinity helps us release the mountain of detrimental consensus reality pressures that have been heaped upon us since birth.

The keys to effective practice that we've explored thus far are challenging. Fearing change and surrendering control are two of the strongest universal fears in the human experience. To that end, keep in mind that inner alchemy is a process, not an event. We do our best with the techniques we learn, which sometimes pans out marvelously, and other times we're not there yet. That's OK. The important thing is to persevere and keep trying our best. In my experience, any progress made in inner alchemy is beneficial, whether we reach where we aspire to be or not.

Relatedly, it's often helpful to see outcomes in inner alchemy along a spectrum. When we see results in binary terms (e.g., success or failure, win or lose), we can disregard our progress, feeling like our efforts were wasted since we aren't where we want to be. It's a huge deal though, for instance, the first time we sense subtle energy, shift a harmful thought pattern, or manifest something intentionally. By accepting that every step along our journey is worth celebrating, we can build forward momentum and have a more fulfilling experience along the way to realizing our intentions. The journey becomes its own reward, and we feel healthier, stronger, and more capable as we walk it.

Another key to effective alchemical practice is the way we mind the tenet of always trying our best. It's important not to have unrealistic, unhealthy expectations of ourselves, which includes avoiding perfectionism. While there may be conceptual perfection, as in mathematics, and ultimate perfection, like divine unity, when it comes to human beings in the world, we're imperfect. We may experience inner perfection in meditation, but humans make mistakes, and aspiring to perfection in practice can create tremendous stress that keeps us permanently dissatisfied with our results. That said, even though practice doesn't make perfect, it does make. What we think and do affects and shapes us, so it's important to cultivate habits of thinking and acting that support our intentions.

A habit is a pattern of behavior that resists being changed or stopped. Regularly performing behaviors, whether in thought or action, creates habits, which makes them easier to repeat. When we consistently do things as well as we can, including our spiritual practices, we create a habit of performing at our optimal level. Though everyone has off days, this type of approach vastly improves our practice level over time.

One of the greatest myths about spiritual practice is that "just showing up" is sufficient, as if simply sitting for meditation will eventually make us enlightened. Unless "showing up" means trying our best in each moment, this isn't enough in my experience to lead to strong results. If we perform practices in a manner that's inconsistent, inattentive, or halfhearted, our results will mirror that (unless we win the lottery of grace). We'll also reinforce being inconsistent, inattentive, or halfhearted in other areas of our lives.

There's a popular saying from Zen teacher Cheri Huber that "how you do anything is how you do everything." How we participate in each moment affects our greater life experience. This doesn't mean we should become perfectionists who feel guilty when we watch movies for a day or don't clean the bathroom, but it's important to recognize that every moment of our lives counts to some extent. Each one holds powerful opportunities for supporting our intentions or not, and there's no pause button in inner alchemy. Everything ends up in the forge. This is one reason why the Little Work is so essential and a messy room isn't just a messy room. To that end, if we want to laze on the couch, better to do so from a set intention than a state of unconsciousness. This way, we reinforce an overall habit of acting with intent in our lives. Without becoming perfectionistic, it's critical to be as impeccable with our thoughts, words, and actions as we can.

The last key we'll explore before diving into creating a daily practice is the importance of having a strong foundation. Magical traditions have sprung up like wildflowers since the occult revival of the nineteenth century. Never in recorded history has there been a spiritual movement that so prominently featured self-directed practice and customization, and why not? This is the Age of Aquarius, the sign of innovation, revolution, and unapologetic individuality. The motion of this age is toward breaking outdated molds, questioning norms, and dissolving archaic boundaries that have outlived their usefulness. In today's world, the Mysteries have gone open-source, with once-cloistered sacred teachings now hidden in plain sight, often just a web search away. We have the freedom to weave a cohesive magical practice from whatever metaphysical elements inspire us. We can also integrate the fruits of contemporary scientific research into our metaphysical work, as I've done by incorporating psychology here. That said, we can also squander time reinventing the wheel or create unbalanced systems that don't work well. Having freedom is wonderful, but we still must know what we're doing.

Another potential pitfall of this novel freedom is that we can practice shallowly. Many practitioners today jump from path to path or practice inconsistently. This is like digging many shallow wells instead of one deep one. Spiritual training is supposed to push us outside our comfort zone, shake up our thought-dependent reality experience, and acquaint us with our shadow so we can fundamentally transform. That doesn't happen if we stop practicing when a path gets too challenging or uncomfortable, which is likely not how our ego would frame this (e.g., "I just don't feel this anymore" is often ego code for "I'm scared of what could come next"). Many of us feel like we're doing poorly or even regressing when we're actually making huge strides, we're just well outside our comfort zone. It's also common to feel like giving up when we're on the precipice of astonishing break-throughs. The Mysteries may be more accessible now, but they're still hidden in that if we don't commit to practice, we won't experience them to much depth.

Inner alchemy happens with persistence and concentration. We must build a rock-solid foundation that we can rest upon and work from. We can customize our path to fit our personal resonance with various metaphysical symbols, iconographies, implements, etc., but we must also stay the course with what we undertake if we want to get anywhere. For me, this foundation is the eight limbs of Yoga. Yoga has been part of Western occultism for over one hundred years, at least since Aleister Crowley integrated it into Thelema. In magic school, I encountered the eight limbs in Crowley's writings around the time I discovered the *Yoga Sutra of Patanjali*, a classic Yogic text that features them. I subsequently embraced the eight limbs and haven't looked back. What this has meant is that regardless of where my eyes wandered metaphysically, I maintained a daily practice anchored within the eight limbs, which has kept me on track.

The eight limbs begin with yamas (restraints) and niyamas (observances). The yamas are ahimsa (non-harming of self and other), satya (truthfulness, integrity), asteya (non-stealing), brahmacharya (living in the awareness of the highest reality), and aparigraha (non-attachment, non-covetousness). The niyamas are shaucha (cleanliness, purity of mind), santosha (contentment), tapas (austerity, self-discipline), svadhyaya (study of the sacred, introspection), and ishvara pranidhana (attunement to the supreme consciousness, surrender and devotion to the divine). The primary purpose of the yamas and niyamas isn't to impose an ethical system upon us. They're for recalibrating our thinking and acting to focus on the divine, process old karma, and minimize accumulating new karma. They keep us on an even keel internally, which supports meditation. In many traditions, brahmacharya involves celibacy. This is to assist Yogis in concentrating on Yoga and facilitate sublimating sexual energy to the higher chakras, not because there's something wrong with sex. Many modern Tantric traditions practice a form of brahmacharya that incorporates sex in a manner that preserves and harnesses sexual energy.

The yamas and niyamas have manifestational significance too. In the Yoga Sutra, it's said that effectively practicing them will remold our lives. For example, when a Yogi is rooted in ahimsa, other people will lose all feelings of hostility toward them. Svadhyaya is said to result in communion with the deeper nature of reality, and asteya brings "all jewels" (which the Yogi, having embraced Yoga, is unattached to). Otherwise, the remaining six limbs relate to meditation: establish a stable meditation posture (asana), regulate your energy through your breathing (pranayama), withdraw your senses from the outer world (pratyahara), concentrate (dharana), perceive the Ultimate with one-pointed concentration during meditation (dhyana), and enter a state of oneness (samadhi).

One needn't hold Hindu beliefs to adopt the eight limbs, aside from some beliefs that are largely universal in mysticism (even if expressed differently), like that everything is inherently divine and we can experience that. In fact, many of the great Yogic texts specifically emphasize deconditioning the mind and transcending thought-dependent reality, which includes moving beyond our beliefs. To quote Sri Swami Chidananda, a venerated Yogi from India, "The application of Yoga is universal. It may be applied within the framework of the religious life, yet it transcends religion. It is supra-religious. Yoga is far removed from any dogma or doctrine. Its basis, in so far as its concepts are concerned, is entirely universal." While approaching and utilizing Yoga with respect for its origins and humility is critical, we must also honor what it is: a path to freedom from thought-dependent reality and ego, a way to union with all things. That said, I encourage anyone interested in Yoga to read classic texts like the *Yoga Sutras*, the *Bhagavad Gita*, and the *Upanishads* and to learn about Yoga's cultural significance and history, so as to practice in a reverential, informed manner. Though Yoga has long been part of Western occultism, it hasn't always been honored and neither has the culture it comes from. It is incumbent upon us to do better.

The tenets of the Little Work emerged from my living the eight limbs of Yoga as an occultist and psychotherapist. I wrote them so others can benefit from my experiences and clinical training, which hopefully means having an easier, simpler, or more efficient alchemical process. Some of the tenets offer a "how" to the "what" of the yamas and niyamas (e.g., "How can I live in the awareness of the highest reality?" "See everything as energy," "Live consciously," etc.), though one needn't embrace the eight limbs to practice the Little Work system. The tenets provide a foundation that can stand alone or be integrated with other approaches.

On a related note, it's also important in this Aquarian era of individuality not to throw out the valuable aspects of external support. Another tenet of the Little Work is to *welcome the support of others*, which can come in many forms, including books, systems, covens, orders, teachers, etc. There's much to gain from the experiences, wisdom, and support of those who've walked the path before us. It can also be difficult to see ourselves without help, especially our shadow. When I was learning how to work with the ego, I benefitted immensely from my mentor in magic school repeatedly pointing mine out to me. My defense mechanisms were also so strong that I didn't realize how raw parts of myself were from the childhood abuse I experienced, but she did. She walked me to the glacier that had formed around my heart and supported me as it melted in tears that flowed almost every day for six months. She helped me learn to love and trust again. Spiritual teachers, mentors, and psychotherapists can greatly facilitate our journey like this and offer us expertise we don't have. If we have the opportunity on the path to work with others whom we trust, that's worth seriously considering.

With whatever approach you choose, whether it's this one or another, I implore you: build a sturdy foundation. Master the basics. When exercises seem too elementary to do as often as instructed, do them until you understand why it was important for you to do them this much. In magic school, that's what I did. I made myself sit with the concepts and perform the tasks regardless of what I thought of them. In light of the results I got, that was one of the best decisions I've ever made.

At first, try practicing a significant amount in a foundational system or series of techniques. Benefit from the work of those who came before. Once we're grounded on the path, we can experiment. Otherwise, practice as consistently as you can. Conditional, inconsistent effort yields conditional, inconsistent results. Most of our outcomes are directly tied to our degree of focus and commitment. Don't take my word for this though. We needn't take anything in magic on blind faith or because someone else said it, but we do need to make the time and effort to find out for ourselves.

CREATING A DAILY PRACTICE

"Give me a place to stand and I will move the earth."
—ARCHIMEDES

If we want magic to be part of our daily life, we must make it part of our daily life. This is where daily practice comes in. Every system of spiritual development I've encountered that has compelling evidence of sustainable, alchemical results emphasizes ongoing practice. The degree and form of practice may differ, but the emphasis on consistency doesn't. The magic that most changes our lives is the one we practice every day.

A plethora of influences constantly bombard us: friends, family, community, colleagues, entertainment, advertising, news media, government, etc. With explicit or implicit suggestions coming from all directions regarding how to think, feel, and act, how can we separate from this onslaught enough to connect with our core and discern what's healthy for us? To do this, we begin by drawing a line in the sand, with all of that on one side and us on the other. This line is the daily practice.

Establishing a daily practice involves creating non-negotiable time for alchemical work each day, which becomes a sanctuary in our schedule. Inner alchemy requires the ability to step back from our day-to-day lives and detach some from the urgency of our thoughts and feelings to work on ourselves. Daily practice helps us cultivate this ability through deciding that, regardless of what's happening in our lives, we'll make time to practice. When we don't step back like this, we can be like an author who's so consumed by a story that they feel more like it's writing them than they're writing it.

The daily practice is where we perform rituals, meditate, and engage in other supportive practices like journaling and reading sacred texts. It's a cocoon wherein the work of inner alchemy begins in earnest, and an oasis from the external demands of our lives. When we practice daily, external forces become progressively less able to seize our attention because we develop the ability to set them aside at will. At first, this usually manifests more in action than internal experience. For example, we turn off our phone when practicing, but the issues of the day still run through our mind. Eventually, we develop to where we can generally release external matters internally too.

By adhering to our daily practice, we demonstrate to ourselves that excepting emergency situations, it's OK to release external demands for a period of time each day. Many of us feel like we must respond to everything that feels urgent immediately, even when this isn't the case. Daily practice helps us become more able to take space for ourselves and let things go, at least while practicing.

In addition to external matters, daily practice also demonstrates to us that we can set our internal concerns aside each day. We can feel intense, distracting impulses and not succumb to them or be mired in a difficult emotion or thought process and choose to focus elsewhere. This doesn't mean we deny or avoid what we feel and don't attend to what we think, but rather that we become able to engage our interior world with intent. Most of the time, what we feel and think can wait until our practice is over, and as we demonstrate this to ourselves, our thoughts, emotions, and impulses increasingly lose their power to hijack our behavior. The ability to feel a strong urge and not follow it expands into the rest of our lives, which is extremely helpful in circumstances where impulsive decisions could harm us, like quitting a job in a passing rage. Our lives begin to feel more stable with the routine of unplugging each day, and our psychic emanation orients itself accordingly. In this breathing room, we can nourish ourselves and perform deep alchemical work.

Many people have profound experiences and epiphanies during spiritual retreats or workshops, but afterward, the transformations that they thought would occur in their lives don't pan out. Once back in the ocean of their old consensus realities, they couldn't maintain what they found in the containment of a retreat or workshop space. Daily practice fundamentally differs from this. It establishes a foothold where we are and builds from there. If we aim to sustainably transform ourselves, it's better to practice daily for just five minutes than several hours once a week. When we do something occasionally, our mind digests the experience as just that, an occasion. With spells, that's what we want because occasions stick out from our status quo, but day-to-day behavioral change is different. Habits shift through consistent repetition of a new desired pattern. If we want to change how we are in our day-to-day lives, we must make day-to-day changes.

For me, daily practice was the pivot point at which my life began transforming. It's where spiritual awakening and deep psychological healing became the texture of my lived experience. I thought I knew so much about spirituality before I practiced daily. I'd philosophized about it for years and practiced some, but the truth is, I had no idea how far down the rabbit hole went, and I still don't. This process has been eye-opening, humbling, awe-inspiring, and priceless, and I doubt I would've experienced most of what I have without consistent practice.

My daily practice hasn't always been easy to maintain. I'd love to say I've unfailingly brought a high degree of attentiveness to it, but I haven't. One of the ego's most common resistance tactics after a daily practice is established is to incite sloppy practice, which diminishes results. At the same time, even in my roughest moments with my daily practice, I can tell that it supports me. A daily practice can serve many beneficial purposes in our lives, but it must exist for this to occur. Though we may skip a day here or there during emergencies (although I still recommend doing something, even a quick ritual), setting aside time each day for inner alchemy is pivotal.

If you find yourself struggling to practice daily, remind yourself why daily practice is important. Everything we do in this system has purpose behind it. One reason I frequently describe the benefits of practice is because I know from psychology that awareness of an activity's potential benefits can help us build motivation to do it. We all know this to some degree from our day-to-day lives. For example, it's easier to motivate ourselves to exercise if we believe that will improve our health and sex life. When we can connect the desire we feel for something with what we must do to make that thing happen, taking those actions becomes easier. One reason I could commit to daily practice was that my psychic senses told me what my magic school teacher had done was real, and if I did these practices, I could have those experiences too. I also sensed that the healing I sought was available in my magic school, or at least that training was a step toward it. Those were my carrots. When we root in our motivation, it's easier to stay on task.

ELEMENTS OF A DAILY PRACTICE

"Look! Even now the king is raining treasure from the palace,
but this gold is only caught by those who make themselves an empty space before it."
—RUMI

In the Little Work system, we perform practices in and out of ritual space. Practices in ritual space, like High Magic and meditation, are like weight training for the subtle body. By practicing daily, we develop our psychic sensitivity and ability to harness subtle energy. We also learn to align our levels of being and ensure that they and our psychic emanation are tuned at least daily, which makes us healthier and more magically effective. We become likelier to notice if our stress level is too high, something's deeply bothering us, or we're starting to get sick, which we can then attend to.

Out of ritual space, we engage in alchemical psychological practices. The more we perform these practices, the more proficient we become in them and the deeper their effects are. In my psychotherapy practice, I often say this is like physical therapy for the mind. As we master these practices, it becomes likelier that we'll reach for them in a difficult moment when they could help us. One of the most universal challenges spiritual aspirants face is that coping tools can vanish from our awareness when we most need them. As upset strikes, we suddenly forget about breathing exercises or meditating on fire and earth for strength and stability. When we weave these practices into our day-to-day lives, they progressively stay in reach when we need them, eventually becoming reflexive.

When establishing a daily practice, the most effective method I know is to start small and build. My daily practice began with just five minutes a day. I never would've thought something so small could revolutionize my life, but it did. One benefit of such a short practice is I could strive to focus throughout it. I believe it's better to start with a brief practice we can bring our all to in terms of attentiveness than a longer one where we lack the stamina to continually try to concentrate. One way we build concentration, aside from harnessing emotion, is through practicing attentively. The mind inevitably wanders during ritual and meditation, but when we do each in short bursts, we have a better shot at continually refocusing it, which increases our ability to concentrate over time.

In my experience, a daily practice in ritual space usually includes the following elements. I provide techniques below for practicing each, but if you already have techniques you feel comfortable with, feel free to keep using them.

Relaxation is emphasized in every system of spiritual practice I know. A salient point to understand about relaxation is that it isn't just a state that comes and goes. It's a skill we can develop that's essential for meditation. Relaxation helps us become present, release tension, and steady our psychic emanation. One exercise I know that helps with learning to relax is called "fourfold breathing," which is a form of pranayama. Fourfold breathing involves breathing rhythmically into our abdomen for a count of four, holding our breath for a count of four, exhaling for four, pausing for four, and then repeating this cycle. If a four count strains you, feel free to use a three or two count instead and build from there. You can also try a four-two-four-two count. We can enhance fourfold breathing to great effect by visualizing golden light filling us as we inhale. Many sages have taught that visualizing ourselves being saturated with golden light is beneficial for our physical and mental health. This could be because of the association between golden light and the sun, the most vitalizing planet. Additionally, we can practice pore breathing, where we imagine breathing energy into our pores. To do this, we first spend a fourfold cycle visualizing all of our pores opening. Next, as we inhale, we visualize our pores (and thus our bodies) filling with golden energy that's unconditionally and infinitely potent. We repeat this with each inhale until the energy saturates us.

Another powerful relaxation technique is called "progressive muscle relaxation," which is often used to treat anxiety and can be paired with fourfold breathing. In this technique, we imagine warm, golden light filling and relaxing our body parts in ascending order (toes of the left foot, left foot, left ankle, left calf, left thigh, right toes, right foot, right ankle, right calf, right thigh, pelvis, etc.). If an area doesn't relax, we imagine our next inhalation entering this area while we tense the muscles there, hold this tension along with our breath, and then release it with our exhale while imagining this area relaxing. When learning this technique, tensing and releasing each muscle group can be best to facilitate experiencing deep relaxation. The goal here is to become able to enter a deep state of relaxation on command. Until we can do that, regularly engaging in relaxation exercises is important. These can be completed in less than ten minutes and performed while in bed before sleeping, and there are many free guided progressive muscle relaxation recordings available online.

Grounding involves releasing excess or unwanted subtle energy, usually into the earth, which is helpful to do before magical work. This energy can come from many sources, like interpersonal interactions, attending large events, sex, emotionally evocative media, etc. To ground, we can visualize roots growing from our feet into the earth and the unwanted energy flowing down these roots and being absorbed. We can also visualize a grounding cord, which is a cord of energy sent from our root chakra into the earth's core. Some people ground after rituals or spells to release any excess energy that was raised and to aid them in reorienting to a non-ritual state. Grounding can also help us feel attuned to the earth and accordingly stable, sturdy, and rooted.

Centering involves aligning our levels of being and bringing our awareness into the present moment. In practice, this generally includes relaxing, allowing our thoughts and feelings to subside, and becoming present within ourselves. Many people use steadying practices to help them center—for example, by mentally scanning their bodies, checking-in with their senses, or witnessing their breath, which helps them become quiet, balanced, and focused. Centering helps us align our subtle body and even out our psychic emanation.

Banishing removes unwanted energies and forces from a psychic space. While grounding removes unwanted energy from our aura, banishing usually expands this to include a larger space and additional things. For example, in the LBRP, we banish a host of unwanted elements from our internal and external space, psychically and psychologically, extending at least to the ends of the circle we cast during the ritual. Another way of banishing is to imagine a ball of bright light in our hands that has the power to banish the unwanted. Then we visualize this ball expanding to cover the entire space we want it to apply to. We can also specify that this energy ball will only banish particular things (as contrasted with the LBRP, which is more blanket). Otherwise, we can use the banishing hexagrams to negate planetary influences and the banishing pentagrams for their respective elemental, astral, and earth-oriented targets.

In addition to banishing, many practitioners also create energetic barriers for containment and protection, called "wards." In the LBRP, the circle we draw serves this purpose, and many witchcraft traditions teach their practitioners to create and perform magic in energy spheres, which are called "circles." A magical circle keeps unwanted influences out while also holding the energy we raise in.

The more we experience a state of consciousness, the easier it becomes to reach that state again. Consistent practice of relaxing, grounding, and centering fosters an ability to relax, ground, and center at will. Additionally, regularly grounding, centering, and banishing gives us a heightened sense of how things affect us on various levels. Many of us are shocked when we deeply ground and banish for the first time and discover that our psychic space was filled with other people's energy. The awareness we get from these practices then makes us likelier to be more intentional with how we engage with things. For example, if we notice ourselves feeling drained after parties, we may interact with partygoers differently in the future.

All of these practices have practical psychological benefits too. Imagining sending our burdens away, unwanted influences disappearing, and ourselves being protected and contained is potent to do even if there were no metaphysical benefit involved. Performing these practices daily enables us to realize that, in most cases, we can clear our internal landscape and experience some peace. The imagination is one of the most powerful tools available to us, psychologically and metaphysically.

To begin each practice in ritual space, I recommend bowing and performing a quick, seated progressive muscle relaxation followed by two to four cycles of pore breathing. This grounds, centers, and energizes us. Then we perform our rituals and meditate, which we'll explore in the following sections. To close our practice, I suggest bowing again, expressing reverence and gratitude.

In this system, we journal about how our practices went after completing them. For example, did we have any noteworthy experiences? How focused and attentive were we? We can track additional information too, like the time of day we completed our practices, the moon phase (or other astrological information), our health status, our emotional state, where we were, etc. Keeping a journal helps us stay mindful of our practice level, observe trends in how we practice, and approach practice with the aim of increasing our attentiveness over time. We also journal in this system about our alchemical psychological practices, which we'll explore in upcoming chapters.

One journaling practice I highly recommend is having a checklist of the spiritual practices we perform with a space to indicate how attentively we performed them. For example: how focused was I in ritual today on a scale between one and ten? The reason for this is the ego's tendency to nudge us toward lackluster practice. When we don't monitor our attentiveness, we can end up phoning in our practices without realizing it, which will diminish our results. Without an objective form of measure like a checklist, it's also easier to lose sight of our practices, only to abruptly realize we haven't meditated in weeks. Additionally, having a checklist full of checkmarks can make us feel like we're on a streak, which provides momentum to persist with our practice level. Once we cross a major threshold, like six months of daily meditation, it becomes unlikely that we'll break this streak.

Exercise

Consider various ways to ground, center, banish, ward, and contain. Practice one in each category.

On Ritual

"Whatever you do, whatever appeals to you,
perform it with all your heart, spirit, energy, and mind."
—DONALD MICHAEL KRAIG

In the magical tradition I trained in, we memorized High Magic rituals and performed them daily. Before joining my magic school, my magic was usually more spontaneous, and the power, depth, and alchemy of practicing memorized rituals daily astonished me. It also facilitated profound healing from psychological trauma. To alchemically transform our mind and equilibrate the elements within, having memorized rituals aligned with these aims is tremendously helpful, like a bodybuilding regimen designed to yield particular results. I encourage any aspirant who's serious about inner alchemy to perform memorized rituals daily.

Additionally, I've never seen anything help people learn to concentrate faster than daily ritual practice. My experience is that when learning to concentrate, it's better to have several things to focus on for a short time (e.g., visualizations, words, actions, etc., during a four-minute ritual) than one for a longer time (e.g., one chakra for thirty minutes). This provides the mind with less opportunity to wander and more touch points for refocusing ourselves when we become distracted. The latter example is somewhat like beginning a weight-lifting regimen with too much weight. Instead of learning to concentrate, we're more likely to just zone out. The concentrating emotion raised in ritual is also harder to muster in a more abstract meditation practice. That said, it's critical in daily ritual practice to avoid mentally drifting off as we habituate to it. Strive to keep your mind alert and focused. Staying present with the gestures, words, visualizations, and energy of the rituals helps with this.

Further, when we feel stillness in ritual, it's important to hold to it. This doesn't mean stopping a ritual to be still, but rather staying still, focused, and present in our mind when there isn't something specific to think about. Thoughts are like a veil between us and the direct experience of the moment. Part of inner alchemy is learning how to expand the experiences of stillness we find so we can experience reality more inherently. Once we reach stillness in ritual, we can have confidence that we'll eventually experience it in meditation too.

In a daily alchemical practice, rituals are the generalized blueprints for our sought alchemical effects. This is like casting major spells every day to transform us and increasingly align us with spirit and archetypal consciousness. The great human archetypes, which are deftly represented in the Major Arcana from tarot, are each part of our psyche. We all have an Empress, Hierophant, and Hanged Man within us, but we haven't necessarily developed or connected with these aspects of ourselves. When we design rituals, we have a powerful opportunity to decide what qualities and archetypes we want to cultivate within ourselves (beyond the Magician and High Priestess, which are part of our ritual attitude). If we want to develop humility and devote ourselves to the Divine Mother, for example, performing a devotional ritual to her each day can mold our reality around this intention. We just have to persist with it until this shift occurs. In my experience, the more we perform rituals with consistency, attentiveness, and care, the more real they feel.

The content of rituals and our actions within them can hugely impact us in myriad ways. For example, in the LBRP alone, magicians grow to the size of the universe, draw energy from heaven and earth, evoke archangels, and align themselves twice with the Tree of Life while vibrating Hebrew divine names. To perform this ritual effectively, we must enter a state of power and awe. By doing this daily, feeling powerful and awed becomes part of our day-to-day life. We incrementally gain access to strength that we didn't feel before. The self-confidence, assurance, reverence, awe, gratitude, humility, and spiritual alignment this ritual instills within us permeates our sense of self.

Ritual can also help us process emotions and increase our self-understanding, similar to how poetry, music, and theater can. Many seasonal rituals that feature metaphors related to the human journey have this effect. Like poetry, ritual can engage our psyche holistically, integrating analysis and imagination, reason and emotion, doing and being, etc. Ritual can be broadly and profoundly healing and transformative accordingly.

Through daily alchemical ritual practice, we equilibrate the elements within ourselves. One way to do this is by having four rituals that each spotlight an element and magical tool, all under spirit. We begin with the dagger, followed by the wand, the chalice, and the pentacle. With the dagger, we banish, which symbolizes using the discerning mind to cut through the illusions of thought-dependent reality as we seek the inspiration air is known for. With the wand, we harness the will, the wherewithal and strength to follow through on our intentions and raise our consciousness. With the chalice, we open ourselves to the celestial waters of the divine with devotion, reverence, and awe. With the pentacle, we stand tall upon the earth in alignment with our spiritual aspirations, firmly and humbly rooted with our soul perched to soar. Depending on our spiritual intentions, we can also create a fifth ritual that specifically spotlights spirit.

Though these rituals generally correspond with one element more than the others, they involve the interworking of each. For example, in the tradition I trained in, the LBRP corresponds with air and utilizes the dagger, yet is a balanced alchemical ritual in and of itself, fully integrating the forces of each element under spirit. It also includes grounding, centering, banishing, warding, and tuning ourselves to the divine. If we only perform the LBRP, we've completed a balanced practice, so please don't feel obligated to create elaborate rituals based on the four elements if that's not what you feel called to do. Start with one and see how you feel. That said, I do recommend that whatever rituals you create maintain an elemental balance. For example, avoid leaning so heavily on water for psychic development that you become disconnected from earth.

If you decide to practice multiple rituals a day, begin with one, and wait a minimum of six months before adding another, six more months before adding the next, etc. Pacing can be a major issue in magical practice (it's one reason for working with teachers). Occult history is littered with practitioners who sped through alchemical systems without sufficiently equilibrating the elements within themselves, only to have their egos win them over and pollute their work. Inner alchemy takes time, and patience is a virtue in magic (impatience is a karmic knot we all must untie). No one can force a bud to flower. What we can do, and aspire to with alchemical practice, is provide supportive conditions for these transformative processes, like placing fruit in a brown bag to ripen faster. The rest is out of our hands. Consequently, we pace ourselves in this system to avoid overstraining. Allowing at least six months before adding another ritual gives us space to gain some proficiency and depth with each ritual too. This enables its effects to permeate our psyche, psychic emanation, and outer world, giving us an experiential awareness of what it does as we notice what changed after preforming it. This forms a solid foundation to build from.

In our subtle body, there's an alchemical energy called "Kundalini" that's usually dormant at the base of the spine. While approaching the Great Work, the Kundalini awakens and ascends an energetic pathway that runs along the spine, called the "shushumna," which connects the major chakras. Ritual and meditation can stir this energy and begin this ascent. One of the greatest metaphysical benefits of having a spiritual teacher is that they can transmit divine energy into us, which is called "shaktipat." For many people, this transmission is what awakens their Kundalini energy and continual shaktipat greatly facilitates its ascent, as well as releasing karma. Initiating into the Mysteries also awakens Kundalini, which is a benefit of joining an occult group. When the Kundalini reaches the crown and stays there, we enter an enlightened state that signifies the completion of the Great Work.

Forcing Kundalini energy to rise can be dangerous. We all have blockages in our chakras that we can clear through ritual, meditation, and alchemical psychological practices. When we try to move the Kundalini without clearing these blockages, the energy can ram into them, resulting in serious health problems. We can usually avoid this issue by performing inner alchemy at a moderate pace, allowing the Kundalini to gradually rise. If you're working unsupervised, I strongly recommend going slower than you think you must when adding to your practice. At minimum, follow the recommendations I lay out here and wait until you feel solid with a ritual before adding another.

To create a ritual for inner alchemy, think about what the divine means to you, and what relationship you want to have with it. How do you conceptualize it, if at all? What evokes a sense of awe and reverence in you? Who do you want to be, in the most undiluted, archetypal sense? Contemplating these types of questions forms the basis for designing rituals, which are a space for poetry and symbolism. In practical terms, recall what we reviewed about spellcraft and apply that too. Also, consider integrating mythological figures or stories you resonate with, thus increasing a ritual's archetypal texture. Because we perform these rituals daily, it's important to design them with practical considerations in mind too (e.g., can we perform them while traveling? Do they require expensive supplies? etc.).

In my daily practice, I perform two original rituals and three classics. The classics are the LBRP (air), the Banishing Ritual of the Hexagram (BRH, fire), and the middle pillar from the Golden Dawn (spirit). The originals are an invocation of the Great Mother (water) and a Kabbalistic overview of the spiritual path that involves tarot (earth).

If you opt to use the LBRP, which I recommend (especially if you're new to magic), perform it at the start of your daily practice. If you don't, consider the elements within it and try to construct a ritual that accomplishes a similar purpose relative to what you seek (or rework it, which we'll learn about in the next section). For the other rituals, I encourage you to research. With the wand ritual, consider reviewing the BRH, or simply meditate on the element of fire and contemplate how a ritual could equilibrate that energy within you. The form is up to you (e.g., you could recite a chant while drumming, dance, sing, etc.). The essential pieces for inner alchemy are equilibrating the elemental energy and attuning to the divine.

A myriad of rituals are available online that we can draw inspiration from, including those of the Golden Dawn and Thelema. Even if you don't resonate with those systems, reviewing their rituals can be helpful because they tend to be well thought out. Some specific works you may benefit from exploring include the Charge of the Goddess by Doreen Valiente, Opening by Watchtower by Israel Regardie, The Book of the Law, and the Golden Dawn initiation rituals. We can also seek inspiration from prayers from various religions, and when it comes to ritual, there's nothing wrong with plagiarism. What matters with a ritual is how it makes us feel, what it conjures within us and connects us to, not originality. To that end, symbols that already evoke a sense of awe, reverence, or mystery in you are probably the best to use.

The Lesser Banishing Ritual of the Pentagram: A Case Study

"Those who regard this ritual as a mere device
to invoke or banish spirits are unworthy to possess it.
Properly understood, it is the Medicine of metals and the Stone of the Wise."
—ALEISTER CROWLEY

The LBRP may be the most famous magical ritual in history. It's one of the best examples I know of a balanced, alchemical ritual, and consequently, we'll explore it in depth to gain more insight into creating balanced, alchemical rituals. Over the years, aspirants have performed the LBRP with substantial variation, even fundamentally altering parts of it. Some replace the Hebrew and archangels with parallel elements from the their tradition (i.e., Druidic, Norse, etc.). I attended a workshop where about nine people performed the LBRP, and their approaches all differed. If you find yourself drawn to this ritual but turned off by parts of it, know that you have options. The original ritual itself was largely assembled from preexisting elements. While I wouldn't recommend refashioning the LBRP without first understanding how it works, there's no need to act like it's a sacrosanct direct download from God. A benefit of performing this ritual is sharing in the energy other practitioners have poured into it. Some even say that the LBRP is a key that can unlock the door to the Western Mysteries energy current.

To begin, here's the ritual itself:

0. Relax and center.

1. Stand before your altar, facing east. Bow reverentially. Pick up the dagger with your right hand (we'll review what type of dagger to work with later). If you don't have a dagger, use your extended and joined index and middle

fingers, keeping your other fingers back, as in a fist. Close your eyes. Imagine yourself growing to the size of the universe, such that the universe is contained within you. For help visualizing this, search for a video called "Powers of 10," which features an animated version of this process. When you reach the limits of the universe, imagine it existing within an orb of white light just above your head. This light is the full power of creation, the might behind the Big Bang.

2. Reach up with the dagger and draw this light into your head, filling it. Rest the dagger's tip on your third eye (i.e., the middle of your forehead just above the eyebrows). Hold the dagger so the handle is well below your forehead (i.e., so it doesn't look like you're stabbing yourself). Vibrate the word, "AH-TAH," which means "unto thee." (Rhymes with "ma" and "ma." Note: people pronounce these words differently. I've also heard this one pronounced "AH TAY" and "AH TOE.") Feel the vibrations in your body while doing this and with each word you vibrate. Intone these words for at least a few seconds.

3. Lower the dagger to your pelvis, imagining a line of white light moving down your body and into the earth. Point the dagger earthward. Vibrate "MALKUTH," which means "kingdom." (Rhymes with "shawl" and "youth.")

4. Touch your right shoulder with the dagger, imagining it filling with white light that branches off from the central line. Vibrate "VE-GEBURAH," which roughly means "power." (Rhymes with "say," "ge" as in "get," "blue," and "ma.")

5. Touch your left shoulder with the dagger, imagining it filling with white light, forming a cross with the other lines. Vibrate "VE-GEDULAH," which roughly means "glory." (Rhymes with "say," "ge" as in "get," "due," and "ma.")

6. Hold the dagger at your solar plexus, which is just under your sternum at the tip of the rib cage, with the dagger pointing up so the blade lies flat against your heart chakra area. Vibrate "LE-OLAM," which means "forever." (Rhymes with "say," "go," and "mom.") Then vibrate "AMEN" or "AUM." Yogis believe "AUM" is the primordial vibration of creation. (AUM is pronounced like "home" without the "h.")

7. Draw a flat banishing earth pentagram in blue flame in front of you (practicing drawing pentagrams against a wall can help with keeping them flat). Be deliberate as you draw. Imagine that the subtle energy's there and try to feel it. Start on your left around hip level and draw upward to just above your head (this is your line size since pentagrams are equilateral).

8. Bring your arms to your side and bend your knees slightly. As you inhale through your nose, rise up with your hands ascending the sides of your body, imagining that you're drawing energy from the earth through your body. When your hands reach eye level, pierce through the center of the pentagram with both of them, which will require lowering your head slightly (your left hand should be in a fist save for your extended and joined index and middle fingers), step forward with your left foot, and imagine the energy flowing out of you and igniting the pentagram. The second the energy moves out of you, vibrate, "YOD HE VAV HE." (Rhymes with "God," "say," "muave," and "say.") These are the four letters of the unspeakable name of God from Judaism (i.e., it's believed to be too sacred to be spoken). Step back and reverse the motion with your hands until they're at your side. Point the dagger toward the center of the pentagram and move ninety degrees to face south, drawing a quarter circle of blue light. The circle's size is up to you. Traditionally, the altar stands a bit east of the circle's center, enabling the bulk of the ritual to be performed in the center. When casting the first pentagram, walk past the altar via your left side to the east point. After completing the circle, walk back to the center via the other side (i.e., clockwise). If your altar is against the eastern wall, treat it as the easternmost point of the circle, performing all but the pentagram casting in the circle's center. Move at a pace that facilitates being deliberate.

9. Draw a pentagram as described above. Vibrate "ADONAI." (Rhymes with "ma," "dough," and "sigh.") This means "lord." Then continue drawing the circle and face west.

10. Draw a pentagram as described above. Vibrate "EHIEH." (Rhymes with "say," "fee," and "say.") This means "I am." Then trace the circle to the north.

11. Draw a pentagram as described above. Vibrate "AGLA." (Rhymes with "ma," "buh" as in "butter," and "ma.") This is an acronym that stands for

"Atah Gebur Le-Olam Adonai" or "Thou art great forever, my Lord." Then trace the circle to the east. Return to the center as described above.

12. Bring your feet together and hold your arms out like a cross, with your left hand in a fist and your right holding the dagger (pointed up).

13. Say "Before me," and then vibrate, "RAPHAEL." (Rhymes with "ma," "bye," and "bell.") As you do this, visualize the Archangel Raphael in front of you in yellow garb holding a caduceus.

14. Say "Behind me," and then vibrate, "GABRIEL." (Rhymes with "ma," "free," and "bell.") As you do this, visualize the Archangel Gabriel behind you in blue garb holding a chalice.

15. Say "At my right hand," and then vibrate, "MICHAEL." (Rhymes with "me," "high," and "bell.") As you say this, visualize the Archangel Michael at your right in red garb holding a sword.

16. Say "At my left hand," and then vibrate, "AURIEL." (Rhymes with "or," "free," and "bell.") As you do this, visualize the Archangel Auriel at your left in brown garb holding a pentacle.

17. Say "For about me flames the pentagram" while visualizing the pentagrams you've drawn.

18. Say "And within me shines the six-rayed star" while visualizing a hexagram (composed of a red upward triangle and a blue downward one) within you with your heart in its center.

19. Repeat steps two through six. Replace your dagger. Bow.

There are many videos online demonstrating how to perform this ritual. I encourage you to watch some while reading along with these instructions.

The LBRP has three distinct parts. The first is the Kabbalistic Cross (the part that's repeated), which features a rough translation of the Lord's Prayer (i.e., "Unto thee, the Kingdom, and the Power, and the Glory, Forever, Amen"). Since Malkuth, Geburah, and Gedulah (also named Chesed) are spheres on the Tree of Life, this process involves attuning ourselves to the tree. Through vibration and visualization, we construct a thought form of it in our aura, which helps us align with its energies and access its myriad uses. Additionally, we draw divine energy down from Kether (to the degree we currently can, which develops over time) and connect with the earth, permeating our bodies with divine energy while rooting ourselves. This process is purifying, aligning, and empowering. It helps clear blockages in the chakras we touch or are near with our hand. In this version of the ritual, that includes all the major ones. Feeling vibrations and visualizing light in these areas helps clear the blockages too. Through vibrating holy names and visualizing divine light, we also raise our vibration.

The more conventional meanings of Geburah and Chesed on the tree are strength/severity and mercy/loving-kindness, and the LBRP balances these forces within us through the heart, which signifies Tiphareth. The transposition of the tree onto our bodies is one reason we hold the dagger with our right hand in this ritual (i.e., on Geburah's side). Through the Lord's Prayer, we affirm our fundamental divinity because, as part of the whole, we are the kingdom, the power, etc. We recognize our nature as a drop in the ocean of undifferentiated oneness, and doing this helps us link with our Higher Self, however we want to conceptualize that. If we end the Kabbalistic Cross with "amen," we affirm, "It is so" (a rough translation of amen). If we vibrate "AUM," we attune ourselves with the primordial vibration of the universe.

Next, we intone Hebrew divine names after drawing the banishing pentagrams. Vibrating these names tunes us to these divine energies across our levels of being. This brings divine energy into our aura, helping purify it and our mind. The pentagrams banish unwanted energies (e.g., astral influences, unsupportive thoughts, energetic residue from others, etc.). As a balanced representation of the elements and spirit, working with the pentagram also helps us balance ourselves elementally. Importantly, this ritual is a banishing ritual because we use banishing pentagrams. With invoking pentagrams, it becomes the Lesser Invoking Ritual of the Pentagram, and most of this ritual is about attuning with the divine, not banishing (although in attuning with the divine, banishing happens automatically). Otherwise, pulling some of the energy we project through the pentagrams from the earth helps us align with the earth and stay grounded.

After this, we evoke four archangels. Evocation involves summoning something externally, like a spirit, angel, deity, etc., as contrasted with invocation. During the archangel evocation, we align with the energies of the archangels (another attunement to the divine) while partnering with them. To that end, this evocation isn't about binding the archangels to our will or anything comparable. We welcome them from a reverential place. Throughout the LBRP, we stand in our power, but not our ego: the might of Geburah tempered by the loving-kindness of Chesed, brought into unity within the heart.

For years, I was ambivalent about this section because it felt too Christian to me (with Christianity being the basis upon which many people challenged my civil rights and worse). Eventually, I connected with it through appreciating that though archangels are prominent in Christianity, they represent forces that predate religious symbolism. These forces are aspects of our psyche, like archetypes, that are beneficial to work with, and this work needn't occur in a Christian-feeling way.

Archangels also exist in the higher planes. Even if the archangels in the higher planes are simply thought forms enlivened by years of focused psychic energy, they're still substantial in their own context. If they're more inherent than that, what appears as an archangel to a Christian might manifest as a deity to a Hindu. Archangels can also be several of these things, like how an image of the Divine Mother connects us to the universal force of Motherhood, higher plane maternal deities, and whatever we imagine mother-ness to be. Moreover, the divine is the divine regardless of what we call it. Though chanting particular divine names may have unique subtle effects, and there are differences between subtle beings at the level of personality (e.g., Zeus isn't synonymous with Michael), the divine ultimately transcends symbolism. This is why swapping out the archangels and divine names in the LBRP is OK: in the LBRP, we aspire to that ultimate level. The names and forms are meant to bridge us there. That said, if you swap the archangels out, replace each archangel with a deity that has a similar-feeling tone, so as to maintain the alchemical balance of the ritual.

When we speak of the hexagram in the LBRP, we acknowledge the Mystery of the merging of heaven and earth. Affirming that "within me shines the six-rayed star" validates that the completed Great Work is already within us; we need only realize it. Other versions of the LBRP use the language "in the column shines the six-rayed star" and "behind me shines the six-rayed star." These refer to the middle pillar of the tree and convey a similar notion since we've attuned ourselves to the Tree of Life via the Kabbalistic Cross.

The LBRP is profoundly alchemical. When performed daily, our thought forms of the divine strengthen and expand, increasingly dissolving ego impurities and clearing chakra blockages. The LBRP incrementally surfaces our karma and psychological issues, as any type of consistent attunement to the divine will.

Aligning with the divine makes whatever stands against this alignment self-evident, like how the mess in a dark room becomes apparent when we turn the lights on. When we're unbalanced toward sluggishness, the LBRP enlivens us. When we're too amped up, it centers us. If you find yourself struggling to stop procrastinating, you can use the LBRP to help with that.

The LBRP also aids us in navigating the ego's resistance to inner alchemy. A primary intention of the LBRP is to banish the inner saboteur from our magical work, mental state, and inner guidance, which is one reason aspirants traditionally learn it early in their training. That said, the ego tends to revolt when people start practicing the LBRP daily, manifesting an assortment of obstacles. This makes sense given what we can see this ritual does, even after just scratching its surface. These reactions wane as we persist with the LBRP daily.

With regard to the previous section, grounding, centering, banishing, warding, and containment are all facets of the LBRP. It works on each level of our being, with things to do, feel, visualize, and say at every step of the process, as well as subtle energy to direct. I've never experienced anything that tones and tunes my subtle body like the LBRP, particularly when combined with the middle pillar, which I encourage you to research.

Exercise

If you opt to try the LBRP, begin practicing it daily. Otherwise, contemplate what you want the first ritual you write for inner alchemy to be like, write it, and start performing it. Reread the section in part one on ritual attitude before beginning your ritual practice.

MEDITATION AND MINDFULNESS

"The world appears to you so overwhelmingly real because you think of it all the time; cease thinking of it and it will dissolve into thin mist."
—NISARGADATTA MAHARAJ

Meditation is one of the most potent practices I've encountered for inner alchemy. It has a myriad of benefits beyond the relaxation and stress reduction it's commonly known for. Meditation involves concentrating on one thing to the exclusion of all else, and the ability to concentrate that we develop during ritual fosters our ability to meditate. What we meditate on depends on our objective, as different subjects garner different results. In Yogic meditation, Yogis often focus on chakras to clear blockages, develop spiritually, and stimulate the Kundalini energy. Some visualize deities or light within while meditating too.

Concentrating on one thing to the exclusion of all else involves excluding our experience of meditation. The aim is to become completely absorbed in our meditation's subject, withdrawn from other sensory or mental activity. To aid in this, we learn to practice mindfulness. Mindfulness is a witnessing state, rooted in the present moment, that's non-conceptual, non-judgemental, and detached from personal identification. In practice, this means if we mindfully eat, we observe what's happening within us while eating (i.e., the sensory information we receive and whatever thoughts and feelings arise). While doing this, we don't identify with our thoughts and feelings (e.g., "this tastes good," "I'm tired," etc.). We simply witness. Mindfulness can be practiced in any area of life.

When we've never practiced meditation or mindfulness and hear someone say "You are not your thoughts and feelings," it's usually counter to our experience. Most of us start mindfulness practice with our thoughts and feelings and awareness being like two clasped hands that feel like a seamless whole. As mindfulness practice acquaints us with pure awareness, these hands start to separate. We begin experiencing that this witnessing awareness is more fundamentally us than our thoughts and feelings, which appear superficial and ephemeral in comparison. The more we practice mindfulness, the further we can separate these hands and the abler we become to pivot into mindfulness at will. This paves the way for profound healing. The ability to detach from our thoughts and feelings and appreciate that they're not what we are facilitates applying alchemical tools in a manner that's difficult to do when we feel smothered or trapped by our thoughts or feelings. Experiencing this novel vantage point also shifts the way we relate to thoughts and feelings (i.e., thoughts and feelings affect us differently when they aren't as close to our center). A mountain lion is less terrifying when it's fifty feet away versus five.

Mindfulness generally features in meditation in two ways. The first is through practicing pure mindfulness meditation, which involves concentrating on mindfulness to the exclusion of all else. We simply close our eyes and witness. The second, which we'll learn here, marries mindfulness with meditating on a different subject through being mindful while focusing on that subject—for example, by concentrating on the heart chakra in the present moment without judgements, identification, or concerns of outcome. As we mindfully focus during meditation, distracting thoughts and feelings fade. We aim in meditation to be relaxed and detached yet simultaneously alert and one-pointed in our concentration.

There are many benefits to meditation beyond what it's commonly known for. As with ritual, a balanced meditation practice can align our levels of being, and repeatedly quieting our mind during meditation releases whatever emotional discord we've accumulated throughout the day. Eventually, meditation becomes like a psychic reset button. The practice of repeatedly quieting our mind can bring tremendous peace to our lives, particularly as we realize we can do this during challenging life circumstances, provided we don't avoid or deny our emotions. We'll explore this more in the water chapter. Additionally, the equanimity we experience during meditation is nutritive and restful. Quieting our mind also evens out our psychic emanation, enabling our energy to flow smoothly, which heals imbalances and supports the manifestation of our intentions.

Otherwise, an attentive daily meditation practice brings us many degrees of awareness. At first, we get to know our thought patterns well, considering that until we can meditate proficiently, we're stuck in our head with our thoughts. When we unconsciously follow our thoughts, we may not realize we have thought patterns, but when we stop biting every hook our mind tosses our way, we can see the cycles play out. Meditation is the first place where many of us experience that thoughts need our engagement to hold sway over us, and when we withdraw it, they weaken or even vanish.

One of the most transformative experiences of my life happened while meditating after arguing with a friend. I couldn't stop thinking about the argument, and I was furious about how it distracted me from my practice. I understood conceptually that these were just thoughts and they needn't capture my attention like this, but I was too worked up to set them aside. At some point, a deep part of myself cried out, "I don't care about this enough to disturb my practice!" and the thoughts about the argument burst like a soap bubble. My mind cleared. These thoughts had felt so substantial, and then they vanished like they'd never existed. I was astonished, and that's just the tip of the iceberg of how meditation can illuminate the nature of thought for us.

By repeatedly redirecting our thoughts to one subject during meditation, we become more able to guide our thoughts in general. Eventually, this enables us to choose what to think about and when, which can be useful if we're struggling to find relief from an upsetting thought. We may not be able to halt a thought process until we've meditated for years, but before then, the mental strength we develop from meditating will enable us to think about topics differently, which affects how we feel. For example, maybe I can't stop thinking about an argument I had yet, but I can think compassionately while I ruminate. This ability to guide thought helps us think more healthfully and align our thoughts with our intentions, which keeps our psychic emanation supportive of them.

Meditation is often where we start experientially understanding that "how you do anything is how you do everything." As we turn inward, the impact of our thoughts and actions becomes clearer, especially as our sensitivity increases, which occurs as our practice deepens. When we eat too much sugar, for example, we feel it. If we had an explosive argument, we experience its echoes. Whatever's amiss in our lives tends to appear during meditation at some point. If we watched a TV show recently, scenes from it might replay in our mind. If we just engaged passionately with a topic, charged thoughts about it will likely show up, and we'll be able to perceive the heft our passion gives them. It also becomes apparent during meditation that focusing on a subject grows that subject within our mind. As our psychic sensitivity develops, we become able to perceive how all of these things impact our psychic emanation. We also start noticing when what manifests around us connects with our thoughts, and how. Through meditation and ritual, we begin feeling our subtle body too. As we feel it, we gain a better sense of what it's doing and how it operates, including how our thoughts and actions affect it. We needn't seek out any of these developments or experiences. They're a normal consequence of learning to meditate, provided we have a consistent, attentive practice.

Many distractions appear during meditation, and the ego is behind most of them. Once we stop following our day-to-day thoughts, the ego may surface unpleasant or thrilling thoughts from the past, including thoughts we've forgotten, or tempt us with ones about the future. For example, suddenly we're thinking about how awful high school was or how exciting travelling abroad would be, for no apparent reason. Sometimes, especially with painful memories, this results from releasing chakra blockages. As these thoughts come, we deal with them like all distractions in meditation: by redirecting our awareness to the focus of the practice. When these thoughts are particularly compelling, we can address them with alchemical psychological practices after finishing meditating. Meditation is often a primary venue for discovering these types of thoughts, which can be karmic knots. Once subconscious material becomes conscious, we can do something about it.

Many new meditators feel like the idea of quieting their mind is hopeless. I epitomized this. Back then, my thoughts raced, my emotions were volatile and extreme, and both felt impossible to rein in. For over seven years, I'd struggled with insomnia involving surging thoughts and emotions (and anxiety and depression since childhood). Then I began practicing intensive Hatha Yoga daily, which cured my insomnia within two weeks and inspired me to study Yoga earnestly. I practiced at that level for about six months and my insomnia never returned. About four months into that, I learned to meditate in magic school and began practicing daily. I started getting the results mentioned earlier, which motivated me to persist with meditation even though my mind didn't quiet for years. The diverse benefits of meditation are worthwhile, whether our mind quiets soon or not.

NAVEL, HEART, AND THIRD EYE CHAKRA MEDITATION

"Your task is not to seek love, but merely to seek and find
all the barriers within yourself that you have built against it."
—RUMI

In the Little Work system, we meditate on three chakras: the navel, located under the belly button about an inch inside the body; the heart, located at the breast bone; and the third eye, located inside the head just above the space between the eyebrows. In a nutshell, this builds the will, opens the heart, and increases our vision and connection to spirit. We also meditate on stillness to explore the deeper levels of our being. Consistently meditating on these three chakras has substantial benefits. When we meditate on chakras, we draw energy to them, which helps cleanse them of blockages. This is somewhat like spraying a dirty surface with a hose. In this metaphor, our attention is the hose and our concentration level is the water pressure, which both correspond with how quickly we clear these blockages.

As I mentioned earlier, everyone begins meditation practice with blockages. Some of these are karmic knots from previous lives, while others originate from our experiences. One of the most common sources of these blockages is growing up in an environment that didn't offer us unconditional love and acceptance, to whatever degree that affected our sense of self-worth. Many of us in the LGBT community were taught there's something fundamentally wrong with us, which can result in navel and heart chakra blockages (because this wounding often makes it harder to love and trust others). These blockages are like psychological splinters of varying sizes that hurt us as we step through life. Regardless of where our blockages originated, chakra meditation is an effective method for clearing them, especially when paired with the psychotherapeutic tools we'll learn.

Clearing chakra blockages doesn't necessarily affect us in linear or straight-forward ways. During meditation, we may feel achiness, coldness, tension, or discomfort in a chakra, and when blockages surface, we may become emotional, which we respond to by remaining focused on the chakra. Memories related to difficult experiences we had in this chakra area can appear, and if they do, we hold these memories in the light of our visualization and continue focusing on the chakra. Importantly, there's nothing forceful in this type of meditation. We relax, stay mindful, and patiently allow our visualization to do its work.

Clearing blockages can also cause difficulties related to chakra areas to man-ifest outside of our meditation practice. For example, after navel meditation, we may find ourselves remembering incidents when we felt shamed or even have ex-periences that evoke this issue. When things like this happen, we apply mindful-ness and other alchemical practices we'll learn later. This is one reason we needn't worry about discerning what to work on in our alchemical process. By energizing our chakras and aligning with the divine during rituals and meditation, the issues we need to address will surface.

As a chakra's blockages clear, it opens. Thankfully, we needn't fully heal or re-solve all of our issues in a chakra domain for this to happen. What we each per-ceive when chakras open may differ, but the experience is palpable. When your heart opens, for example, you'll know.

In this system, the first chakra we meditate on is the navel, the seat of our ego and will. Feeling persistently ineffectual, insecure, powerless, or weak-willed indi-cates the presence of blockages here. An open navel signifies someone who is largely at peace with themselves and strong-willed. If they need to stand up for themselves, they can, even if they feel apprehensive in doing so. Many of us have blockages here from being encouraged to be other than we are (i.e., richer, smarter, thinner, etc.). Meditating on this chakra awakens courage and the confidence to be and accept ourselves. If we meditate on the navel in isolation, it can become unbalanced, manifesting in selfishness, vanity, and narcissism.

One reason we meditate on the navel, as well as perform strengthening rituals, is that many of us live in places where we must be strong and able to establish firm boundaries in order to be healthy and practice inner alchemy. With an open navel, we can handle adversity and protect ourselves from being taken advantage of. Also, every spiritual aspirant needs a strong will to keep themselves from getting knocked off the path.

The second chakra we meditate on is the heart, which is the seat of love within us and where we connect with others. It's the first chakra above the individual ego's concerns. When we grow up in an environment that prominently features emotional or physical violence, conditional love, greed, or selfishness, it's normal to have blockages here. Called the "Lotus of the Heart" in some Eastern traditions, the heart chakra connects us with higher consciousness, being the veritable seat of the soul. Kabbalistically, the heart is where heaven meets earth in Tiphareth, the central sphere of enlightened consciousness on the Tree of Life. Through meditating on our heart, we can find this sanctum within ourselves.

As the heart opens through meditation, devotional rituals, acts of compassion, and affirmations, we discover an inexhaustible source of love within that can help us heal and transform. Consistently connecting with this source roots us in unconditional love. One of the metaphysical secrets of well-being is that we don't need anything from others in order to feel good, which is the opposite of how most of us are conditioned. This doesn't mean we don't need other people. It means the validation we've been taught to seek externally can be found within, and we can feel love simply by meditating on love. This love doesn't wax or wane, though our perception of it can. Unlike external validation, which we may have to jump through hoops to get, this love comes with no strings attached. It's a fundamental part of ourselves. We simply tune to it and it's there.

By rooting in this love, we automatically become less attached to how others think of us and less dependent on them emotionally. This love increasingly frees us from any felt need to please others or find our sense of self-worth in relation to them (by wanting their attention, comparing ourselves to them, etc.). We become able to connect with others authentically, and in our fullness, love unconditionally.

As the heart opens, we also become able to psychically connect with life. Feeling the spirit within ourselves enables us to feel spirit elsewhere. With this sensitivity, we can perceive the divine light in others, as well as how disconnected they are from it. Unhealthy mental, emotional, and behavioral patterns, which generally come from living in societies that are alienated from nature and otherwise dysfunctional, are like visible veils atop this light. As we remove these veils within ourselves, it becomes apparent how they obscured us from this light. This helps us become compassionate with others because we recognize that they're unaware of their effulgence, like we were, and much of the harm in the human world stems from this lack of self-awareness. If a critical mass of people found the inner light, most of the world's ills would wither away.

In developing this sensitivity, however, we also gain a greater sense of what people feel underneath their exteriors, beyond standard empathy. Having this information, which comes unsought, can lead to a difficult adjustment period. For example, we may have a friend we thought was easygoing who we discover is insecure and resents us. It's critical not to interpret more from these perceptions than is justified (e.g., "She resents me" doesn't mean "She wants me to fail"). Alternatively, we may discover that an ostensible sourpuss has a heart of gold.

We may not always abide in this open-heartedness. Egos usually feel threatened by the freedom and acceptance of this state, despite how blissful it is, and act accordingly. But once we reach this river within, we never forget it's there. We can't fall under a consensus reality spell that tells us we're unworthy to the degree we could before. We also can't fall into the belief that others are fundamentally evil when we know we're all divine and that most of just haven't experienced this truth. Importantly, this open-heartedness doesn't make us weak, sentimental, or overly accommodating of others' dysfunction. Instead, it enables us to navigate ignorance without losing perspective. We know we're under a collective spell of self-deception, and it's part of our duty as magical practitioners to break it.

The last chakra we meditate on is the third eye. This chakra connects us to higher vision and the higher planes. Through the third eye (and the heart), we receive guidance from our Higher Self, which can help us determine how to proceed in life. The third eye can also aid us in gaining insight into our karmic cycles and having experiences like astral projection. For those of us who aspire to the Great Work, third eye meditation helps us raise our resting awareness up the chakras en route to the crown. Many practitioners have spirit guides or ascended masters they work with, and the third eye is the conduit through which this occurs. It's critical when meditating on the third eye (or any chakra) not to lust for the experiences it can give. This can cause tension that results in psychological or physical problems, and this lust also keeps us from concentrating one-pointedly and being in the present moment. If we notice ourselves doing this, we relax and mindfully refocus on the chakra at hand.

When starting a meditation practice, it's normal to experience some mental tension as we learn to concentrate one-pointedly without tensing the area we're focusing on. Getting a handle on how to do this can take time. That said, if you experience headaches or pain in the third eye area while meditating on it, meditate on the heart instead. Most teachers I've encountered teach that heart meditation is safe. Some say this is because the heart is the central point of the chakra system and opening it balances the lower chakras while expanding our consciousness to integrate the energy of the upper chakras. Once your heart opens, try meditating on the third eye again. Until then, use the time you would've spent meditating on the third eye to meditate on the heart (e.g., double your amount of heart meditation).

Meditating on the navel, heart, and third eye chakras for the same amount of time each day (or more for the heart than the others) composes a balanced practice. Unless we're meditating on all seven chakras, I was taught to meditate on the other chakras primarily if there's an issue with one of them. For instance, if we experience sexual dysfunction, we can meditate on the sacral chakra. Because we feel when chakras open, we'll likely know when we've achieved our desired result there (and our sex life will improve accordingly too). If we continue meditating on this chakra, it can become unbalanced (e.g., leading to hyper sexuality that interferes with work performance). Because of the potential for subtle body imbalances, it's generally better to meditate on an element rather than a chakra if we seek temporary support in a situation. For instance, if we lack confidence before a difficult conversation, we can meditate on the alchemical symbol for fire instead of the navel.

How to Meditate

"Happiness is your nature. It is not wrong to desire it.
What is wrong is seeking it outside when it is inside."
—RAMANA MAHARSHI

To practice meditation, first select a posture. Two appropriate postures for beginners are shared below. Though these postures are precise, approach them with a sense of ease. Ideally, attend a meditation class to ensure your posture is correct. Sitting in an incorrect posture, especially repeatedly, can lead to injury.

The pictured posture below is the Burmese posture. For this posture, sit on a cushion such that your hips are higher than your knees. If you're sitting on a circular meditation cushion (zafu), sit on the front third of it. Straighten your back while maintaining ease in your body. Cross your legs in front, resting the heel of your front foot above the ankle of your back foot. Place your palms face down on your knees or thighs, whichever is more comfortable, or with your right hand resting on your left palm with your thumbs touching, in the navel area (pictured). Each time you sit, alternate the leg you place in front.

You can also meditate in a chair. To do this, place items under its back legs to create an angle that enables your hips to be higher than your knees or buy a cushion designed for postural support while sitting in a chair. Don't sit deep in the chair unless doing so still allows for correct posture. Straighten your back while maintaining ease in your body. Place your feet on the floor, approximately hip width apart, and your palms face down on your knees or thighs.

Figure 12: Burmese Posture

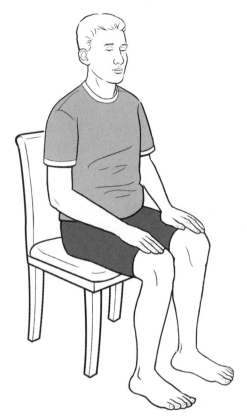

Figure 13: Meditation Posture in a Chair

While meditating, breathe through your nose and into your abdomen, allowing your breath to naturally govern itself, which may take a few sessions to acclimate to. If you want, you can practice fourfold breathing at the start of meditation to help yourself relax. You can also practice fourfold breathing throughout meditation, provided it becomes automatic. Before meditating, center yourself. If you experience difficulty centering, breathe into your abdomen for five to ten breaths, imagining warm, golden relaxing light there or do a quick progressive muscle relaxation.

Next, bring your awareness to the navel. Visualize a fist-sized orb of golden light there, like a small sun, for the designated amount of time. Then do this in the heart. While in the heart, consciously tuning to love can be beneficial—for example, by recalling the last time you felt unconditional love and allowing this feeling to fill you. Next, meditate on the third eye in the same manner. In each section, imagine the golden light radiating into every cell of your body. If you're devoted to a primary deity, you can visualize this deity in the orbs of the heart and third eye. Whenever you find yourself distracted, softly guide your awareness back to the chakra at hand.

While meditating, concentrate as best you can without tensing yourself. Feel the presence within, and seek the stillness beneath mental, emotional, and physical activity, like listening for the sounds within a quiet room. When we meditate, we incrementally perceive our subtle body, but this is less likely to happen as quickly or at all if we don't attend to what we feel. If you don't feel anything at first, don't worry. Just continue focusing on feeling as much as visualizing. Eventually, we reach a "sweet spot" in meditation where it feels blissful. Once we do, the desire to return to and deepen this state helps us motivate ourselves to continue meditating. After meditating on the chakras, meditate on stillness within, allowing the practice to settle and expand. To end the practice, wiggle your fingers and toes and bring your awareness back to the room. If possible, remain silent for ten minutes or so after meditating.

There are several techniques I know that facilitate building concentration during meditation. One is counting. It becomes apparent in meditation that the mind can think about more than one thing at a time, albeit not well. We can focus on a chakra, for example, yet also find ourselves running through our grocery list, eventually losing touch with the chakra altogether. When you catch yourself distracted from a chakra, try anchoring your attention in it by internally counting in cycles from one to ten, alongside visualizing the golden orb. Once you feel stably focused on the chakra, stop counting. If you become distracted again, count again. The reason for cycling from one to ten is if we count indefinitely, we're likelier to zone out. Having to remember to restart counting at ten helps us stay present. Similarly, if you're visualizing a deity within a chakra, you can internally offer it mantras or prayers to help steady your focus, stopping once your focus stabilizes.

Another technique that can help us build concentration is performing an internal guided meditation. At each section, we can think something like, "visualize a golden orb in the navel, feeling the power of will…" etc., which can help anchor us in the practice. This should be brief and only repeated in a section if we find ourselves highly distracted (e.g., "bring your awareness back to the radiating orb…") because guided meditation can be too stimulating. In my experience, counting is generally better for refocusing because it's less involved and stimulating.

An additional technique that can aid with increasing concentration in meditation is staying mindful of breaks. A break occurs whenever we become distracted during meditation. Breaks are either physical or psychological. Any bodily motion unrelated to breathing is a physical break. The ego tends to manifest many types of sensations to cause physical breaks. This is one reason ensuring we have correct posture is critical. When we sit properly, we can be more certain that any aches or pains we feel aren't indicative of a potential injury from postural misalignment. Upon feeling an urge to move during meditation, we relax and refocus on the meditation's subject. With time, these disturbances diminish and our attention progressively withdraws from the physical level.

A psychological break is any thought or feeling we have during meditation that isn't part of the practice. These were described earlier, and the salient point is to see these as breaks and strive not to indulge them. No matter how compelling thoughts or feelings are, the response to them is singular: refocus on the meditation's subject, using mindfulness to let these thoughts and feelings fade as much as possible. We may also experience psychic phenomena during meditation (or what appears to be this), like overhearing a stranger's thoughts. The response to these experiences remains the same: refocus on the meditation's subject.

To further strengthen our meditation practice, it's beneficial to reflect on our concentration level in our journal, track it in our checklist (e.g., on a scale from one to ten), and note any clear breaks we experience. This helps us stay mindful of the need to minimize breaks and practice at the highest level we can. As far as I know, tracking breaks came from Aleister Crowley, and I think it's a tremendous practical contribution to meditative work. While these observances may seem draconian, fundamentally, they're about practicing well. I've known many long-term meditators who've never experienced strong, sustainable results, and I think that's largely from inconsistent and unfocused practice. These are ways to avoid that.

Now that we've reviewed the elements of a daily practice in ritual space, we can assemble one. In this system, that involves:

Going to a quiet space in which you won't be disturbed for the duration of the practice (silence any phones).

1. Bowing.

2. Relaxing, grounding, and centering with fourfold pore breathing, using progressive muscle relaxation if needed (a fast version can be done once we're adept at relaxing, where we spend one cycle of four on our legs, one on our pelvis, our torso, etc.).

3. The LBRP or a self-created ritual that includes banishing, warding, containing, and aligning with the divine.

4. Three other alchemical rituals and one dedicated wholly to spirit, if desired. Wait at least six months before adding each additional ritual.

5. Navel, heart, and third eye chakra meditation. After four weeks of ritual practice, begin daily meditation if you feel ready and able to commit to it. Start with two minutes per chakra, in the navel, heart, and third eye order, preceded by about ten seconds of centering and followed by two minutes of stillness. When you've completed this practice at least six days a week for four weeks, increase the time in each chakra and stillness by one minute if you want to and feel ready. If you subsequently miss more than four consecutive days of practice, subtract this added time. Continue adding time in this manner (i.e., moving from eight minutes to twelve, sixteen, twenty, etc.). Stop increasing your chakra meditation time after reaching ten minutes per chakra, adding further time to the stillness section alone. In my experience, ten quality minutes per chakra is sufficient, and transitioning between sections too often prevents the depth that can be experienced with prolonged focus on one subject. There are several meditation apps available that can keep time intervals like this. I use a chime recording I made on my computer that sounds when it's time to switch chakras. Having to check a clock or reset a timer while meditating is inadvisable, given what a significant break that poses.

6. Bowing again.

7. Journaling.

SACRED SPACE

"The generation of atmosphere, the aura of the uncanny,
is one of the most important secrets of magic."
—DOREEN VALIENTE

In addition to daily practice, designating a specific place in our home for rituals, spells, and meditation is also beneficial, which is a way of creating "sacred space." Sacred space is space that feels sacred to us, and it can be internal or external. Ritual, meditation, and alchemical psychological practices are ways of creating internal sacred space. We create external sacred space through acting in, and caring for, a space in a sacred-feeling manner. External sacred space can be permanent or temporary. For example, when we cast a circle, we create temporary sacred space.

To evoke the feeling of sacredness, many people decorate their sacred spaces with items that feel sacred to them, like art, candles, crystals, and statues. When determining how to decorate a sacred space, we can ask ourselves questions like: what makes me feel holy? Filled with awe? Wonder? Mystery? What do I love? What makes me feel nourished and supported? As long as we feel sacredness when we enter a sacred space, we've effectively created it.

Many magical practitioners create permanent sacred space in their home, the centerpiece of which is often an altar. An altar is a surface that's used during rituals and spellwork or otherwise aligned with magical intent. In addition to this primary altar, some practitioners have separate ones dedicated to other things, like the four elements, deities, love, prosperity, etc. Altars can be whatever size and shape we want, though considering factors like sacred geometry and how tall we are can be beneficial (i.e., how far do we want to have to bend down to pick up magical tools?). If an altar table isn't an option, a dresser top can be used or even a cloth that's taken out during magical practice and then put away. In ceremonial magic, the altar is traditionally made of wood and formed of two stacked cubes, which symbolizes the Great Work. Regarding where to place items on an altar, layouts vary between magical traditions. I encourage you to find a layout that resonates with you or create your own. I generally place tools elementally (i.e., the chalice in the west/water, etc.).

Creating and maintaining sacred space helps us sustain, augment, and contain our magical work. Our altar physically represents the reality we seek to create as a magical practitioner, and performing our spiritual practices in the same place or with the same setup helps us connect with them more readily. One explanation for this comes from the psychological phenomenon called "classical conditioning."

Classical conditioning, roughly put, is a learning process wherein a neutral thing becomes associated in our brains with something that elicits a particular response in us, such that the neutral thing then elicits this response too. This is probably best illustrated by example, the most famous of which is that of Pavlov's dogs. Ivan Pavlov, a Nobel Prize–winning physiologist, conducted an experiment in which he always sounded a metronome just before feeding some dogs. Eventually, whenever the dogs heard the metronome (neutral thing), they salivated (particular response) because their brains associated the metronome with food (thing which already elicited the response).

Humans can also be classically conditioned, and psychologists have found that this associative learning process has applications far beyond the borders of Pavlov's experiment. Generally speaking, whatever we simultaneously experience becomes associated in our brain, particularly if this simultaneity happens repeatedly or with extreme emotion. Once these associations build, each element can summon the other connected ones, like how sounding the metronome made the dogs salivate. This holds for sensory information we take in, thoughts, feelings, and anything else we register experiencing. For instance, if my grandmother often made me silver dollar pancakes that she served on crotched placemats, the sight of either may bring her to my mind and evoke emotions I associate with her. I may also feel uncomfortable visiting a restaurant I frequented with an ex because of the association between it and the relationship for me. There's a popular saying, "Neurons that fire together, wire together," which encapsulates and simplifies this phenomenon.

When we create sacred space, we use classical conditioning for our benefit. After practicing in a sacred space regularly, our altar, magical tools, etc., become like the metronome did for Pavlov's dogs. We then reflexively shift into a state of reverence and alignment upon entering our sacred space, consistent with what we've reached in our practices. Even when we don't feel like practicing, the associations we have with the space can help us focus and engage.

One reason using items that already feel sacred to us is helpful when creating sacred space is that they link our sense of the sacred with this novel space, which jumpstarts our sense of its sanctity. Because of classical conditioning, it's important to only use our sacred space and magical tools for metaphysical work. Utilizing them for other activities would weaken the desired associations. For example, if Pavlov also sounded the metronome before walking his dogs, that would've diluted their association between it and food. If we must use a sacred space for multiple purposes, it's critical to have elements that are only utilized during our practices, like an altar cloth we solely use for magic.

Beyond classical conditioning, our sacred space also becomes infused with the subtle energy of our practice. It starts to vibrate higher as we repeatedly perform rituals and meditate within it. Anyone with developed psychic sensitivity can feel the difference between a statue in a Hindu temple that's been consistently used in ritual and one that hasn't. Palpable vibrations emanate off of these statues. This holds for our sacred space too, which becomes charged and energetically aligned as we use it, like a battery we can draw from or a note whose pitch we can match. This is another reason to only use our sacred space and the items within it for metaphysical work, if possible. Using these things for other purposes will shift their energetic charge. Relatedly, many people charge or consecrate their magical tools, which fosters a sense of these tools' sanctity and purpose. Consecration rituals can range in complexity, and I encourage you to explore some online. An example of a simple consecration ritual is holding a tool, visualizing it filling with purifying light, and then charging it like we would a crystal.

Regarding what tools to use, it makes sense for inner alchemy to have a balanced representation of the elements (i.e., a dagger for air, wand for fire, chalice for water, pentacle for earth, and candle for spirit). Aside from the specification that the dagger have a double edge and the pentacle have a pentagram or hexagram on it, there's ample room here for personalization. Many people have found creative ways to make these tools on a budget and posted articles about that online.

In addition to an altar and magical tools, it's worth having clothing we specifically wear for metaphysical work (unless we prefer being nude). The clothes from our day-to-day life are psychologically associated with it. Since we seek to experience something else in our rituals, wearing our normal clothes during ritual doesn't make sense. Conversely, wearing ritual attire alerts us that we've left our status quo. It can also help us enter archetypal consciousness. For example, dressing like a mage can make it easier to feel like one, which facilitates us stepping into that role. Regarding what to wear, I think that's largely a matter of personal preference, though many practitioners traditionally favor robes and cloaks.

The more sacredly we treat a space, the more sacredly we'll perceive it. This relates to the psychological impact of treating something sacredly, which reinforces its sanctity in our mind, and the metaphysical impact of how this attitude orients our psychic emanation. Taking a few conscious breaths upon entering a sacred space while allowing ourselves to feel its sanctity can aid with this.

Devoting space in our home to magic is a powerful testament to how important magic is to us. Doing this also affirms that we can construct a supportive environment for inner alchemy. Sometimes this begins with a small section of a room or items we must pack up after our practice, and that's fine. Staking a claim for our magical life in the physical world, regardless of how, is the most important act here. Then we build from there.

Observances for Attuning to the Natural World

"Every act in life may be dedicated in such a way
that living itself becomes sanctified and transformed."
—ISRAEL REGARDIE

In addition to our daily practice, there are other observances we can undertake to help us attune to the divine, which increasingly bring the sacred into our mind and day-to-day life. These also aid us in staying focused on our alchemical work and practicing aligning our levels of being, concentrating, and perceiving and directing subtle energy.

The first observance provides multiple opportunities for alignment each day: praying over food. Although it's self-evident, it's worth appreciating that after air, food is our primary energy source, and we can't live without it. Eating affirms our place in the natural world, and it provides an opportunity to feel humble, grateful, and reverential accordingly.

During food prayers, many people charge their food with subtle energy. To do this, hold your hands over your food and imagine golden light flowing from them into the food, amplifying its ability to nourish you. Some people also imagine filling their food with love or other qualities.

Here are some examples of food prayers. Feel free to write your own.

"From forest and stream; from mountain and field; from the fertile Earth's nourishing yield; I now partake of divine energy; may it lend health, strength, and love to me. Blessed Be."
—Wiccan prayer from *Living Wicca* by Scott Cunningham

"This food comes from the earth and the Sky. It is a gift from the entire universe and the fruit of much hard work. I vow to live a life that is worthy to receive it." —Buddhist prayer

"Now that I am about to eat, O Great Spirit, give my thanks to the beasts and birds whom You have provided for my hunger; and pray deliver my sorrow that living things must make a sacrifice for my comfort and well-being. Let the feather of corn spring up in its time and let it not wither but make full grains for the fires of our cooking pots, now that I am about to eat."
—Native American prayer

Another powerful observance is adoring the sun four times a day, which comes from Aleister Crowley's *Liber Resh vel Helios*. When we adore the sun, we face a given direction, assume a particular posture, and offer words related to the observance. Each of the four adorations corresponds with an element and has a specific posture and set of words, which should be memorized. We perform these adorations in order from east, where the sun rises, to the south, west, and north. After adoring, we make the Sign of Silence, by placing our left finger to our lips, as if saying, "Shhh." Though this practice comes from Thelema, these postures originated in the Golden Dawn. Feel free to create others if these don't resonate with you.

In Thelema, adorations are used to anchor the Great Work in an aspirant's mind throughout the day. They also help us align ourselves with nature through connecting with the sun and its rhythms.

Here are Crowley's adorations:

Figure 14: Adoration Postures

Sunrise (East, Air):

> *Hail unto Thee who art Ra in Thy rising, even unto Thee who art Ra in Thy strength, who travellest over the Heavens in Thy bark at the Uprising of the Sun. Tahuti standeth in His splendour at the prow, and Ra-Hoor abideth at the helm. Hail unto Thee from the Abodes of Night!*

Noon (South, Fire):

> *Hail unto Thee who art Ahathoor in Thy triumphing, even unto Thee who art Ahathoor in Thy beauty, who travellest over the heavens in thy bark at the Mid-course of the Sun. Tahuti standeth in His splendour at the prow, and Ra-Hoor abideth at the helm. Hail unto Thee from the Abodes of Morning!*

Sunset (West, Water):

> *Hail unto Thee who art Tum in Thy setting, even unto Thee who art Tum in Thy joy, who travellest over the Heavens in Thy bark at the Down-going of the Sun. Tahuti standeth in His splendour at the prow, and Ra-Hoor abideth at the helm. Hail unto Thee from the Abodes of Day!*

Midnight (North, Earth):

> *Hail unto thee who art Khephra in Thy hiding, even unto Thee who art Khephra in Thy silence, who travellest over the heavens in Thy bark at the Midnight Hour of the Sun. Tahuti standeth in His splendour at the prow, and Ra-Hoor abideth at the helm. Hail unto Thee from the Abodes of Evening!*

Crowley's adorations utilize Thelemic symbolism, which features Egyptian deities. Unless you resonate with these adorations, I recommend writing your own. Because we adore four times a day, adorations provide a powerful opportunity for aligning with our alchemical intentions (and they can be written accordingly). In *Modern Magick*, Donald Michael Kraig integrated elemental work more explicitly with adoration practice, which I've taken a step further. I directly connect with the elements during my adorations for greater attunement with nature and elemental equilibration. They're also a reminder for me that each moment provides opportunities for approaching the Great Work, and a way of aligning with that intention.

These are my adorations:

Sunrise (East):

> *Hail to the powers of air and inspiration at the rising of the sun. May each thought be dedicated to the Great Work and placed at the feet of the Divine Mother.*

Noon (South):

Hail to the powers of fire and creation at the midcourse of the sun. May each word be dedicated to the Great Work and placed at the feet of the Divine Mother.

Sunset (West):

Hail to the powers of water and intuition at the setting of the sun. May each feeling be dedicated to the Great Work and placed at the feet of the Divine Mother.

Midnight (North):

Hail to the powers of earth and formation at the midnight hour of the sun. May each action be dedicated to the Great Work and placed at the feet of the Divine Mother.

Whenever possible, perform adorations outside. When performing them inside, visualize the sun to connect with solar energy. For example, when facing east, imagine the sun is rising and feel its rays saturating you with vital, golden energy. At noon, imagine the sun is overhead, shining upon you. At sunset, imagine it setting, and at midnight, visualize the sun beneath your feet radiating upward. After this, you can also visualize the respective elemental symbol at your chest alongside your body being made of the element. For instance, a blue downward triangle for water and your body made of ice, steam, etc. Then make the Sign of Silence. If you have a devotional practice with a deity, you can also bring your hands to your heart and take the elemental symbol, then visualize the form of the deity and offer it to them before concluding with the Sign of Silence. Because this practice is so brief, I recommend lingering in these visualizations until they feel substantial. Though it's best to adore at the specified times, there's still benefit in performing adorations a bit late or early. Many people set noon and sunset adoration alarms on their phones, while performing sunrise and midnight adorations upon rising and before bed. After each adoration and prayer over food, try to experience a few moments of stillness.

Beyond adoring the sun, many magical practitioners also observe the moon cycles. In Wicca, holding ritual observances on the full moon is traditional. There's a powerful ritual called "Drawing Down the Moon" wherein a practitioner draws the essence of the full moon within. This invocation can be profoundly alchemical. I encourage you to research it if it appeals to you. Otherwise, creating spells or rituals each month that work with the lunar cycle and relate to our intentions and alchemical journey can also be potent.

In addition to the moon cycles, many practitioners observe the annual solar progression through the zodiac and seasons. Many religious traditions find significance in the equinoxes, when the days and nights are of equal length, and the solstices, the shortest and longest days of the year. In Wicca, this cycle is represented in the myth of the Goddess, who moves from maiden to mother and crone, and the sun god, who dies and is reborn each year in accord with the seasons. These observances are also tied to agriculture (e.g., the first harvest, second harvest, etc.). Many Pagans work with the myth of Persephone and her annual underworld journey too.

Figure 15: Wheel of the Year

Astrologically speaking, the solstices and equinoxes correspond with the sun entering the cardinal signs (i.e., the sun enters Aries at the vernal equinox, Cancer at the summer solstice, etc., as pictured in figure 15). Many solstice and equinox observances align metaphorically with the seasons. For instance, rituals at the beginning of spring can focus on new life after winter, deriving wisdom from experiences had during winter, planting our intentions, etc.

The remaining four holidays that are traditionally observed in Wicca—Beltane, Lammas, Samhain, and Imbolc—occur near the midpoints between the solstices and equinoxes. These holidays have traditional and astrological significance, which often overlaps, and consequently, many people observe them on the exact astrological midpoint days. For instance, astrologically speaking, the veil between the worlds is the thinnest when the sun is at fifteen degrees Scorpio, so it makes sense to observe Samhain then. The same holds for celebrating Beltane, a fertility holiday, when the sun is at fifteen degrees Taurus. Observing these holidays at the apexes of the fixed signs also affords us strong, focused elemental energy that can be harnessed.

Working with the seasonal holidays can greatly aid in inner alchemy, as there's astrological support for different aspects of it during them (i.e., renewal on the Winter Solstice, making peace with what's passed on during Samhain, etc.). If we can fit a working with the astrology or a seasonal metaphor, it'll align with the holiday's energy. Otherwise, observing the Wheel of the Year can also help us feel more connected with nature.

Exercises

1. Select or write a food prayer and start using it with every meal.
2. Begin practicing the fourfold adorations after selecting or writing ones that resonate with you.
3. Plan a ritual or meditation for the next full and new moon.

CONTAINING THE WORK AND PSYCHIC BOUNDARIES

"Environment is stronger than willpower."
—PARAMAHAMSA YOGANANDA

Before leaving the topic of daily practice, it's critical to consider the importance of containing alchemical work. Nineteenth-century occultist Eliphas Levi wrote of the four powers of the Sphinx, which are also known as the four words of the Magus: to know, to dare, to will, and to keep silence. These have become foundational conditions in many magical traditions, and Levi appears to be where they entered popular occult consciousness. In *The Dogma and Ritual of High Magic*, he wrote that these are "indispensable conditions" in attaining the knowledge and power of a magician.

There isn't a consensus between traditions on what these conditions signify. The first three, however, have some self-evident value. Knowledge is beneficial in what it enables us to do (i.e., we can learn how things work, how to do things, broaden our mind, etc.) and how it conditions us. When studying occultism, we feed our subconscious thoughts that eventually reprogram it, thus influencing our perception of reality. While studying Hermetic Kabbalah, for instance, a day usually comes when we start recognizing Kabbalistic correspondences all around us because everything can be positioned on the Tree of Life. Since increasingly perceiving the divine everywhere is part of completing the Great Work, this is tremendously helpful.

We must be daring when undertaking a magical path to step outside our comfort zone and veer from cultural convention into the unknown. We must also be daring to explore our shadow and address what's in it, and to tug at the threads of our thought-dependent realities. In *The Ritual of Transcendental Magic*, Levi wrote that "in order to dare, we must know; in order to will, we must dare." Knowledge fosters our daring through acquainting us with some potential benefits of alchemical work, which helps us motivate ourselves to undertake it.

Will is required for completing the Great Work because it's a mountainous journey outside the shelter of convention. There may be times when our feelings insist that we turn back, yet we must push on. That's how a dark night of the soul can feel. We need willpower to do anything we intend, but we need an abundance of it when feeling that deflated. If we aspire to the Great Work, we must develop willpower to where it's unconditional, beyond the reach of our feelings.

Lastly, we come to keeping silence. This is the condition I've seen people struggle with understanding the most, and that was true of me when I joined my magic school. I thought the veil of secrecy was archaic, especially since almost everything we practiced was published. I didn't understand the value of containment then and how keeping silence connects with it.

Inner alchemy is fragile work, as is magic. Both depend on us thinking and acting in unconventional ways and tuning our psychic emanation to particular configurations. Consequently, we need assurance in what we're doing, that it's beneficial, effective, and real, as well as to devote substantial time and energy to it. To do this, we must establish a protective container for our efforts to gestate in, like a caterpillar's cocoon. We forge this container by creating boundaries in our lives that foster metaphysical work. These help us protect the energies we're cultivating and shaping and keep our mind supportive of our workings. Keeping silence in and of itself accomplishes much of this need, especially where others are concerned.

The human mind is extraordinarily susceptible to influence. There's only so often we can hear someone naysay what we believe in before we start doubting ourselves unless we consistently rebut their perspective (this is the illusory truth effect in action). When we share our metaphysical work with others, we risk the assurances mentioned above. I encounter this issue as a psychotherapist when a client learns a new technique and tells their spouse, only for their spouse to think it's silly. The client then returns feeling discouraged and for the technique to work now, we must undo the effects of the spouse's opinion. Regarding magic, we may tell a friend a result we had only for them to call magic absurd and leave us questioning our experience.

For various reasons, others can feel and behave antagonistically toward our alchemical work. Some may be attached to people remaining as they are, and as we change, they feel unsettled. Some might feel like our transformations involve an implicit judgement of them for not working on themselves as we have, which they resent. Some may try to reduce or minimize our results because their ego feels threatened by our accomplishments. Even friends who are normally supportive may unintentionally push against our process if they subconsciously worry that our alchemical work endangers our friendship with them (which is a valid concern). Occult practice may also be against people's religions, and some might even persecute us if they learn we're into it. Regardless of the whys, these types of dynamics aren't worth risking and they're wholly avoidable. When we don't tell others what we're doing, we don't have to deal with whatever they'd think or feel about it. I learned to keep silence the hard way through experiencing most of these scenarios.

Even if we try to share our alchemical process with others, they won't understand unless they've done something similar. Talking about a metaphysical experience with someone who hasn't had it is like describing sex to a virgin. It's generally best to say nothing, lest they develop an unnecessary, inaccurate opinion about metaphysics. As inner alchemy transforms our lives, others may notice and ask what we're doing. From that openness, it makes sense to share a bit because this path might be right for them too. But even that is done with an understanding of the limits of what can be communicated with words.

Metaphysically speaking, not involving others in our magical work means we won't have to deal with their energy affecting what we intend. Others have the power to offer counter-emanations to ours, although this is seldom to the degree of what we're offering unless they're fixating on us. Why subject ourselves to the possibility of this resistance unnecessarily?

Despite all of this, humans crave connection and sequestering ourselves is too much to ask of most of us. Not sharing with our loved ones what is, or will likely become, the most important process in our lives is tough to swallow. This is where spiritual community comes in. We can identify others doing similar work whom we can connect with, which can help us stay aligned, validated, and focused on our path. This is a huge benefit of membership in a coven or order.

There are additional aspects to keeping silence and the other three conditions too. One of these is to strive for inner silence, which we usually discover in ritual and meditation. This state is exalted throughout the mystical traditions of the world, and when we experience it, we understand why.

Beyond keeping silence, another crucial aspect of containment is being mindful of environmental influences. Our subconscious mind is like a sponge that absorbs information from our environment without discernment. Consequently, being as intentional as we can about what's around us is critical. To harness the suggestibility of the subconscious, we come to the next tenet of the Little Work, which is to *surround yourself with what you want to become*, with people and things that affirm your intentions. When we don't surround ourselves with what we want to become, it's difficult to reach an escape velocity that overpowers the influences around us that invalidate our intentions. We're more likely to match our status quo and stay in patterns that keep us where we are. Surrounding ourselves with resonant art, books, films, etc., helps the qualities we want to embody seep into our subconscious mind, which greatly aids in manifesting them in our lives.

Exercises

1. Consider where to find spiritual community.
2. Examine your surroundings. Are you surrounded by what you want to become? If not, what's one thing you can do this week to start changing that?
3. For the foreseeable future, try to read at least ten pages of material that validates your spiritual path daily. With mystical material, experiment with doing this in a semi-trance state.

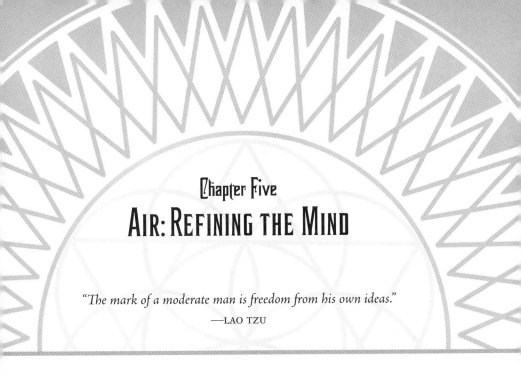

Chapter Five
Air: Refining the Mind

"The mark of a moderate man is freedom from his own ideas."
—LAO TZU

For the rest of this book, we'll journey through the elements, learning practices for developing and equilibrating them within ourselves. Through these practices, we can give ourselves a greater sense of ease on the physical plane and orient our psychic emanation to support our intentions, thus paving the way for deeper work.

Each of the following chapters features specific qualities to develop for equilibrating and cultivating its respective element. We accomplish this through dutifully performing the practices contained therein, which earns us a magical tool. For air, this tool is the dagger. Earning the dagger primarily involves two tasks: training ourselves to think supportively and freeing ourselves as best we can from unsupportive, inaccurate thoughts we already have. We accomplish the latter through developing and applying discernment. Once we've earned the dagger, it helps us deflect the onslaught of influences trying to guide how we think. It also aids us in exposing the ego and keeping the ego at arm's length. The dagger is the synthesis of what we've learned about how the mind works, harnessed for our healing and transformation.

To develop discernment, it helps to understand what discernment is. Per the New Oxford American Dictionary, discernment is the "ability to judge well." To judge well, we must think clearly and accurately, which includes distinguishing between fact-based observations and opinions. For example, "I was twelve minutes late" is a fact-based observation, whereas "Being late means I'm unreliable" is an opinion. Judging well also involves reducing bias in our thinking through applying critical thinking to our thoughts and feelings and exploring other perspectives with an open mind. Somewhat confusingly, this is the opposite of what "being judgemental" means. Being judgemental involves unfairly criticizing something, which discernment is an antidote for. When we discern, we stay mindful that something isn't true simply because it seems true. Many people believed the world was flat because it appears flat. Many feel blue is a masculine color because they were conditioned that way. In this system, we use discernment to remove as much unhealthy conditioning from our thoughts as we can, stepping increasingly into inherent reality.

The tasks for earning the dagger are facilitated by three core practices: a compassionate mindset, a learning outlook, and affirmation. Each of these involve discernment, and another facet of discernment in this system is applying our wisdom and experiential spiritual understanding to our thoughts and feelings. When we don't integrate wisdom and spiritual insight with fact-oriented thinking, we can end up with perspectives like "People are fundamentally untrustworthy." This arguably stands up to reason, but it mistakes the level of ego for the bigger picture.

Developing a Compassionate Mindset

"You may call God love, you may call God goodness.
But the best name for God is compassion."
—MEISTER ECKHART

The integrated discernment we cultivate in this system is called "compassion." In many spiritual traditions, compassion means far more than its dictionary definition of concern or pity for the suffering of others. Beyond pitying suffering, it's understanding that suffering, and our own, as deeply as we can. When we incorporate our wisest, most accurate understanding of suffering with the insights we gain from opening our heart, we get compassion. In a nutshell, compassion is the synthesis of love and wisdom, the marriage of an open mind and open heart. We recognize the nuance at play in what we experience and observe while staying grounded in love and our profoundest spiritual insight. Compassion can radically transform people, and in inner alchemy, it's the philosopher's stone.

With compassion, we don't just hear of someone committing murder and assume he's deranged. We look at the whole story: the boy whose father abandoned him, whose mother died shortly thereafter, who was in and out of foster care, who came from an impoverished area with underfunded schools where joining a gang was normal, whose society implicitly suggested that people of his race are second-class citizens, etc. Compassion involves stepping out of our frame of reference and trying to really bear witness to others, intellectually and emotionally. There's a cognitive fallacy called the "fundamental attribution error" where a problem's cause is unduly attributed to a person's internal qualities over external factors. The man in this example? "He's a bad seed." In reality, barring environmental factors, he probably would've led a healthy life. Compassion calls us to recognize the complexity of situations like these when evaluating them. It asks that we see the big and little pictures and thread them together with the unconditional love that comes from attuning to the divine.

Importantly, compassion doesn't absolve people of all responsibility for wrongdoing. We aren't solely the products of our circumstances, but it's also inaccurate and unfair not to weigh the factors that influence behavior. This holds for us too, and compassion can alleviate some of our shame or guilt about our past actions by reminding us that we're human and outgrowths of our circumstances. In our inexperience, we couldn't have always known the best course of action to take, and we may have experienced many compelling influences and urges to take a different one. We don't even fully mature brain-wise in terms of ability to regulate impulse and emotion and assess risk until around age twenty-five. We can't reasonably consider our past actions without weighing factors like these.

I say that compassion is the philosopher's stone because when we place it on ourselves, it relieves suffering and dispels ignorance, and as our suffering and ignorance resolve, we move closer to the divine. Many of us are empathetic, understanding, and forgiving with others, especially loved ones, yet harsh with ourselves. Compassion neutralizes this. A project of ours falls apart and instead of condemning ourselves, compassion says, "It's OK to feel upset. This experience doesn't make you a failure. Nurture yourself and take it easy tonight." Then we feel better. Not all better, but better to where an experience that might've once catalyzed a descent into depression now results in a rough couple of days. This kind of thinking takes practice, particularly since it must be sincere to work, but once we get there, our relationship to our emotions and thought-dependent self-concepts changes tremendously.

This was at the heart of my journey. I was unwaveringly hard on myself, and if I didn't meet my astronomical standards, I felt worthless. I was so wounded from being repeatedly told while growing up that I was fundamentally flawed that I'd overcompensated with a perfectionism that made me good at most things yet horribly insecure. Then I read the Tao Te Ching, which my intuition guided me to, and reading from it daily became part of my practice for the next five years or so. The first time through it, I was rocked by this quote: "Compassionate toward yourself, you reconcile all beings in the world." I started practicing self-compassion each day, and it proved true. As I accepted and made peace with something in myself, I could do so with others. Through introspection, I recognized the violence and destructiveness in my thinking, which resulted mainly from the abuse I survived as a kid and how sick the society I came from was. I'd known this intellectually for years, but it was different to pick the muck of that treatment off myself and stop unconsciously blaming myself for how those experiences had shaped me. In understanding the violence within myself, I understood much of violence in general, which has deepened with my psychotherapy practice.

Many people speak of the ills of the world and "senseless violence" as if they can't understand where these ills come from. Barring antisocial personality disorder, where violence and amorality do seem to spring from nowhere and metaphysically, I'd say it probably results from karma from previous lives; human behavior isn't senseless. It makes sense if we're willing to explore the shadow and understand what drives people over the edge. Most often, there's a cycle of pain at work. The people in question were hurt deeply, sometimes continually and pervasively. Their actions extend from this in some manner. If we want to heal on the societal level, factors like this must be addressed. Compassion calls us to recognize that when someone is sick, we blame the illness, not the person, and if we want them to heal, we must treat the illness. Compassionate thinking, combined with High Magic and Yoga, is how I successfully treated the cycle of pain and violence within myself.

When my heart opened and I experienced the divinity within, another puzzle piece fell into place and I saw more of the big picture. There was nothing to gain or be or do to make myself worthy. I already was, and nothing could ever change that. Humans are the only beings on earth that struggle with justifying their existence. Nature just lives. The inherent reality is that being alive justifies existence, regardless of what consensus realities might teach.

When we practice compassion, we see the world as it is as best we can, accepting it and humanness accordingly. Accepting humanness generally means applying the wisdom most of us already have about life to our thoughts—for example, that everyone makes mistakes, everyone is unique, people are highly influenced by their upbringing, no one is always right, etc. In my experience, the touted virtues of many of the world's religions naturally emerge if we focus on compassion: patience, forgiveness, unconditional love, contentment, gratitude, serenity, etc. When we know we aren't our story, and increasingly experience that everything is divine, we don't have to work at these types of qualities. They just come. We can practice these virtues, and that's helpful to a point, but none of them need be forced. They'll emerge when it's time.

Approaching each moment with compassion, to whatever degree we can, helps us navigate difficult situations. It makes us more understanding of others, which enables us to better engage with them, and it helps us accept our humanness, which brings us greater peace. Difficulties are far more manageable when we don't judge ourselves as we stumble or for feeling however we do. We also get up much faster once we stop kicking ourselves when we're down. That said, it's important to appreciate the distinction between being compassionate with ourselves and being too lenient, which can become an issue if the inner saboteur tries to exploit the practice of self-compassion (e.g., where it suddenly becomes a little too OK that we didn't meditate this week or haven't looked at our goals in months). A primary way to avoid this trap is to mind the tenet of always trying our best, and the biggest red flag to watch for is compassionate thinking being used to consistently rationalize or excuse a lack of effort toward our intentions.

We can cultivate a compassionate mindset by training ourselves to:

+ Clarify the facts of circumstances and consider them from a diverse assortment of angles to achieve maximum accuracy.
+ Give careful attention to the distinction between fact, interpretation, and opinion.
+ Recognize the context and history that bears on situations.
+ Apply empathy.

- Apply our spiritual beliefs and insights and our wisdom and values while minimizing assumptions.
- Listen to our intuition after we've developed the discernment to do this effectively.
- Use accurate language.

In a nutshell, a compassionate mindset is one in which we think in a fact-oriented, empathetic, accurate, spiritually-connected, and wise manner. This brings us to two more tenets of the Little Work, to *view everything with compassion* as best we can, and to *apply discernment to each thought and feeling*. This may seem like a big production, but in my experience, it just takes consistent practice. Even a little each day can make a huge difference.

———

In CBT, identifying common cognitive distortions (also called "unhelpful thinking styles" or "thinking errors") helps people learn to think more accurately and healthfully. These distortions were identified and initially researched by psychiatrists Aaron Beck and David Burns. Knowing these distortions aids us in recognizing and dismantling them within ourselves. Below are some examples of distorted thoughts and healthy alternatives to them. While reading these examples, consider the different impacts between the initial thoughts and the alternative ones, and how they could influence perception. The language we use to describe things also profoundly shapes how we experience and internalize them. If we use language that oversimplifies, we have a greater likelihood of experiencing and understanding things simplistically. Consequently, a key part of compassionate thinking is training ourselves to use accurate language. Also, please note that the alternative thoughts below aren't insincerely positive. They're more accurate takes on the situations.

———

Here are the common cognitive distortions:

Black-and-White/All-or-Nothing Thinking: Thinking without gray areas. This frequently involves inaccurately applying adverbs like "always" and "never," whether explicitly or implicitly. *Examples*: "All men are jerks." "If I'm not perfect, I'm a failure." "Everything sucks." *Alternative Thoughts*: "Some men are jerks." "Making a mistake doesn't make me a failure." "Multiple difficult things are happening in my life right now."

Overgeneralizing: Drawing patterned conclusions with insufficient justification. *Examples:* "Everyone's rude in New York." "I'm terrible at this job." (After making some mistakes my first week.) *Alternative Thoughts:* "I've met many New Yorkers who behaved rudely." "I'm making many mistakes. Hopefully, I'll get better as I learn."

Mental Filtering/Tunnel Vision: Attending to only what validates certain beliefs we hold. *Example:* "People's praise for my article was insincere. I can tell from their critical feedback that they thought it stunk." *Alternative Thought:* "My article had strengths and weaknesses, which people expressed."

Disqualifying the Positive: Making the positive not "count." *Examples:* "I'm a loser. That PhD I earned? It wasn't very hard to obtain." "I don't care that he's working on himself. He's a terrible person." *Alternative Thoughts:* "A lot of time and effort went into that PhD." "I struggle to believe that he could change, but he does appear to be trying."

Labeling: Applying an inappropriate designation based on insufficient evidence. *Examples:* "I yelled at my husband. I'm a horrible wife." "I know we just talked once, but what a creep!" *Alternative Thoughts:* "I feel terrible for yelling at my husband. How can I try to avoid doing that again?" "He spoke so disrespectfully. I wonder what that was about?"

Mislabeling: Applying ill-fitting language to a situation, often with exaggeration. *Examples:* "He still hasn't picked a career path. That man can never make his mind up about anything!" "I'm an anxious person." *Alternative Thoughts:* "It seems like he struggles with making difficult life decisions." "I'm a person who has anxiety."

Personalizing: Tending to believe things are about oneself with insufficient evidence. Also, feeling responsible for situations over which we have little authority. *Examples:* "Why does the waiter resent me so much?" "Did you see that look? She can't stand me." "I can't believe my daughter did that. I failed as a parent." *Alternative Thoughts:* "I wonder what's going on with the waiter. He seems upset." "I wonder what's up with her. That felt like a nasty look!" "My daughter is an adult who makes her own choices. I'm not responsible for everything she does."

Jumping to Conclusions (usually as Mind Reading and "Fortune-Telling"): Examples: "He hasn't said anything, but I can tell he's holding a grudge." "She just cancelled at the last minute. I knew she didn't like me." "This is doomed to fail. I just know." *Alternative Thoughts:* "Something seems off with him. I wonder if he's holding a grudge." "She just cancelled last minute. I wonder what's going on." "I feel like this is doomed, which is unsurprising given the disappointments I've had in my life. I'll try not to assume the worst."

Catastrophizing: Assuming the worst will occur. *Examples:* "I just felt pain in my stomach. It must be cancer!" "She hasn't texted me back in two hours. She must want to break up!" *Alternative Thoughts:* "If this pain continues, I'll see my doctor." "I wonder why she hasn't texted me back?"

Minimizing: Underplaying the importance of a situation, usually as a defense against difficult emotions. *Example:* "I know we were just robbed. It's fine. Whatever." *Alternative Thought:* "We were just robbed. I think I'm in shock. I'll be present with what I feel about this, whatever it is."

Emotional Reasoning: Because I feel it, it must be true. *Examples:* "My boss treats me like this because he wants to fire me." "See that dark sky? This day will be dreadful." "I feel drawn to this painting of Marie Antoinette. I was her in a past life!" *Alternative Thoughts:* "I feel like my boss wants to fire me." "Dark skies can make me feel so down. I'll prioritize self-care today." "I feel drawn to this painting of Marie Antoinette. Maybe I was her in a past life."

Shoulding: Imposing punitive standards that disregard the complexity of life. *Example:* "I should always be on time." *Alternative Thought:* "I can't control things like the freeway. I can only do my best to be on time."

Blaming: It's everyone's fault except mine (or the opposite). *Examples:* "Everything bad about my life is the government's fault." "My relationship would be wonderful if I wasn't so terrible." *Alternative Thoughts:* "The systems in my country don't provide adequate support and opportunity for its citizens. This is terrible and really makes my life harder." "Each member of a relationship contributes to it. Even if the issue is mostly mine, I'm doing my best with it and my partner is choosing to stick around."

Fallacy of Change: I will feel better when someone/something changes. *Example:* "Meeting my soul mate will make me happy." *Alternative Thought:* "Another person can't be the source of my lasting happiness, although a relationship can be deeply satisfying."

Exercise

Each day for the next week, take at least three thoughts you have and respond to them with compassionate thinking. Identify any cognitive distortions or other problematic elements in them too. Here are some compassionate thoughts that might help with this:

+ That was the best I could do in that moment.
+ It makes sense that I could feel and act that way given what I've lived through.
+ When I look at the big picture, I see where everyone was coming from.
+ Others taught me not to like and respect myself, not me.
+ I'm a human being. It's OK for me to make mistakes.
+ No one is always right.
+ If I'd understood the situation better, I would've acted differently, and I will in the future.
+ I've learned what I can from this. Beating myself up more isn't going to help anyone.
+ I'm in a difficult situation. Feeling difficult emotions about it is normal.

CULTIVATING A LEARNING OUTLOOK

"The mind is but a set of mental habits, of ways of thinking and feeling, and to change they must be brought to the surface and examined."
—NISARGADATTA MAHARAJ

Compassionate thinking is the primary tool we use in the Little Work system to address our unsupportive thoughts. The main way we discover what these thoughts are is with a learning outlook. Having a learning outlook means approaching life with the intention of learning from whatever we can. There's always something to learn from what's happening around or within us. Sometimes we learn in the conventional manner, like by developing new skills, studying unfamiliar concepts, or analyzing external trends. Other times, we learn about our inner workings through contemplating our thoughts, feelings, and actions. With a learning outlook, we acquire wisdom through consistently exploring how our inner world and the world around us operate, as well as by reflecting on our experiences.

One of the most famous phrases associated with the Western Mysteries is "know thyself." Though there are layers to this proposition that become apparent over time, knowing ourselves initially involves discovering what's happening across our levels of being as best we can. We put an end to unconscious, autopilot living, training ourselves to be present and introspective instead. We ask ourselves questions like, "What thoughts are active within me, consciously and subconsciously?"

A host of opportunities for personal transformation become available through tuning in to ourselves, as we explored earlier when learning to monitor our energy. For example, we might notice how tired or anxious we are, simply because we're paying attention. It's difficult for these insights not to influence our behavior, particularly as they build. The first step of developing a learning outlook is cultivating this self-reflectiveness. Then we deepen our self-awareness by seeking to understand what motivates our thoughts, emotions, and actions.

We can learn a lot about ourselves by examining what we perceive. Perception is like a mirror, not necessarily because we're like what we see, but because our perceptions reflect our conscious and subconscious beliefs. For example, if I perceive danger upon seeing tall men walk toward me, what beliefs might foster that reaction? Every reaction we have indicates something about our psychological makeup, and understanding how we think and why we react to life as we do provides us with insights we can use when cultivating compassion. To that end, rather than take our thoughts, feelings, and actions at face value, we analyze them with a learning outlook. We needn't do this with all of them, but anything that evokes a significant emotional reaction within us is worth exploring. To do this, we engage in a process called the "downward arrow technique" in CBT, where we ask questions that reveal the deeper levels of our thoughts, feelings, and actions. Questions like: "Why might I be thinking, feeling, or acting like this?" "What thoughts, beliefs, and experiences might've inspired this feeling or behavior?" "What might this thought, feeling, or action signify?" and "Where does that significance come from?" While doing this, we aim for the root of the thought, feeling, or action.

For example, let's say I feel highly anxious after not receiving a prompt re-sponse to a text message I sent a friend:

"What's this anxiety about?"

"I'm worried she won't text back."

"Which would signify?"

"That she doesn't want to be my friend?"

"Has she given you any indication of that?"

"No."

"Can you think of thoughts, beliefs, or experiences that might've inspired this reaction?"

"I've lost friends over the years. I worry I might lose more."

"What does losing friends signify to you?"

"Loss of companionship."

"What does loss of companionship signify to you?"

"That I'm not worthwhile."

"Why might it mean that?"

"If people don't want to spend time with me, something's probably wrong with me."

"Has anyone given you a reason to believe something's wrong with you?"

"Yes. I was bullied in school."

With this insight into what's happening under the surface, I can apply com-passion to each layer of the reaction, helping shift unhealthy patterns of thinking, feeling, and acting.

Without performing alchemical work, we're likely to remain at the mercy of how external forces shaped us. We'll keep feeling, for example, like we're incom-plete without an ideal lover or undesirable if we're overweight. We'll continue inadvertently validating the ways we've been conditioned away from our authen-ticity. Many of us also have lingering subconscious beliefs from childhood that don't match our adult now. Children can easily develop beliefs like "When people don't like me, that means I'm bad" and "The only way to meet my needs is to do what others say." Beliefs like these can influence our perceptions, emotions, and ac-tions without us realizing it. If we don't adopt a learning outlook (or another com-parable practice), we're also unlikely to recognize the deeper motivations behind our actions. As we apply a learning outlook though, they become apparent. For example, if we're frustrated about work and unconsciously vent that by snapping at our partner, this will become clear with introspection (e.g., "Why do I keep snapping over little things?" "I'm stressed from work").

To address beliefs we were conditioned into, we can ask ourselves questions like "Where did this belief come from?" "What effect does believing this have on my perceptions and actions?" "How does believing this make me feel?" and "Why might this thought not be true?" After examining a belief, we can consider what we want to believe about the related topic now, assuming we feel a change is warranted. This generates beliefs that gradually become how we feel and subconsciously think about this topic if we continually remind ourselves of them when it comes up. For example, whenever we feel incomplete without an ideal lover, we challenge that feeling by affirming a thought like "No relationship can make me feel whole, and I recognize that my belief that one can comes from conditioning."

Identifying our beliefs brings them into our conscious mind, which enables us to work on them. For example, when I initiated into Hermeticism, I didn't know I had low self-esteem. My insecurities were too buried beneath defenses. After analyzing my thoughts, emotions, and behaviors, I could see my insecurities, which I could then address. Without this insight, I was more apt to reinforce my defenses, particularly when faced with adversity, which is what usually happens when people don't know how to healthfully process emotion. Instead of realizing, for example, that "Because my father abandoned me, I subconsciously believe all men will," our romantic relationships simply fall apart. We can't figure out why we keep freaking out when someone gets close to us, but the answer is right between our ears. It's our trauma, which the ego uses to keep us from what it fears.

To that end, one of the most useful aspects of a learning outlook is that it unmasks the inner saboteur, enabling us to strategically navigate ego resistance. A powerful question to incorporate into a learning outlook is "What's the ego's motivation here?" To build on the example from above, "My relationships keep falling apart." "What's the ego's motivation here?" "To keep me from being hurt like I was before." "What fear is the ego using?" "Abandonment." Then we can address this fear with compassionate thinking, affirmations, and the practices in the water section. Eventually, we'll likely become able to have a relationship without these derailing emotions, and until then, we at least recognize where they come from, which still enables us to have healthier relationships.

A learning outlook also helps us identify cognitive distortions. When we don't know we think distortedly, cognitive distortions tend to run rampant. After naming them, they're easier to recognize and challenge—for example, by thinking something like, "That was overgeneralizing. I'd better qualify this statement."

Another aspect of a learning outlook is analyzing behavioral or emotional trends, as in the example above about relationship sabotage. This is where we develop insights like "When I'm exhausted, I become grouchy," "I backpedal whenever people disagree with me," and "Every time I succeed, I take a slightly self-destructive action." Some of these may be learned behaviors. With the latter example, examining deeper may reveal something like "Because of mistreatment in childhood, I feel I don't deserve success." Once we recognize trends like these, we can do something about them. For instance, the latter example is from my life. After working with a learning outlook for a few months, I noticed that I almost immediately engaged in a disappointing behavior after a success or breakthrough. Rather than celebrate my progress, I became mired in shame or guilt. By catching my inner saboteur in the act like this, I could plan differently for the future. The next time I had a success, I made a point to lay low for a while after celebrating it. As I stopped falling for this trap, it disappeared, which is what happens when we don't bite the hooks the inner saboteur throws our way. It moves on to something else.

Applying a learning outlook also involves observing how our thoughts, emotions, and actions affect our energy and influence our psychic emanation. In meditation, this information is a side effect of the practice. With a learning outlook, we seek it out.

An additional dimension of a learning outlook is identifying karma. Until we're enlightened (and some say even after), there's always at least one karmic issue afoot in each moment of our lives. In my experience, these aren't always readily distinguishable from the psychological issues we've explored in this section, and we needn't fixate on parsing this out. When alchemy is our aim, this all becomes one big process. That said, sometimes we clearly see karma at work. For example, if three people imply that I'm selfish over a few days, that's probably karma (and worth sitting with). If I make an uncharacteristic series of inattentive blunders throughout a month, that's probably karma. By engaging in inner alchemy, we invite these kinds of experiences, so it's important to avail ourselves of them. If we don't, we can get stuck where we are, or have these experiences escalate in intensity until we get the point.

Karmic processing can involve making meaning from the events in our lives by finding significance in them, which has psychological benefits. This includes recognizing the personal development opportunities presented by situations. For example, rather than simply losing my job and going on unemployment, I also see an opportunity to reflect on my career. The end of a dysfunctional, long-term relationship also becomes an opportunity to learn to pay better attention to my emotional needs and advocate for them. This isn't the same as the notion that "everything happens for a reason." It's about the fact that we can find an alchemical angle in most experiences. This can be a potent way of navigating adversity because rather than simply feeling defeated, miserable, etc., we become stronger, wiser, and more resilient because of how we face it. When we learn something from an experience, the learning becomes associated with it, sometimes even overshadowing it in our memory. That said, as I mentioned earlier, when we're in great pain, this needn't be forced or rushed.

Regarding events happening for a reason, we can look at karma that way, particularly in that our past experiences contributed to us being who and where we are today, which can be explored on a strictly psychological level too. We can also see what comes to us as being for our evolution and try to gain insight into how, which can foster a deep sense of peace. But because karma can't be understood with the rational mind, the "reasons" we find will be limited by our current level of perception. That said, we could see the surfacing of karmic knots as happening for a reason, although the underlying reason would be the same: that's part of evolving. However we want to make meaning in life is ultimately a personal decision though, and making meaning from our experiences can greatly enrich us. As we release our karma and psychological baggage, we become clearer, lighter, and freer.

As has probably become apparent, applying a learning outlook requires self-honesty. We don't have the option to ignore the shadow during inner alchemy. Denial, avoidance, defensiveness, and unconsciousness are off the table, which means we must accept our issues as they are. Acceptance is a critical ability to develop for inner alchemy. Essentially, it involves admitting the reality of something, and it doesn't mean we don't want that thing to change. For example, if we feel jealous, we admit that without rationalizing about it because we're embarrassed about feeling jealous. This raises another tenet of the Little Work, which is an amendment of an earlier one: *accept change and where you are*. When we don't accept where we are (emotionally, physically, etc.), and start working on ourselves there, it's difficult to work on ourselves effectively. For example, if we won't admit that we feel hurt, how can we deal with that pain, much less recognize how it causes us to behave and think toxically? Without accepting where we are, we're more likely to continue spinning defensive illusions about ourselves. With acceptance, we can examine situations more fully and figure out what to do about them from a place of understanding. This helps us get a clearer sense of our options, which can include seeking help. A person who recognizes that they're emotionally wounded, for example, is more likely to try psychotherapy.

While growing up, our subconscious likely erected defenses that we don't realize are there, particularly for those of us with psychological trauma, like in the earlier example about abandonment. This can include having cover stories about ourselves. In my case, after the abuse I survived, I developed a tough exterior. Unbeknownst to me, it was a façade. My inner child remained a sobbing clump. Consistently applying a learning outlook exposes illusions like these, which enables us to address what underlies them.

Exposing our defenses and exploring our shadow can be painful. Who wants to realize, for example, that they're deeply insecure? Judgemental? Selfish? I certainly didn't. This work can feel like ripping a bandage off to treat the infected wound beneath it. We acclimate to this process though, becoming increasingly more comfortable with it. We also pace ourselves when exploring difficult emotions, which we'll learn to do in the water section.

Though peering beneath our defenses is difficult, if we want deep freedom and healing, we must. Also, we can draw considerable strength for this from ritual and meditation. These practices fortify us to walk into our shadow and integrate what we find there into our self-understanding.

Consistent application of a learning outlook shows us that we're not our thoughts, and as we repeatedly meet our thoughts with compassion, our future perceptions change. Another tenet of the Little Work, which will take on different levels of meaning over time, is to *let go of what you believe you are*. If it's a thought-dependent part of you, it doesn't have to persist, or at least hold the sway over you that it does now.

Exercises

1. For the next week, write a daily journal entry where you apply the downward arrow technique to at least one substantial emotional reaction you had each day.

2. Moving forward, review the day's events each evening with a learning outlook in a journal (or whenever is convenient for you—in magic school, I wrote on scraps of paper throughout the day and typed them later). Answer questions like, "What can I learn from my experiences today?" "What would I do differently in the future?" Note any patterns or trends in your thoughts, feelings, and actions. Record any epiphanies you had about yourself or otherwise. If you noticed resistance from your inner saboteur, document it.

3. Complete a major events timeline and environmental factors analysis. Exploring the impact of significant past experiences and environmental influences can help us understand how we think, feel, and act. Identifying these connections to our past facilitates self-compassion and a realization that we often see our circumstances in light of previous experiences.

To begin this exercise, create a document and write out each year of your life as a heading. Depending on how your memory works, grouping sections based on life events may be helpful (e.g., high school, first apartment, etc.). In each section, list the major events you remember from that time that occurred in your life or influenced you. Include events like "Began attending elementary school," "Shared in the national grief over a war," and "Won a talent competition." Also include events like "Befriended John, who was my best friend for eight years," "My parents divorced," "Lost my grandmother to cancer," etc. These can be as seemingly minute as "Had an argument with my ex-girlfriend that I still feel guilty about." The relevance here is the impact an experience had on you. These scenarios stick out in our mind. If you already know some ways an event has affected you long-term, note that (e.g., "Was held back in first grade and have had low self-esteem ever since"). Include all significant losses on this timeline, as well as your accomplishments and times you felt you failed. After this, indicate any major environmental influences you recall, and connect these to significant events where applicable (e.g., "Was taught by my religious community to feel shame about my sexuality, which negatively influenced my early experiences of sex and dating").

Internal Sacred Space and Affirmation

"Make a castle of your mind."

—BUDDHA

The last primary practice for air in this system is affirmation. Affirmation involves intentionally thinking in a manner that supports the manifestation of a sought reality. Affirmation practice can include thinking specific thoughts, called "affirmations," and initiating general trends in our thinking through practices like a compassionate mindset.

Whenever we think, we add to, reinforce, or chip away at stories we hold about reality (or create new ones), which can help or harm us. To facilitate inner alchemy, we stay mindful of this and don't just allow thoughts to run wild within ourselves. Instead, we explore them with a learning outlook, considering their purpose and effects. It's common knowledge that if we eat junk food and don't exercise, our physical health will suffer. This is true at the mental level too. Thinking junk-food thoughts and not exercising our mind is bad for our mental health. Consider how you feel watching a distressing film. How would you expect to feel after thinking similarly distressing thoughts? In this system, we discover what thoughts and tendencies of thought are healthy for us and guide our thinking accordingly.

With a learning outlook and compassionate mindset, we transform what's already happening within our mind. With affirmations, we consciously build something new, and this includes reading sacred texts that foster our spiritual beliefs. These practices collectively create internal sacred space and orient our mind to support our alchemical intentions.

Some people feel like thinking with the intention of shaping reality is phony, but we've shaped reality with thought without realizing it since childhood. Our thought-dependent realities weren't real for us at some point. Just because we were too young to witness our thoughts coalescing into these realities doesn't mean they didn't. When we practice affirmation, we take ownership of this process and use it with intent.

As we experience our reality shift through practices like High Magic, meditation, compassionate thinking, and spells, we gain a greater understanding of how perception works, as well as perception's malleability. Watching an element of a consensus reality crumble within us, while understanding that's happening, weakens the ability thought-dependent realities have to enthrall us. They stop seeming as real. As this occurs, affirmations become increasingly powerful for us because we know our reality isn't as solid as we believed, and it can be reshaped accordingly.

Most of us come to the Little Work with beliefs that don't support our well-being in several areas of life. For example, consider what happens if we have thoughts about money that don't support financial prosperity. We might make a product and undercharge for it or hesitate to ask for a raise we deserve. We might reconcile ourselves to the notion that nothing much will improve for us financially, which tunes our psyche and psychic emanation accordingly. If we continue feeding these beliefs, our financial status quo will likely persist.

When we tidy up our thinking in an area by affirming perspectives that align with our intentions, our experience of it can profoundly change. Over time, our perceptions, actions, and feelings start following our affirmed perspectives, and our psychic emanation begins manifesting accordingly. What comes to us changes, as well as how we utilize it, and there's tremendous opportunity there. Even pivoting from a thought like "I'm terrible with money" to "I'm terrible with money, but I also haven't studied financial management" opens hundreds of doors of possibility that were closed to us before. There's a huge difference between the finality of "I'm terrible with money" and the possibility of "I lack financial management skills." This shift makes us more likely to walk through one of those doors, which could lead to skills that revolutionize our relationship with money.

At first, the alchemical mental processes in this chapter can feel intimidating and overwhelming, like how arriving at a huge, overgrown garden and being asked to tend to it could. Like with that garden, the initial weeding and preparing of our mind requires substantial time and effort. Afterward, the process is more about maintenance. Getting to know ourselves takes a while, but eventually, we have a general sense of what makes us tick and what does and doesn't support our intentions. Once we know our habitual thoughts, feelings, and actions, how our history shapes our perceptions, what our insecurities are, etc., and have set up supportive thinking habits, this process becomes far less involved. It becomes more like weeding a garden, and it doesn't require micromanaging every moment of our thinking. Most days, we just water the plants and pull any weeds we notice. Then we can plant what we want in this fertile soil, understanding that what we attend to with thought will grow within our experience, psychologically and metaphysically.

PRACTICING AFFIRMATIONS

"Believing takes practice."

—MADELEINE L'ENGLE

A formal affirmation practice involves reciting affirmations we want our reality to mirror with a conviction that these thoughts are true or could be. We identify a shift we want to make in our beliefs or an intention we want to launch, formulate a thought that fosters that, and then repeatedly think this thought while feeling that it's true. While doing this, we align our being with the intention of the thought, like when casting spells. This plants and waters the thought in our mind and attunes our psychic emanation to it. Usually, the beliefs we'll seek to change become apparent while exploring our reactions with a learning outlook.

Affirmations continue our journey of developing the ability to concentrate one-pointedly, and affirming with focus and attentiveness is critical. This is like the difference between the potency of telling someone "I love you" for the first time versus saying it halfheartedly while watching TV. The aim is for these thoughts to reverberate powerfully within our being.

In this system, we use affirmations to establish healthy mental patterns that aid us in manifesting our intentions. Doing this doesn't involve denying or avoiding difficult situations and emotions, which could result in cognitive dissonance. For example, if we feel like our job is crushing our soul, affirming "I love my job" isn't going to help us function healthfully. An appropriate affirmation instead could be something like "I'll make the most of this job while I'm here."

Affirmations in this system are fact-oriented, which is part of where their power comes from. When we anchor affirmations in facts, it's easier to believe them. This minimizes cognitive dissonance, making it likelier that they'll work. For example, the most powerful affirmations I created for my anxiety disorder were "I have effective coping skills" and "This feeling is a symptom, not a fact. It doesn't make a concern legitimate." Regarding the former, anxiety made me feel like I couldn't handle adversity, but when adversity appeared, I navigated it well. Per the latter, anxiety made me feel like whatever it said was true, and it rarely was (e.g., "This itch is cancer"). Consequently, these affirmations were both factual: I have effective coping skills and anxiety gave me feelings that misrepresented inherent reality. By affirming these thoughts consistently, I eventually reached a place where they'd pop into my mind as soon as I felt anxious, making me far less likely to validate my anxious thoughts and feelings. These affirmations, combined with mindfulness and my other alchemical work, have hugely mitigated an anxiety disorder that ravaged my life for years. They were vastly more effective for me than a traditional affirmation like "I'm safe in all situations," which felt untrue.

Relatedly, affirmations traditionally take bold tenors like "I love and approve of myself" and "All is well." If we experience cognitive dissonance affirming sentiments like these, doing so can have the opposite of our desired effect. To navigate this, we can create affirmations that are closer to where we are in our beliefs with the intention of climbing a ladder of affirmations toward our sought shift. For example, if "I love and approve of myself" feels insincere, we can start with affirmations like "I have admirable qualities" and "Others taught me not to love myself, and I can release that conditioning over time." Then we affirm these daily until we feel like they're true (or mostly true). After that, we create a new affirmation that continues up the ladder toward "I love and approve of myself." For instance, "I can have flaws and still deserve unconditional love." We keep climbing until one day, "I love and approve of myself" rings as true as anything else to us, and trust me, that's a remarkable day.

This approach circumvents the issue of needing to affirm in the present tense, which is traditional in affirmation practice, because these affirmations evolve. We explored this issue earlier with the example of "I will be healed" versus "I am healed." As a reminder, affirming "I will be healed" can ceaselessly push our healing into the future, while affirming "I am healed," if we don't believe that, can generate enough cognitive dissonance to sabotage our intention of healing. It's OK to affirm "I will be healed" though if a week later we switch it to "I feel myself healing" and continue building from there.

Affirmations utilize the illusory truth effect and confirmation bias for our benefit. Once our subconscious integrates affirmed beliefs, it filters reality to validate them, and our psychic emanation manifests accordingly. Our work is to reach this tipping point, as well as continue affirming if we're immersed in a consensus reality that pushes against our affirmed perspectives.

Another important consideration in affirmation practice is to avoid using language that inadvertently reinforces what we seek to change, which usually involves excluding unwanted elements from affirmations. For example, an affirmation like "I'm not afraid of intimacy" evokes our fear of intimacy and history of that fear, even in its seeming negation. This anchors that fear in our conscious mind and associates it with our present moment experience. This affirmation may summon doubts that overshadow our hope of feeling safe being vulnerable. Meanwhile, "I'm open to intimacy" reinforces the hope without evoking the history. Feel the difference between "I'm stronger than depression" and "I'm strong." Imagine thinking both a hundred times a day and how different the result would be (and that's just on the psychological level). This isn't usually an issue with spells since they're more of an occasion, but with daily affirmations, it's critical to take care not to reinforce unwanted elements. This concept aligns with the classic adage, "What you resist, persists." A major exception to this is affirming a truism or fact that can help us amend distorted thinking about a topic. For instance, "Millions of people have recovered from depression, so there's hope for me," "With billions of people on earth, I can find another relationship," and the example I shared about anxiety being a symptom of a disorder.

Another exception to this is reminding ourselves of past successes, lessons learned, or values-driven beliefs. For example, affirmations like "It's OK to disappoint people who have toxic expectations" or "I healed my relationship with my dad, so I can heal this" can support change. Unless we want to constantly remember our experiences of adversity or suffering, affirmations that include unwanted elements are intended for short-term use. But acknowledging the strength evidenced by our survival and resilience is a potent part of empowerment, and it can help us grow stronger.

Excluding unwanted elements from affirmations doesn't mean we hide from our past difficulties or deny them. We just don't actively affirm these elements, and when we think about them, we do so with a compassionate mindset. Wading into suffering without compassion tends to create more suffering in our mind. When we apply compassion, it integrates our past difficulties with our alchemical process over time.

Altering thought-dependent realities, particularly to where our perceptions shift, takes time. The thoughts we've inadvertently affirmed throughout life are often pervasive. We'll also almost inevitably fall back into old, unhealthy habits or patterns, but this doesn't mean our work has been for naught. It just means there's more to be done in an area. By affirming fact-oriented, supportive thoughts and meeting our prior beliefs with compassion, our unhealthy thinking patterns erode. That said, some mental illnesses include unhealthy thinking patterns that only appear when people experience symptoms (e.g., like during a manic episode). These thinking patterns are highly resistant to change, and this isn't what I'm referencing here. Even then, many people still find significant benefit from affirmations and compassionate thinking, particularly in helping them support themselves during episodes and when they aren't symptomatic. By consistently practicing affirmations and compassionate thinking, we eventually think compassionately by default. When we reach this state, our mind has become the dagger.

Exercise

Complete a formal affirmation practice at least daily. This should take no more than three minutes. As you apply a learning outlook, identify thoughts that would be helpful to cultivate for your intentions (e.g., "My job is a personal growth opportunity" or "I can develop healthy relationships skills"). For now, create affirmations about unconditional self-love and gratitude. If you're unsure where to start with this, one can be an affirmation listed earlier, and another can be "I'm grateful for food, shelter, and clothing." We can also create affirmations that align with our spiritual beliefs and intentions (e.g., "The divine is everywhere," "May my work serve the highest good," etc.) to increase their presence in our conscious mind and perceptions.

Here's a process for creating an affirmation:

1. Identify a belief you want to change (e.g., "I'm not worth anything").
2. Identify the theme(s) of this thought (e.g., sense of personal value).
3. Identify the spectrum of feelings along this theme (e.g., "I feel valueless" to "I'm indisputably valuable").
4. Use your feelings to identify your place along this spectrum (e.g., "I feel like I have some worth").
5. Design an affirmation that's an emotional step higher than that (e.g., "My self-worth can develop from where I am").
6. Recite this affirmation four or more times a day until it feels true. Then, create a new affirmation that's closer to where you want to move with this issue (e.g., "My self-worth grows daily").

We can also make affirmations that help us release chakra blockages. Here are themes that fit the chakras:

+ Root: physical vitality, confidence in health
+ Sacral: sexual comfort, deserving pleasure, deserving passion
+ Navel: self-esteem, self-confidence, asserting oneself
+ Heart: love, compassion, gratitude, intuition
+ Throat: self-expression
+ Third Eye: vision, imagination, creativity, insight, intuition, psychic ability
+ Crown: trust in the divine, surrender to the divine

While performing chakra-related affirmations, it can be beneficial to place our hands tenderly on the body areas that correspond to the chakras we're affirming about and imagine energy flowing from our hands into those chakras.

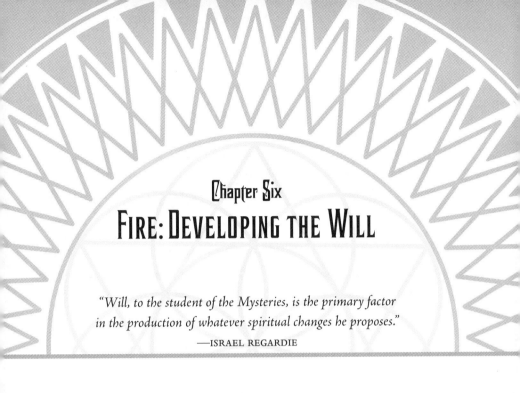

Chapter Six

FIRE: DEVELOPING THE WILL

*"Will, to the student of the Mysteries, is the primary factor
in the production of whatever spiritual changes he proposes."*
—ISRAEL REGARDIE

The next element in our alchemical journey is fire, the home of the will. On a basic level, the will is the part of us that initiates action. Without a will, we wouldn't be able to act on our behalf, even to survive. On the surface, will is what enables us to set a course and follow it. More deeply, it's also the part of us that desires to tread that path, which is where the motivating energy to do so usually comes from. The will affirms "I am," "I want," and "I need," and consequently, it's connected to the ego. It keeps us alive.

All conscious action involves deciding to do something and then doing it. The more outside our status quo an action is, the more willpower taking it generally requires unless we have a huge motivating desire involved. To realize the intentions we seek, some of which are likely well outside our status quo, we must develop our will by earning the wand, which is the magical tool connected with fire. To do this, we practice following through on our word, root in our authenticity, clarify our values, connect with our desires, learn to set healthy intentions, and develop the courage to act when afraid. We also become adept at changing.

In this system, we strive to live in a state of connection with passion and purpose. For many of us, this begins with making a habit of asking ourselves what we want. When we have a healthy connection to will, we feel comfortable answering that question. The first time I directly asked myself what I wanted, I felt audacious. I'd been taught on some level that facing desire so nakedly was selfish, and following the abuse and dehumanization I experienced, part of me also didn't feel like I deserved pleasure. But asking myself what I wanted, and heeding the answers that came from that, dramatically improved my life, especially as doing so became a regular occurrence. I also realized I'd already lived much of my life in alignment with desire, just without recognizing it. For example, what food to eat, which movie to watch, which friend to call, etc. (i.e., "What do I want to do now? And now?") My free time was largely spent pursuing wants, but because I felt uncomfortable exploring desire, this was mostly unconscious. Even while engaged in activities that weren't pleasure-driven, desire was involved (e.g., "I want to succeed at work," "I don't want to upset my mother," "I want to help my friend," etc.). By not owning desire, I became highly susceptible to external influences that normalized certain desires. I started wanting things that, upon reflection, I didn't really want, and in today's world, there are thousands of influences telling us what to want.

Without discovering what our sense of purpose calls for, which can start with asking ourselves what we want, we can spend our lives largely fulfilling the desires of others without realizing it. We may find ourselves in a life we thought would satisfy us that doesn't, like a CEO who quits her job to become a monk. There's a part of us that knows our next best step and dream to pursue though. We just have to learn to connect with this part of ourselves and believe we deserve to follow its guidance.

A mind that's loaded with conflicting desires creates a jumbled psychic emanation and expends considerable time and energy fumbling between day-to-day choices, much less long-term ones. When we tune in to ourselves, clarify our values, and understand why we want what we want, much of this equivocation fades. We can then harness our will to live increasingly in alignment with our intentions.

With a developed will, we become able to act in support of our intentions regardless of how we feel. Many of us surge with passion when an epiphany dawns on us and make bold proclamations (e.g., "Things are going to change for me after this workshop!"), but then our motivation dies shortly thereafter. Our ego asserts itself and the inertia of our status quo overwhelms our intentions. A developed will enables us to keep this fire burning.

The wand may be the trickiest tool to wield because we can fall under the spell of egoic power and lose our way. Many have before. Discernment and compassion are critical here so we don't tumble into the lower chakras as our power builds, favoring selfishness, greed, etc. To that end, a key part of equilibrating fire is anchoring ourselves in the higher purpose of our work, which we perform in service of something greater than our individual ego. At the very least, we have some aim of connecting with our authenticity, which aligns us with the highest good, and broadening our horizons. With the philosopher's stone of compassion in one hand, we can hold the wand in the other without becoming corrupted.

Owning Our Personal Power

"We cannot do without power
but it must be allied with Love or with Wisdom."

—UNKNOWN, AS QUOTED IN *ASPECTS OF OCCULTISM* BY DION FORTUNE

To healthfully develop will, it helps to explore the topic of power further. Power is the ability to act or do something in a given manner, or the capacity to influence or direct something. There are many types of power, and we can have varying degrees of it. For example, we can have power internally, socially, culturally, professionally, etc., and power dynamics can be formal or informal. In a work hierarchy, we might have power over our direct reports while being under our supervisor's authority, which are formal power dynamics. In our family, we might have power over our younger siblings, which is usually informal (especially once all are adults). Additionally, we might hesitate to disagree with an aggressive friend or do something that's unacceptable in our community because of fearing conflict or criticism, which are informal power dynamics.

Many people feel like power is an ugly word, and power can certainly be abused. However we feel about it, power is part of life, and some of the worst abuses of power occur when people have power and don't accept it. Better, for example, to be a parent or employer who owns their power and uses it appropriately than to act like a friend only to pivot into authoritarianism.

In this system, we cultivate personal power, which is the power we have and the degree to which we understand and own it. This includes our sense of agency, or ability to act and make choices. The word "understand" is present because understanding our power enables us to use it in particular ways. For example, if I don't understand that I can shift my perceptions by changing how I think, or I do to a limited extent, doing so is only within my personal power to the degree of my understanding. Part of applying a learning outlook is gaining a sense of our personal power.

Every situation involving people can be viewed in terms of power. Though constantly thinking about power can harmfully warp our psyche (i.e., by making concerns about power overshadow the other aspects of our experiences), ignoring it is unwise. Understanding power dynamics helps us achieve our intentions, and in some situations, keep ourselves safe. For instance, let's say we seek a promotion at work. A wise employee with this objective will learn their boss's expectations and how not to threaten their boss's sense of power. Then they can work in a manner that pleases their boss and lines them up for promotion. Though many of us would rather do and say what we want when we want, which is normal, a person who understands power dynamics will be more strategic when seeking something from a situation. Importantly, this isn't synonymous with being manipulative because there's no intent to take advantage of another. This is about understanding how a system operates and using that knowledge for our benefit. Unless we're going to dismantle that system, it behooves us to figure out how to ethically work within it to reach our goals.

When developing personal power, we can do it from two primary vantage points: the ego and the heart. The latter vantage point fosters inner alchemy, while the former hinders it. These vantage points needn't be wholly exclusive though. For example, a balanced ego calls us to care for ourselves, set boundaries, and claim a seat at the tables in our lives, which are healthy things to do. The issue arises when the ego isn't guided and tempered by the heart's compassion, which is a visible problem in much of today's world. An unchecked ego operates from a place of lack and fear and generally seeks to dominate. When we live primarily from this vantage point, we see our worth in terms of what we possess and control. Unbalanced fire in its extreme, which is unchecked ego, can result in someone who destroys lives, literally or figuratively, without remorse, who makes decisions in the name of power and greed without concern for others. This is the Devil from tarot, set loose upon the earth.

The alternative is operating from a heart-centered place. The heart sees the bigger picture of life, feels the suffering of others, and lives in connection with the divine. It recognizes the abundance in nature, as well as the potential for creation.

The heart asks: "Why are people starving when there's plenty of food to share?" and "This is good for me, but will it harm others?" A heart-centered person understands that their worth has nothing to do with externality or dominating anything. They also appreciate that they aren't worth more or less than anyone else. Free from the falsehoods that accompany those misperceptions, they're able to serve a higher justice. This is the Magician and High Priestess, who live empowered lives in alignment with their deepest authenticity, which necessarily results in a desire to serve. A heart-centered person doesn't feel put out by helping others without clear self-interest, and the heart doesn't need an empire to feel fulfilled. The simple act of being kind is enough.

Living primarily from the ego or heart isn't usually determined by a single choice. At first, it's generally more of a process, and this can be tricky because it's not about forcing ourselves to be virtuous. As our heart opens through spiritual practice, living in a heart-centered manner becomes easier, and how to becomes clear. When our resting awareness stations in the heart, this becomes how we are most of the time.

In each elemental chapter, we'll explore the subject of acceptance. In the air chapter, we reviewed accepting where we are psychologically. Another critical piece of acceptance is accepting what is, the circumstances in our lives. Accepting what is doesn't mean we like, condone, or don't seek to change it. It means we aren't in denial about situations being what they are, which facilitates us determining what to do about them. For example, treating illness, whether mental or physical, is generally hindered to the degree that denial about the reality of the illness is present. Accepting what is also involves striving not to avoid the problems in our lives, which is important because, as with illnesses, many problems worsen when they aren't addressed. With situations we struggle with, we have two practical choices if we want to feel better: change them or change our relationship to them. This hearkens back to the famous Serenity Prayer by Reinhold Niebuhr: "Grant me the serenity to accept the things I cannot change, courage to change the things I can, and the wisdom to know the difference."

If there's a condition I want to change, I consider my options. If I can change it how I prefer, and doing so is warranted, I will. If not, I try to make peace with it or improve it in other ways, making it as comfortable for myself as possible. For example, if I don't like my job but feel like I can't quit, can I improve my day-to-day experience (e.g., by listening to music)? If I have a mental illness, can I seek help to mitigate my symptoms?

When we don't accept what is, many of us tussle with reality, engaging in thought processes that, while understandable, are upsetting and generally unhelpful: "I can't believe this." "What did I do to deserve this?" "What bomb will drop next?" "Here's another day of this garbage." Etc. The first two examples can sometimes facilitate processing shock or grief about difficult life circumstances, like being diagnosed with a serious illness, but not indefinitely. It's one thing to express and honor the devastation we feel about a situation and another to engage in an ongoing battle with its reality that increasingly does little but upset us. When we accept what is, we let this fight go, which facilitates us recognizing and clarifying our choices (i.e., identifying where our power is). For example, let's say we're stuck in traffic. Instead of writhing in frustration about how terrible this is for hours, we just accept it. Then we process our frustration in a healthy, compassionate manner, which we'll learn to do in the next chapter, and move on. "Now what? I guess I could reflect on my goals and do affirmations."

Pushing against a situation's reality creates stress, which can have damaging effects on our subtle body and mental and physical health, especially if this stress is frequent. Our stress about difficult situations can actually result in worse consequences than the situations themselves, or exacerbate these situations further. For example, chronic pain that we accept and mindfully witness is less debilitating than chronic pain we resist, which is a research-supported assertion and part of why mindfulness has become so popular.[5] As someone who has multiple chronic health conditions and daily chronic pain, I can attest to these benefits. Accepting these issues made them far more bearable for me. This doesn't mean I don't have difficult days, but when I do, they're nowhere near what they were before I learned acceptance.

As magical practitioners, we can also use magic to try to change unwanted situations we don't see a path out of. Making peace with situations as best we can is important in this too though as that diminishes any attachments we have to

---

5. La Cour, Peter, and Marian Petersen. "Effects of Mindfulness Meditation on Chronic Pain: A Randomized Controlled Trial." *Pain Medicine*, Volume 16, Issue 4 (2015): 641–652. And Rodriguez, Tori. "Pain Acceptance Linked With Reduced Disability, Pain Interference in Migraine." Clinical Pain Advisor. April 4, 2017. https://www.clinicalpainadvisor.com/migraine-headache /migraine-sufferers-may-benefit-from-acceptance-and-commitment-therapy/article/648142/.

results, which could derail the working. Also, when we accept a difficult situation, to whatever degree we can, it consumes less of our internal resources (i.e., the mental and emotional energy spent resisting its reality). This energy can be then used for other things, including the spell that gets us out of it.

Otherwise, another important aspect of owning our personal power is using empowered language when we decide not to do something. Rather than "I was too tired, so I couldn't do that" we can say something like "I chose not to do that because I was tired." This type of linguistic shift fosters a greater awareness of our personal power. Sometimes we're at the mercy of our circumstances (e.g., "I missed the appointment because my car was rear-ended," "I had the flu," etc.), but mostly, when we don't do something, it's because we decided not to. Doing it might've been uncomfortable, but this doesn't mean we couldn't have. When we allow excuses, rationalizations, or justifications to supersede that truth, we become more at the mercy of external conditions and how we feel. The reality our subconscious projects will be one where we feel like we lack agency in those situations. By saying something like "I was upset last night, so I opted not to call her back" rather than "I was too upset to return her call," we reclaim our power.

One reason exploring issues of power is important is that while growing up, we lack it. Children generally aren't allowed to make important decisions on their behalf (e.g., they don't get to pick their schools, choose how they spend much of their time, etc.). Consequently, we can enter adulthood with inaccurate concepts of power that are beneficial to release. For example, we may feel powerless in a situation because that's how we felt in a comparable one growing up, when really, we have many options. We may also feel like we'll get hurt if we stand up for ourselves because that's what happened in our childhood home. By assessing our power with a learning outlook, we're more apt to notice issues like these and update our sense of agency to match our adult now.

In general, it's important to appreciate the power we actually have, not just what we feel we have. There are people who've packed a suitcase and left their lives behind. In the 1950s, Peace Pilgrim literally walked away from her life, penniless, and she never looked back. I'm not recommending we do that, but we do have the power to make bold decisions, especially if we're willing to be uncomfortable. That person who drives you nuts? In most cases, you could cut them from your life. That job you hate? You could quit. You could never speak to anyone you know again. You have that power. Actions like these might lead to consequences we're unwilling to entertain, but there's a difference between can't and won't. When we don't appreciate that we have power like this, we can feel more trapped in circumstances than we are.

In inner alchemy, a developed will is usually more about the power we know we have than the power we use. Others almost never see this degree of power, and we may appear calm and easygoing, which in most cases, thanks to our alchemical work, we are. But we know what blazes beneath our surface, and when that will is needed, it's there. We can become an irresistible force or immovable object on command. We can raise mountains with a will like this. We just don't because we're wise enough to understand that mountains are best left be.

Exercises

1. Think of the domains in your life (i.e., work, home, community, etc.) and consider the power dynamics in them.

2. Assess your strengths. One aspect of developing personal power is acquainting ourselves with our strengths. Everyone has strengths. When we recognize our strengths, we reinforce them, which increases our self-confidence and ability to act on our behalf. Some strengths are clear-cut, like physical strength or stamina, while others may be less so. For instance, a strength of yours could be the support you've consistently shown your friends. There's no such thing as an insignificant strength. To begin this exercise, recall the strengths you've exhibited in each life domain (e.g., family, friends, romantic relationships, work, health, community, hobbies, etc.) and list them. To facilitate this, consider the following questions:

   • What have you survived that was difficult to make it through? What strengths helped you with that?

   • What have you completed that was tough to finish?

   • How have you helped others in a way that indicates strength?

   • What strengths do others see in you (or what might they see)?

   • What do you do well?

   • What do you like about how you treat others?

   • What do you like about how you live?

   • What do you like about yourself (or what would you like about someone who's exactly like you)?

When you feel weak, read through this list. Add to it as you recognize additional strengths.

3. Another strengths-related exercise, which comes from solution-focused brief therapy, is to look for exceptions to our thoughts of weakness. For example, if we have a thought like "I can't care for myself," we try to remember instances when we cared for ourselves effectively. Then we examine what was different then versus now. Perhaps we cared for ourselves well when we had more free time before starting a demanding job. Considered this way, it's not that we can't care for ourselves, but more that our circumstances make doing so difficult. This exception then becomes a pivot point for changing our inaccurate belief. Can you think of any exceptions like this in your life?

An additional way of seeking exceptions is to remember instances when, because of unusual circumstances, we behaved in a manner we normally feel unable to. For example, a person who compulsively eats might believe they're powerless over food, yet be able to restrain themselves when they're at an event and it's not time to eat. This exception demonstrates that they actually can control themselves around food. The trick is to find a way to bring this strength into the circumstances they struggle with.

Will Development Exercises

"Thus bind thyself, and thou shalt be for ever free."
—ALEISTER CROWLEY

To build personal power, we cultivate the will. Without a developed will, this book's information will mostly stay conceptual, and for inner alchemy, we need more than that. In my experience, there are two salient aspects of will development. One is learning to harness our desire for an outcome to motivate ourselves to act toward realizing it, which is addressed in the next section. The other is becoming able to act simply because we will it. Both help us achieve our intentions and are developed in this system. The latter is critical for situations where our motivation resists being stoked.

On the surface, developing the second type of will is simple. To build our ability to follow through on intentions, we practice setting intentions and following through on them. This strengthens our "will muscles" and establishes a habit of following through on our word. Because our brain strives to keep habits, creating this habit provides us with momentum behind seeing our intentions through.

The most effective technique I know for cultivating this habit is will development exercises, which stem from Aleister Crowley's work, as detailed in *Liber III vel Jugorum*. Will development exercises are exercises performed for at least seven days that involve intentionally changing our behavior at the level of thought, word, or action. For instance, we might journal for fifteen minutes a day or meditate on a tarot card for one minute each morning. These may seem insignificant, and if they were isolated, they might be, but when performed week after week, they exponentially grow the will.

Crowley's approach to will development was extreme. He recommended cutting ourselves whenever we miss the mark with these exercises. His approach was as much about subjugating the ego as developing will, so his exercises were more continuous than most of the ones I include (e.g., "Throughout the day, don't cross your legs"). Crowley's recommendation was to train ourselves as animals generally were in his time, to "beat a disobedient dog." While his approach was unnecessarily severe, he wasn't totally off base, which later research in behavioral psychology illuminates.

B. F. Skinner, a prominent twentieth-century psychologist, famously researched operant conditioning, a learning process in which behavior is conditioned through utilizing pleasure or pain (i.e., reward or punishment). For example, if we want an animal to sit on a couch, we can give it treats when it does. If we want it to stay off the couch, we can spray it with water when it sits on the couch. Though humans are more complex than animals, we still respond to operant conditioning. If we punish ourselves when we do something we don't want ourselves to do, we can develop an aversion to doing it. Even the thought of it may fill us with dread.

This is actually one of the main problems with Crowley's approach. Skinner found that when using operant conditioning in people, punishment often resulted in aversive feelings toward the object of the conditioning. For example, a child who's punished for not completing their math homework can come to dislike math and subconsciously associate math homework with punishment (which is classical conditioning). In contrast, rewarding a child after they complete their math homework can associate math homework with the reward for them. They may even look forward to doing it.

Punishing ourselves during will development exercises can make us averse to them and inner alchemy, which is the opposite of what we want, so we don't do this in the Little Work system. There's also no sense in hurting ourselves in the aim of well-being. Instead, we can reward ourselves for completing will development exercises (or following through on other intentions), and when we don't complete an exercise, we don't get the reward. In my experience, not receiving the reward is usually sufficient "punishment."

Over the years, I've also had considerable success with assigning rewards to major projects I anticipated experiencing resistance to completing. For instance, to motivate myself to finish my final papers in graduate school early, I pledged to reward myself with a new musical instrument. This was a splurge I wouldn't normally have bought, and selecting rewards we wouldn't otherwise give ourselves (or would feel apprehensive giving ourselves) can highly stoke motivation. Clearly, this approach only works if we don't give ourselves rewards when we don't earn them. The aim is to show our ego that if it gets out of our way, it'll get something it wants. If we cave in instead, it'll continue trying to derail us as it sees fit.

Regarding the exercises themselves, Crowley recommended doing them for seven days or more. In my experience, seven days is a sweet spot. Most of us already conceptualize a week as a discrete event and can digest the notion of acting differently for seven days. For example, rising two hours earlier for a month might sound extreme, but for a week, it's probably manageable, though this would be too intense at first. I recommend starting small with these exercises in terms of the time and energy they require and building from there. This makes us likelier to complete them long enough to begin experiencing their benefits, which provides motivation to persist with them.

One of these benefits is that will development exercises build our sense of self-efficacy. We gain a growing assurance that we can do what we intend to since every week, we intend something different and do it. Another benefit is that will development exercises make us more comfortable with change by accustoming us to it in small doses. After doing these for a while, we can make small to moderate changes without getting the same kind of psychological resistance we would've before. Even our resistance to bigger changes decreases. Doing something different each week helps us break our inertia and trust that it's OK to do different things. These exercises keep us from nesting in our comfort zones, particularly when we start picking difficult ones.

Will development exercises also increase our awareness. Having something out of the ordinary to focus on heightens our attention. It makes the day stand out because we must remember the exercise and do it, and with the lengthier exercises, that can involve significant remembering. These exercises nudge us to be more present, which helps us generally be more present and less habituated in our day-to-day life.

Habituation is one of the greatest causes of unconsciousness, and many of us zone out in a variety of situations, like when driving a familiar route. Will development exercises are like little alarms that go off to wake us up. A daily practice isn't enough to stave off this tendency to go unconscious because it too can become routine, even with solid results. However, when we combine will development exercises with ritual, meditation, mindfulness, and a learning outlook, they snap us out of unconscious, autopilot living.

Because of how we react to them, these exercises also help us become more aware of our psychological makeup. For example, there might be some we struggle to complete or even forget about, while others are easy for us. This is valuable information. It helps us increase the accuracy of the picture we have about our strengths, weaknesses, and interior world, as well as see how our ego reacts to different things.

In terms of designing these exercises, it's critical for the first six to eight months to perform ones that have minimal emotional significance, like Crowley's "avoid crossing the legs." When we involve subjects we have an emotional charge with, our emotional resistance will factor in on top of the standard ego resistance to performing these exercises. This can make it far harder to complete them, leaving us less likely to select more and experience their intended benefits. For example, if you have challenges with cleaning up, don't pick will development exercises that deal with this at first (e.g., "Do the dishes daily").

Once we've firmly established the habit of completing weekly will development exercises, we can use them to help us achieve our intentions. We simply start designing exercises that relate to our intentions (e.g., "I'll work on my taxes for twenty minutes a day"). The strong inertia of our habit will help us push through any resistance we feel to seeing our intentions through. We can also use these exercises to audition new behaviors without the emotional heft of a lifestyle change. For example, if we want to become vegan, we can audition veganism for seven days. If that works out, we can try seven more. This way, we sidestep the substantial resistance that can accompany a bold pronouncement like "I'm vegan for life" and sense of failure if veganism doesn't pan out for us. We can also renew will development exercises until they become habits, though once we're repeating one week after week, we must add another to continue gaining the benefits from novelty listed above.

After we cultivate a high degree of will, we can employ will development exercises to aid us with issues we struggle with emotionally, and we can also make will development exercises heftier. While writing this book, for example, I set a daily minimum of writing 2,500 words. For most of my schooling, I procrastinated on writing assignments, but through inner alchemy, I developed the ability to stop procrastinating at will, which largely came from will development exercises.

From now on, select a will development exercise weekly. I recommend undertaking these exercises for at least a year, ideally indefinitely, but how far you want to take this path is up to you. Begin with exercises that don't require more than five minutes per day. Strive to have an even mix between thought, word, and action exercises. Eventually, it can be beneficial to have more than one will development exercise at a time. For example, you could have one devoted to a goal and another that's more neutral.

If you perform these exercises weekly, you'll make a habit of following through on your word, trying new things, paying more attention, doing something regardless of how you feel, and feeling capable. All of these habits will help you realize your intentions. Below are will development exercises you can try, arranged by degree of difficulty. They can be mixed together (i.e., you don't have to stop doing beginner level ones simply because you can handle advanced ones), and feel free to design your own. These are just to get you started and facilitate the Little Work.

All of these are performed daily for a week:

Beginner

Tie your shoes starting with your right foot first.

Eat with your non-dominant hand during one meal.

Make your bed.

Open and sort the mail.

Write down money spent.

Write down all major emotions you felt.

Make a short to-do list and prioritize the items on it.

Before bed, think of three things you feel grateful for.

Study an astrology sign, planet, or house. This should take no more than ten minutes.

Unlock things with your non-dominant hand.

Think about your strengths at least once.

Read ten pages of a book.

Draw a tarot card and look up its meaning.

Draw the symbol for the element of air and meditate on it for three minutes upon rising.

Draw the symbol for the element of fire and meditate on it for three minutes at noon.

Draw the symbol for the element of water and meditate on it for three minutes at sunset.

Draw the symbol for the element of earth and meditate on it for three minutes before bed.

Practice thinking compassionately at least three times.

Intermediate

Handle a piece of paper once (e.g., if you open a piece of mail, deal with it in that moment).

Wash the dishes.

If you have a doubtful thought, consider the facts for and against it.

Practice mindfulness at least three times (e.g., when eating, doing chores, etc.).

When faced with a task, estimate how long it will take. If you estimate less than five minutes, do it if you can.

Say "compassion" in conversation at least once.

Put away one item whenever you enter a room (where appropriate).

Smile at every stranger you see and nod or say hi, unless you feel unsafe.

Check social media a specified number of times and no more.

Every time you enter the bathroom, clean something within it.

Change the verbal greeting you normally use.

Do something you enjoy each day.

Set guidelines for when you can take breaks while completing tasks (e.g., "I can check my phone after I fold the next ten pieces of laundry," etc.).

If you start reading or writing a paragraph, finish it before taking a break.

When facing a to-do list, start with the item you least want to do.

Look for opportunities to be of service to others and take them without credit (e.g., pick up litter).

Eat a piece of fruit daily.[6]

Tell someone who doesn't usually hear from you that you love them.

Complete one self-care activity daily.

Pay attention to when others use speech that evidences cognitive distortions.

Go for a walk.

Take a different route to a familiar place.

Advanced

When you feel the urge to procrastinate, do the thing. Now.

Abstain from desserts with white sugar.[7]

Put things away immediately after using them.

Do one thing per day related to your goals.

Don't use the word "always."

If you struggle with cleaning dishes, limit yourself to using two sets.

Plan and take a trip with a substantial itinerary.

Change the size of your handwriting or how you write the letter "a."

Don't use the word "hate."

Reach out to someone you haven't heard from in years but miss (just one person, but this can be planned over the course of the week).

Complete tasks that require fifteen to twenty minutes without taking breaks.

Mindfully witness your prominent emotional reactions.

Center yourself hourly.

Look for the divine in everyone you see, including yourself in the mirror.

Try to sense the divine in everything.

Perform an action that's outside your comfort zone.

---

6. If you have an eating disorder, avoid exercises related to food.

7. Ibid.

Avoid using some common word, such as "and," "the," or "but"; use a paraphrase.[8]

Avoid using the pronouns and adjectives of the first person; use a paraphrase.

Avoid lifting the left arm above the waist.

Avoid crossing the legs.

Avoid thinking of a definite subject and all things connected with it, and let that subject be one which commonly occupies much of your thought, being frequently stimulated by sense-perceptions or the conversation of others.

SELF-DISCIPLINE

"It is always easier to fight for one's principles than to live up to them."
—ALFRED ADLER

Once we've developed willpower, we can act on our intentions regardless of what we feel or think in most cases, which is self-discipline. Many recoil at the word "discipline," which is understandable given what it can mean. In the Little Work system, discipline isn't about punishment, obeying orders, or becoming unspontaneous, rigid, and inauthentic. It's simply about self-control, which is crucial for inner alchemy because behavioral change requires consistency. Discipline gives us the ability to commit to our practices.

In this system, discipline arises from will development exercises and a refined awareness of how an action contributes to manifesting or sustaining something we want, which we explored earlier. For example, by appreciating that studying business will help us realize our dream of opening a metaphysical store, we generate energy to study business and our resistance to studying it diminishes. When struggling to motivate ourselves to do something, we can contemplate its benefits in this manner.

Conceptualizing discipline like this is important because of how the subject of discipline will nest in our psyche and reverberate in our psychic emanation. If we see discipline as being about rigidity and burdensome structure, it'll dry us up. If we see it instead as a means of facilitating our intentions, that sense of purpose will shine within us. In both cases, the outward actions can be identical ("Perform rituals daily," "Journal nightly," etc.), but internally, one aspirant rides a wave of accumulating vibrancy, while the other is like a dimming lamp.

---

8. This and the rest of the suggestions below are Crowley's.

Even with a refined awareness of why we want something, we can still struggle to motivate ourselves to act on behalf of this intention because of emotional resistance. For example, I might want to change careers, yet also be terrified of that change's implications. The ego then raises resistance: "Let's watch TV instead of thinking about this...for the rest of the year." "Let's worry to where we become too afraid to seriously consider this." This is where the discipline from will development exercises comes in. We meet whatever resistance arises within us with compassion and care while continuing on our course. As we stop biting these hooks of distraction, they weaken. A moment comes when we sit down to do something we've procrastinated about and just do it because we said we would and that's that, which is tremendously freeing. This ability can atrophy if we shirk our attentiveness and intentionality in day-to-day living though, like how a neglected garden can easily become overgrown.

If you go full tilt with this system, you'll regularly encounter the ego. It'll become apparent that the ego has a "whatever works" policy. For example, if it can derail us with casual sex, we may find ourselves hypersexual. If we always skip our practices when our friends want to socialize, we can find ourselves with a full social calendar and no time for ritual. It's critical to stay mindful of this and hold to our intentions.

Mysteries paths have always required self-discipline. When we aren't able to set aside our moment-by-moment impulses enough to dive within, we can't sustain the level of practice and alignment necessary for deep inner work. We may be metaphysically gifted enough to still have some profound experiences, but we can't seal the deal. We're too at the mercy of our ego, which resists going where High Magic takes us. Even from a less lofty vista, if we want healing, transformation, and freedom, we must consistently pull thought-dependent reality weeds out of ourselves, which requires discipline.

As we develop discipline, day-to-day tasks become much easier to perform. The days of losing track of bills or struggling to do dishes dwindle. Our self-confidence grows as we take charge like this. We start trusting that we can do what we seek to, which opens us to possibilities that previously felt inaccessible and makes us likelier to capitalize on the opportunities we find. Maybe attending night school felt impossible before, for example, but now it seems doable.

Another way we can work with ourselves that involves discipline is through developing rules. In this system, rules are simply behavioral guidelines we set to support an intention. For example, "I practice daily without fail," is a rule I've up-held since 2005. Without this firm commitment, I'm sure I wouldn't have prac-ticed some days. Instead, I practiced sloppily at times, but better to have held this line than risked losing consistency in my practice. If there are behaviors you feel would be healthy for you to uphold, you can try making a rule about them, be-ginning with a weeklong will development exercise (e.g., "I don't check my phone during dinner"). These rules become part of the cocoon we create to contain our alchemical work, and we can always ditch them if we want, so there's no need to feel overburdened by them.

INTENTIONAL ACTION

"Accustom yourself continually to make many acts of love,
for they enkindle and melt the soul."
—TERESA OF AVILA

An intentional action is any action we take with intent, and as we explored earlier, intention is magical. Will development exercises are one example of intentional action, but more generally, intentional action in this system is about becoming as thoughtful and present with our actions as we can. This includes considering the impact our actions have, how efficiently we do things, how to best engage with our environment, etc. We establish as much finesse in action as possible, under-standing that "How you do anything is how you do everything," and our actions can hugely impact our well-being, intentions, and psychic emanation.

An important part of well-being, as well as a flowing, vital psychic emana-tion, is self-esteem. We primarily gain self-esteem in this system through tun-ing in to our heart and spirit and approaching life compassionately. This way, our self-esteem isn't rooted in fluctuating conditions, like how others think of us, or our performance level. At the same time, our actions can contribute to how we feel about ourselves. It's hard to feel good about ourselves if we consistently act against our well-being or conscience. Consequently, a core facet of intentional ac-tion is using a learning outlook to ascertain what feels healthy for us and acting in alignment with that as best we can. We recognize that each action can move us toward or from well-being. Relatedly, some intentions will require us to act dif-ferently in our lives, sometimes even demanding that we stop behaviors that don't serve us. Contemplating how to do this, setting out to do it, and doing it, are all aspects of intentional action. As long as we don't fall into perfectionism or feeling shame or guilt regarding our unhealthy behaviors (especially ones we struggle with stopping or are addicted to), this can be a profoundly healing practice.

When we consistently feel bad about ourselves, we filter reality in a manner that validates that perspective, which our psychic emanation then matches. In my experience, as compassionate thinking helped me feel better about myself and I became more consistent and intentional with my actions, my life began to flow. It was like the difference between living in a dank room that's cluttered and disorganized versus a sunny one that's tidy and thoughtfully arranged.

Intentional action is where we practice responding rather than reacting to situations, which is a popular concept in the coaching world. When we react, we reply to external stimuli in a reflexive manner. These reactions, which can manifest as thoughts, feelings, or actions, are rooted in past experiences and conditioning. For example, if someone insults our intelligence and we immediately yell at them because this is a sensitive issue for us given past experiences, that's a reaction. Conversely, when we respond, we choose how to address external stimuli instead of being reflexively controlled by it. To continue with the example, we may still feel livid if someone insults our intelligence, but we meet that feeling with a pause, wherein we decide how to proceed.

Willpower and mindfulness foster this ability to pause. In this system, we use a learning outlook to explore our thoughts and feelings when we have a strong reaction to something. For instance, we discover why someone insulting our intelligence hurts us so much (e.g., community influences that synonymized worth and intelligence, harsh treatment from our parents if we didn't get excellent grades, etc.). We then remind ourselves what we want to believe instead—that intelligence doesn't indicate worth—and offer ourselves compassion. All of this helps us become able to leave a room rather than fall apart if someone insults our intelligence.

Making a habit of responding increases our personal power. It enables us to stop being at the mercy of external stimuli. Though this is often more of a process than an event (especially with strong emotional reactions), every bit of progress with this is freeing. A reactive part of us is like a marionette others can control. In the water section, we'll learn how to cut these strings, but fundamentally, it's critical to cultivate the habit of pausing and considering how we want to respond to situations. This is easier to establish by practicing with non-antagonizing day-to-day events, and the stronger this habit becomes, the likelier we'll be to pause when we feel like reacting. For example, we can make a habit of taking a moment before answering questions. Internet debates can be excellent for practicing responding because we're sequestered enough to pause and process our emotions before engaging further.

Metaphysically speaking, responding helps us involve our energy with intent in situations, retaining much of it within ourselves. When we react, our energy surges toward whatever prompted our reaction. This is part of the energetic psychology behind why some people enjoy being provocative. They can feed off the energy and sense of power in getting someone to react to them, even when that reaction is violent.

When we respond, our energy doesn't get involved in someone else's dysfunction. If someone says something provocative and we calmly disagree, the situation usually diffuses because they didn't get what they sought from us. Even if they rage at this, we're still protected because our energy is mostly contained within, and we've set the tone rather than fallen in line with theirs. Relatedly, part of intentional action is considering where our energy goes in exchanges with others and how to best utilize it.

Exercises

1. Consider where you can conserve energy through intentional action, or where you might want to show up differently.
2. As a will development exercise, practice pausing before responding to situations in your life, beginning with ones that aren't very emotionally evocative.

CLARIFYING VALUES

"As soon as you trust yourself, you will know how to live."
—JOHANN WOLFGANG VON GOETHE

The Little Work system centers upon training ourselves to live in a manner that supports our well-being and intentions. Thus far, the main intention we've focused on has been performing the Little Work itself. Beyond that, this system involves creating a life that feels fulfilling to us individually. To do this, it's essential to clarify our values and ethics, which inform that process.

Loosely defined, values are the guiding principles we have about life in terms of things like "right" and "wrong." Ethics are the translation of values into codes of conduct for how to behave appropriately. Believing that people should be free to act as they please provided they're not hurting anyone is a value. A code of ethics that integrates this value could include staying out of people's business as long as they aren't harming others.

While growing up, we're exposed to many people's values and ethics, sometimes contrastingly. For instance, our family's values might've differed from our society's, especially if we're immigrants (e.g., there's huge cultural variation regarding the value of the extended family). Our family's values might've also contrasted with those of people from a different religion than ours. Perhaps our parents taught us that all life is equally divine while others were told that human life is holier than animal life.

Without a clear articulation of our values, we may be unaware of what they are, or at least what values are active in our subconscious. For example, our society may have fed us the notion that "wealth determines personal worth," and though we disagree with this, it's active in our subconscious enough for us to feel somewhat deficient if we're not wealthy. Other times, we may have values like "Everyone deserves respectful treatment," which we're aware of and strive to embody. Many of us begin inner alchemy with a mixture of conscious and subconscious values, and a key part of it is sifting through them to release those that don't fit us.

On a basic level, doing what we believe is right feels good, while doing what we believe is wrong doesn't. When our behaviors align with our conscience, which is essentially the voice of our values, they feel good in the moment and after. Consistently acting from our conscience builds our sense of integrity, enabling us to stand firmly behind our decisions, which fosters harmony within our subtle body and psychic emanation. A difficulty here though is that what feels like our conscience can be manipulated by external influences. For example, if we grew up hearing that casual sex is sinful, we may feel shame upon having healthy sexual fantasies. Clarifying our values helps us recognize and release conditioning like this, as does the ongoing practice of a learning outlook.

In today's world, many of us frequently face values-based predicaments—for instance, where some necessities of life are produced in conditions that conflict with our values, yet we lack the resources to buy premium alternatives. Additionally, conflicts between our values and society's values can be difficult to resolve, particularly when a societal value is linked with something we want. For example, we may believe our society's beauty standards are toxic, but we also can't individually transform these standards. Because we naturally desire sex and other benefits that frequently accompany being conventionally attractive, we may continually struggle with the pressure to conform to these standards. Situations like these are often difficult to process. It remains critical to be compassionate with ourselves as we do our best.

Other times, we may have a subconscious belief rooted in trauma that contrasts with a value of ours. For example, we may believe that "everyone's worthy" while having trauma that predisposes us to feel otherwise about ourselves. This may incline us toward self-harming behavior, even superficially, because part of us feels that we deserve to suffer. We'll learn how to address this in the next chapter, but fundamentally, we champion our value and offer ourselves compassion when we don't live up to it.

In contemporary substance use treatment, there's an intervention called "harm reduction" that rests on the notion that even if someone can't stop a harmful behavior yet, they can likely reduce its harmfulness. For example, someone might not be ready to quit heroin, but they can go to a needle exchange for clean needles. In our lives, we may struggle to stop harmful behaviors, yet find ways to mitigate their harm, which can improve our health and how we feel. For instance, I've dealt with binge eating disorder since childhood. Reducing the amount of food I eat during a binge and stopping shaming myself for binging has helped me substantially. Compassion aids us in navigating the dissonance between a value like "The body is a temple" while treating ours otherwise, which may be such ingrained behavior that it takes years to end.

Without clearly articulated values, we can expend significant energy wondering how to navigate difficult situations or even best use our time. Though some situations may inherently warrant contemplation in determining how to best respond to them, most don't. When we know what we believe is generally beneficial to do, most courses of action that align with that are apparent with little reflection. For example, if I know certain behaviors conflict with my values, I needn't contemplate whether to date someone who frequently engages in them. This holds for many levels of decision-making, and the resources we save by avoiding lengthy, stressful, and emotionally charged decision-making processes can be funneled elsewhere. Frequently being in a more conflicted state also negatively impacts our psyche, subtle body, and psychic emanation. Consistent vacillation makes it harder to flow with what we intend, and regular uneasiness, worry, and uncertainty can tank our manifestations.

In mystical systems where aspirants aspire to the Great Work, values and ethics are intentionally aligned with that aim. The yamas and niyamas and the Eightfold Path of Buddhism are two examples of this. These codes of ethics enable aspirants to minimize the accumulation of new karma while burning through what's already there. They help aspirants step back from the external world and cut the tethers within them that their egos use to distract them from the path. The intent is to not make waves, internally or externally, so aspirants can concentrate one-pointedly on the Great Work. Principles like non-harming, integrity, non-attachment, and non-stealing insulate aspirants from the drama of the world.

To get a sense of how this works, let's consider the Yogic value of non-harming, which is paralleled in the Wiccan Rede ("An it harm none, do as ye will"). Harming another produces psychic and psychological effects, which, depending on our conscience, can actually be more harmful than the act was for the other person. Not to mention that we must also experience the effects of any worry we have about the other seeking retribution, the harm that could come from them doing so, and the karma of our action (in this life or another). Consequently, harming people can hugely impact us. Conversely, by embracing non-harming, save for when harm is necessary for defense of self or the vulnerable (which is an exception many Yogis and Wiccans make), these issues leave our lives. When we know violence isn't our answer, we eventually stop asking ourselves the question. We have fewer antagonistic emotional conflicts until we're generally clear, which substantially opens our psychic emanation for our intentions and supports diving deep in meditation (and we haven't even considered the benefits of non-harming that accompany striving not to harm ourselves). Regarding the benefits of another Yogic value, integrity, Mark Twain famously said, "If you tell the truth, you don't have to remember anything." Managing lies occupies our mind, sapping energy that could be better devoted to spiritual practice. It creates stress and disharmony on the psychological and subtle level.

Whether we believe the level of detachment Yogis strive for is appropriate for us or not, it's important to recognize how our actions affect our psyche and subtle body. It's worth considering the consequences of potential actions: how we might feel after, if they'll linger with us, etc. Acting in alignment with our values fosters well-being, and our values are ours to determine. Even among mystical traditions, values can differ. For example, in Yoga, eating animals is thought to increase karma and impede meditation. In other traditions, eating animals reverentially is part of honoring the circle of life.

Clarifying our values helps us insulate ourselves from consensus reality values that don't match ours. For example, I've turned down lucrative promotions because I didn't want to work sixty hours a week. Having previously articulated my values around money and free time, which diverge from my society of origin, made it easier for me to turn down those promotions.

Here are some values-related beliefs we may have internalized from others:

+ When in pain, "walk it off."
+ Taking time for ourselves is selfish and self-indulgent.
+ What we produce determines our worth.
+ Women should sacrifice everything for their families.
+ Our value relates to how physically attractive we are.
+ Career is more important than relationships.
+ We're incomplete without a romantic relationship.

Here are some we may favor instead:

+ People can live as they choose as long as they don't harm others.
+ All of nature is imbued with divinity.
+ All life is inherently worthy.
+ The body is a temple.
+ Service to humanity is service to the divine.
+ Everyone has a right to guide their path.
+ We each have a right to healthy boundaries and self-care.
+ We can honor our desires without being selfish.
+ Abiding self-worth comes from within.

Reflect on how differently the beliefs in the first and second list could shape someone's experience of reality. This is part of why clarifying our values is so essential.

Exercise

List your values in your journal and consider how to behave in alignment with them. To do this, think about what feels right or important to you in the various life domains. For example: family, physical well-being, emotional well-being, relationships, parenting, friendship, employment, recreation, personal growth, education, spirituality, community, citizenship, government, etc. Answer questions like "What's the value of family?" "If I lived 100 percent within this value, how would I behave?" "What's a healthy family dynamic?" Tuning in to our spirit and heart is important when reflecting on values, as is separating ourselves from external conditioning. A learning outlook can aid us greatly in this as we explore each area.

AUTHENTIC LIVING

"To be yourself in a world that is constantly trying to make you something else is the greatest accomplishment."

—RALPH WALDO EMERSON

Articulating our values paves the way for us to live authentically, which means in alignment with our values and what we deeply feel is beneficial or important for us to do. Each of us has an innate sense of who and what we are. As we clarify our values and remove the external conditioning we've received that doesn't serve us, we become able to live in alignment with that sense. This results in a vitality that is satisfying and life-giving.

At the start of inner alchemy, we may struggle to tell the difference between a conditioned impulse urging us one way and our authenticity pointing us another. Much of this issue resolves as we get a sense of what drives our thoughts, feelings, and actions through diligently applying a learning outlook. Meditation and ritual also help us reach a static center within that's inherently authentic and not thought-dependent. As we experience this center, we can feel if we're moving toward or from it, with or against it. That's a general guideline for authentic living: are we moving toward or from the divine? This brings us to another tenet of the Little Work: *center in your authenticity.* When we find our authenticity, we do our best to build our lives around it.

Many contexts can foster inauthentic behavioral patterns, including family, community, culture, religion, and society. The further we are from our authenticity, the worse we tend to feel. Many of us begin inner alchemy with inauthentic behavioral patterns in several, if not many, domains of our lives. For instance, there may be certain roles we're supposed to play or limits we're supposed to adhere to, with significant consequences if we step outside of them. Forces of bigotry may cause us to legitimately feel like we must toe the line to be safe, advance professionally, receive fairer treatment, etc. Psychological trauma may incline us to live inauthentically if it makes us feel unsure about trusting ourselves (e.g., if childhood abuse convinced us we're incapable of doing anything right). We may even come from an unconventional family where we're encouraged to "rock the boat," but only within acceptable confines.

Trying to be something we aren't is one of the unhealthiest forms of stress in life. When I was a closeted teenager trying to be heterosexual, that felt like violating my soul. While some stress is inherent in being human (e.g., growing pains, illness, aging, etc.), it doesn't take effort to be yourself. Making too much effort to be something is a clue we're being inauthentic. Anxiety, stress, depression, and frustration are common symptoms of inauthentic living, all of which can create or worsen physical health problems. Sadly, inauthentic living is so normalized that we may think feeling like this is inherent to adulthood, but it isn't, as inner alchemy will show us.

Sometimes living authentically involves following our inner North Star to make bold changes. It can also involve listening to the internal guidance encouraging us to care for ourselves better. Other times, authentic living is more about our mental state than what we're doing. In societies, we all must do things we wouldn't do if there were no cost to our standard of living. We put on social costumes and jump through hoops that are thought-dependent creations of others. All of that could collapse in an instant, and it's empowering and healing to understand that we needn't define ourselves by these thought-dependent realities. That said, we'll likely continue participating in these realities, so the question isn't just how to live authentically, but also how to live authentically while doing things we wouldn't organically choose to do. This is a place where the Little Work system comes in.

There can be many motivations for performing an action, and shifting our mindset about an action can yield a profoundly different internal impact when performing it. In this system, we learn to integrate our actions with our values and overarching alchemical process, which leads us to feel like we're living authentically. For instance, I turned my career into a primary setting for practicing inner alchemy. My experience of work dramatically improved when it went from being something I had to do to being a core part of my spiritual practice. Many adults feel the most inauthentic at work. In the earth chapter, we'll explore specific techniques to align jobs with inner alchemy so we can feel authentic at work.

Some people balk at the notion of living authentically because "If I said what I want to, I'd get fired," or some comparable sentiment. Living authentically isn't synonymous with living impulsively. It's not a license to do whatever we feel. Some behaviors are unhelpful, inappropriate, or unethical, and a behavior superficially feeling authentic doesn't make it authentic. For example, hitting someone while enraged might feel authentic, but this is the level of ego, and authenticity is deeper than that. The same holds for an impulse that says, "I should eat this entire cake. Now." In this system, we examine these impulses for understanding and learn to respond to them by acting in our best interest. Even an Aries, a born warrior, won't endorse reactive violence if they're living authentically. When an aggressive response is warranted, it'll come through wisdom, not reactivity. Once we connect with our heart, which is a fundamental aspect of authentic living, we'd never choose to hurt someone for any reason other than necessity. We may still struggle with behavioral patterns that harm others (authentic living is often more of a process than an event), but we recognize these as something to heal, not reinforce.

Exercise

In your journal, reflect on your day-to-day life areas. Where do you feel authentic or inauthentic? Where you feel inauthentic, how might you change your behavior to feel more authentic? Where that's not an option, how can you align behaviors with your intentions to facilitate feeling authentic?

CLARIFYING INTENT

"Desires are the pulse of the soul."
—MANTON

As we strive to live authentically, we naturally investigate our wants. Throughout our lives, many sources have encouraged us to want particular things, which we explored earlier. This conditioning can be so strong that we feel like we need something that's unnecessary for living and actually has superficial value to us. Part of living authentically is discovering what we authentically want and releasing wants that don't serve us.

As a kid, I dreamed of buying a mansion, which was the prevailing fantasy among my peers. We were immersed in media that presented luxury as a primary indicator of success. When I reached adulthood, other aspects of this fantasy struck me. Who was going to clean that mansion? What would I do with all that space? I realized a small house in the woods was more my style.

To liberate our authentic desires from unhealthy external influences, we can examine our wants with a learning outlook. For example, by exploring what they mean to us, what value we see them providing, etc., which helps us release wants that don't serve us. Many are usually there because of things like advertising, other forms of media, and cultural norms. Some of us also want things because we believe they'll ameliorate psychological trauma. For instance, some people yearn to be famous or rich because they believe, often subconsciously, this will make them feel valuable after having grown up with low self-esteem. As wounds like these heal during inner alchemy, our desires can change dramatically. Things we may have desperately sought can feel insignificant, and others we wouldn't have looked at twice at can seem profound.

Regarding my experience with this process, years of Yogic practice, which involved recognizing that material things won't give me lasting satisfaction, purged many of my wants and left me living simply. This purge jettisoned any desire I had to climb the corporate ladder. These preferences, which don't reflect my upbringing, have enabled me to live comfortably with a moderate salary. Meanwhile, I used to want every book, "As seen on TV" item, and candleholder in creation. I still love books and candleholders, but the voracious drive to consume that constant advertising conditioned into me is gone. This is the type of freedom that comes with inner alchemy, and you don't have to want what I want. The salient point is for you to decide what you want, to cut whatever puppet strings are within you and desire authentically.

Exercise

Over the next week, whenever you feel a strong want, examine it. Consider if this desire aligns with your intentions and values. Oftentimes, consistently realizing we don't actually want something or that it's unhealthy for us is enough for us to release the want.

Effective Decision-Making

"It is through solving problems in accordance with the highest light we have that inner growth is attained."
—PEACE PILGRIM

Understanding why we want what we want, articulating our values, and prioritizing living authentically aids us in making decisions that support our well-being and intentions. Options that best foster our intentions become far more self-evident. That said, our decision-making process itself might need some tinkering. When we don't use an effective decision-making approach, we can unnecessarily expend time and energy that we could utilize elsewhere, and we're likelier to experience upset and overthinking. Chances are, if we haven't consciously developed decision-making skills, we aren't acting as effectively or efficiently in this area as we could.

My decision-making approach is simple. When faced with a tough decision, I ask myself, "Is there a bottom line or deal breaker here?" For example, when selecting a graduate program, the factors that mattered most to me were quality and cost. When I was admitted to UCLA, I instantly accepted because, as an in-state student, it was the best program with the lowest cost I applied to. I didn't stress about the other programs because this one met my bottom line far better than they did.

We may not emotionally want decisions to be this straightforward, but they often are. If we get offered a job abroad, but we know we don't want to live that far from our family, the decision's made. Why agonize over an option we won't pick? An essential aspect of inner alchemy is recognizing that some thought processes aren't worth continuing. We can question a thought process's value while engaged in it, and if all it's doing is making us regret not moving abroad, for example, we can stop feeding it. The mental control we develop during ritual and meditation facilitates our ability to do this, and it's worth appreciating how unhealthy these kinds of thought processes are, psychologically and metaphysically. If we can't find a healthy justification for a thought process, moving away from it is best.

If there isn't a bottom line or deal breaker that spotlights an option, the next step is to weigh the pros and cons. Writing these out can be helpful because of the perspective that comes when thoughts are contained on a page. There, we can look at our thoughts as a unit or in contrast to each other in novel ways. This usually yields new insights regarding how to proceed.

To make this kind of list, we can draw a line down the middle of a page (or make two columns in a computer document), with one half of the page being for pros and the other for cons. Then we write all the pros and cons we can think of. During this process, a preference often becomes clear. If one doesn't, the next step is ranking the pros and cons (because some are likely more compelling than others). To return to the school selection example, saving money was more important to me than location, though both factors were important. Assessing the weight of the pros and cons helps make a best-fitting choice apparent.

If a decision remains unclear, we can see if we have an intuitive take on what to do or seek outside input. It's important to tread carefully with intuition until we've developed the discernment to use it effectively though, which we'll learn to do in the water section. Our "guidance" telling us not to live abroad, for example, may be our ego fearing bold change. Otherwise, some decisions don't have an apparent best-fitting choice, which warrants a deeper contemplation of options.

Decisions may also hugely impact us emotionally and part of this decision-making process is exploring our emotions and possibly some anticipatory grieving if we decide to move on from something. When we feel attached to something, the prospect of letting it go can be profoundly difficult. Not moving on from something when it's time can cause massive stress though, especially if it's prominent in our lives, which takes a psychological, metaphysical, and sometimes physical toll. This can be like forcing ourselves to wear clothing that's too small as we continue growing. We'll learn techniques for processing situations like this in the next chapter. The salient point here is that we acknowledge and honor our emotions while making decisions. For example, leaving a relationship may clearly be the healthiest choice for us, but this doesn't erase our grief about doing that or the importance of processing that grief. After making these types of decisions, I often write detailed, fact-based explanations of my reasoning behind them. If I later find myself longing for what was, I reread these explanations, which helps me feel sure of my decisions.

One of the most important acts in decision-making is aligning ourselves with our decisions. When we make decisions we feel fear around (which is normal with bold decisions), our ego may try to convince us we made a wrong choice by criticizing our new circumstances. Given that there are usually elements to criticize (or praise) in most situations, finding reasons to second-guess decisions isn't difficult. Since whatever we focus on becomes a larger part of our psychological experience, second-guessing ourselves can escalate an inkling of doubt into a perceived certainty. A situation with loads of potential can suddenly feel like a horrible mistake, and our critical thoughts and feelings become a self-fulfilling prophecy that makes it one. Unfortunately, our psychic emanation will start manifesting in alignment with these doubts, reinforcing the notion that we messed up. Consequently, it's critical when making big decisions to remember how the ego works and that how we think influences whether a decision feels right or wrong. We can take care not to inadvertently sabotage ourselves by investigating the legitimacy of any doubts that surface following changes. Change is often jarring, and doubts about a change may have more to do with stepping out of our comfort zone than the change itself.

Doing our due diligence is important while making decisions. Afterward, it's beneficial to trust our discernment, align with our decision, and appreciate the upsides of what we chose. Fear might make our old circumstances look better than they were and our new ones worse than they are, which doesn't mean we made a mistake. If we strive to stay open for a significant period of time but still feel unhappy with a change, we can pursue other options.

Another common pitfall in decision-making is waiting indefinitely to begin something because we feel like we're in the wrong time or place. This rests on the notion that there's a right time and place, and there often isn't. This doesn't mean there aren't better times and places. For example, certain industries cluster in particular cities and if we want to work in them, we should probably move to one of those cities. That doesn't mean we can't begin whatever we intend where we are though. If we orient ourselves to "waiting," we run the risk of waiting indefinitely.

When we have a goal we feel doesn't fit our circumstances, we can take advantage of the opportunities that exist where we are to work toward it (e.g., planning, developing skills, etc.). Most circumstances have some fruitful elements we can use to aid in manifesting our goals. When we hold a goal in our mind with this kind of openness, we become likelier to notice the opportunities related to it around us and manifest in alignment with it. We may see a flyer for a class related to a goal, a friend may move to the city we were hoping to and invite us to visit, etc. This is also an area where we can utilize spells to move a matter forward.

Making decisions that we can confidently stand behind is important because our decisions are critical to our life courses. Despite what some practitioners proclaim, opportunities can be fleeting. We don't get to have another senior year of high school, and no matter how healthy we feel, we don't get to be twenty-one again. Circumstances change. The passage of time enriches life and gives it depth, as does the weightiness of having to craft our lives from what we find before and within us. When we deny the consequences that accompany choices because "there are infinite possibilities," we detach from the reality of the human experience. Magic is powerful, but natural law has limits, and there's an elegance and serenity to that. Knowing that we acted with integrity and thoughtfulness can comfort us when decisions don't go as we'd hoped.

When we practice High Magic and meditation effectively, they bring us perspective about life. Rather than enter into denial about our options, we witness the human story as it is. Observing this story pivots us into a part of ourselves that's deeper than the mind. As we get acquainted with this part of ourselves, we find an increasing peace with whatever happens.

Exercise

Reflect on some difficult decisions you've made. How might those processes have differed if you'd used this decision-making approach?

Goal-Setting

"Put things in order before they exist."

—LAO TZU

As we develop self-discipline, we become able to stay on course with change initiatives. When we want to launch a large one (e.g., moving to a new city or switching careers), turning it into a goal can greatly aid in making it happen. A goal is an intention we aim to realize through action.

The most helpful method I know for creating effective goals is called "SMART." SMART is an acronym that stands for specific, measurable, attainable, realistic, and time-bound. This technique transforms vague goals into practical action plans. For example, someone might have the goal "I want to improve my health," which is unclear. What about their health do they want to improve? How? SMART goals answer these questions. A SMART take on this goal could be "I want to improve my fitness by doing cardiovascular exercise for forty-five minutes, five days per week, for the next year."

This goal is specific because it answers what and how (i.e., improved fitness through exercise). It's measurable because we can track whether we exercised as planned or not. A goal is attainable if it's possible to achieve it. In this case, are we physically able to exercise like this? Goals are realistic if it's probable that we can follow through on them. For example, can we feasibly commit the time and energy to work out this much? This goal is time-bound because it answers when and for how long.

Vague goals that aren't SMART, like "I want to develop spiritually," can be useful umbrella goals provided we create SMART goals in service of them. For example, some SMART goals for spiritual development could be: "Each day for the next three months, I will meditate for five minutes and do a ritual" and "I will read four books on spirituality this year by reading at least twenty pages per week."

When creating goals, inquiring "What's the path of least resistance to achieving this?" is often helpful. Because we generally experience resistance to change, anticipating resistance and planning around it can facilitate efficient use of our time and energy. There are usually multiple trajectories to a given destination, each of which can evoke different degrees and types of resistance. For instance, if we want to travel, we could fly, take a train, drive, etc. Each approach has different costs, benefits, and amounts of resistance.

While brainstorming options for a goal, one usually generates less resistance within us as compared with the others, which often means it poses the minimal risk or threat to our status quo. This option generally involves the least energy and emotional upheaval too, which all correlates with reduced fear and probability of egoic sabotage. Consequently, thinking through how to SMART-ly achieve goals with minimal resistance decreases stress and increases our likelihood of accomplishing them.

If we feel overwhelmed by what we have to do for a goal (or the goal itself), we can try to break it into more comfortable parts with partializing. A more complex instance of partializing than we explored earlier is using categories while planning a family trip (e.g., transportation, accommodations, activities, and food options). In these respective categories, we list the relevant tasks (e.g., "transportation" includes "research flights," "compare flight costs," "purchase flights," etc.). Without partializing, we might feel overwhelmed thinking through these logistics. By organizing our planning with these categories (and documenting it), this process can feel more manageable.

Goal achievement involves a synergy of the elements within ourselves. We envision with air, feel into being with water, desire with fire, and stay on task with earth while spirit nourishes the entire process. In my experience, goal-setting can be profoundly magical, especially if we involve spells or vision boards in it. By setting goals, we emanate energy that starts aligning forces behind them.

Psychologically speaking, SMART goals feel more achievable than non-SMART goals because they're composed of doable action steps. This helps us motivate ourselves to work toward these goals and removes doubt from our mind and psychic emanation that could sabotage our goal achievement process. As we achieve goals, we gain confidence that we can set big intentions and realize them. This greatly enhances our concept of what's possible for ourselves and expands the reach of our magic. It's astonishing where we can end up by achieving small goals and building from there.

Exercise

Brainstorm some goals for yourself and try to make them SMART. If you resonate with goal-making, consider setting goals each New Year's (while the sun is in Capricorn). A balanced approach to goal-setting can involve considering the elemental domains of life and what we seek to accomplish within them. For example:

+ Air—creativity, education, intellectual development
+ Fire—adventure, initiating large projects, recreation, travel
+ Water—arts, family, mental health, relationships, self-care
+ Earth—career, finances, home, material goods, physical health
+ Spirit—inner alchemy, magic, service

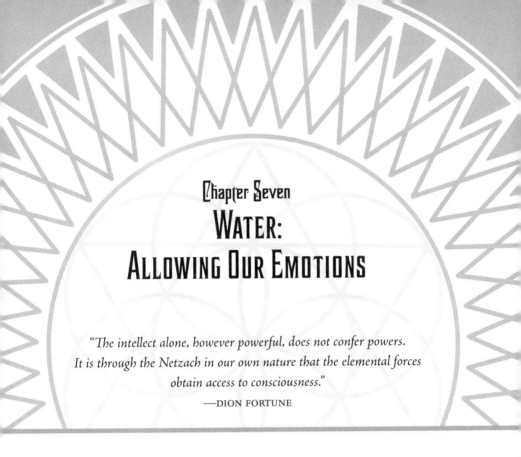

Chapter Seven
WATER:
ALLOWING OUR EMOTIONS

"The intellect alone, however powerful, does not confer powers.
It is through the Netzach in our own nature that the elemental forces
obtain access to consciousness."

—DION FORTUNE

With a developed will and compassionate mind, we move to water, the home of feeling. Without the power of the wand and the discernment of the dagger, it's easy to get caught in the undertow of our emotions. With unbalanced water, we can experience a flow of unstable or codependent relationships, mental illness, and even health conditions that baffle modern medicine. Water must be tempered by air for balanced perspective, bolstered by fire so we can brave difficult emotions and our shadow, and contained by earth so we're not so absorptive that we lose our sense of self.

It's ironic that emotionality is often equated with weakness because feeling is the threshold to our greatest power, wellness, awakening, and peace. We tangibly connect with energy and spirit through feel, and if we don't attend to how we feel, we're unlikely to adequately develop subtle perception. Otherwise, emotion is the lifeblood of magic. We shape magic with thought and sustain it with will, but emotion is what animates it. Nothing compels us like how we feel, and nothing affects our subtle body like emotion. A thought without emotion behind it lacks power, but a burst of rage, flood of tears, or wave of certainty? These profoundly impact our psyche and psychic emanation and can boost or bust our magic. Without emotion, High Magic and spellwork is dry and often ineffective. On the other extreme, when we're at the mercy of our emotions, we can be buffeted about in many directions, scattering our energy and derailing our spells. As we learn to harness emotion instead and induce concentration through it, our magic flourishes.

The magical tool of water is the chalice. To earn the chalice, we cultivate ourselves in key ways related to emotionality. First, we develop a healthy, mature relationship with emotion. This involves accepting the realities of emotionality and learning to process and express emotions healthfully. This also includes incrementally working through any unprocessed emotions we have stored within us. All of this helps us keep our day-to-day emotionality either aligned with our intentions or addressed such that it doesn't sabotage them. Unfortunately, since many of us didn't grow up with models of mature, healthy emotionality, water can have the steepest learning curve of the elements. It's often where we're the most underdeveloped, whether we tend to feel numb to our emotions, overwhelmed by them, or somewhere else along that spectrum.

Another task in earning the chalice is learning how to go a different way than how we feel in order to stay aligned with our intentions while still honoring our feelings. We also learn to harness emotion to support our intentions, which we covered in the sections on spells, rituals, and affirmations. As we gain fluency with our emotions and strong discernment, we work on developing our intuition too.

Despite what many of us were told while growing up, how we feel matters. It indicates where our energy is focused, as well as how our thoughts and feelings are shaping our experience of reality. When we don't process emotions healthfully, they can become like infected wounds, and psychological trauma exerts power over us wherever it's prominent and untreated, especially if it's unidentified. In this system, we learn how to tend to these wounds and develop the ability to prevent more from occurring through healthfully processing our emotions day by day. Once we mature emotionally, emotions make us strong, not weak.

We can perform every ritual in existence, but it's ultimately the feelings of awe and devotion that open us to the celestial waters. We hold our chalice humbly, in love with the divine like nothing we could've imagined, and it fills with nectar. As we drink from it each day, we increasingly perceive divinity everywhere, gaining a fundamental gratitude and reverence for life.

UNDERSTANDING EMOTION

"We are but shadows—we are not endowed with real life,
and all that seems most real about us
is but the thinnest substance of a dream—
till the heart be touched. That touch creates us."
—NATHANIEL HAWTHORNE

Before exploring how to process emotions in a healthy manner, it's beneficial to learn about them. There's no consensus within the psychological community regarding what emotions are and what constitutes a healthy relationship with them. I work with emotions under the umbrella of feelings and find value in differentiating between emotions and other feelings in the following way, as well as acknowledging how feelings can be conditioned:

- Emotions are what we feel in reaction to events, circumstances, information, etc. For example, someone yells at us and we feel hurt, or we watch a melancholic film and feel sad. Thinking can also evoke emotions—for instance, thinking about social injustice and feeling angry or remembering a lost love and feeling wistful. Many emotional reactions are shaped and even created by our perceptions and interpretations and can therefore be conditioned, which we'll explore in depth in this chapter. We all begin inner alchemy with emotional conditioning from our upbringing and other experiences. Emotions are the feelings that respond most clearly to thinking in the moment, as most of us know from having been upset and expressed our emotions only to feel differently.

- Intuition is guidance we receive from higher parts of our being. It's knowledge that comes to us without rational thought or inference. For example, we may feel guided to read a certain book. Intuition is beyond conditioning, but because our mind filters intuitive information, our interpretations of intuitive information can be distorted and biased.

- Instincts are a largely innate form of guidance, inclining us to behave in certain ways, which animals also demonstrate. We have survival instincts, parental instincts, gut feelings, etc. An example of instincts in the animal kingdom is birds building nests. When our survival instincts are active, we may feel intense sensations and emotions in the aim of self-preservation. Many believe our instincts stem from our ancestors' experiences and are difficult to change. Even so, conditioning can affect instincts. For example, growing up in a racist society can cause our survival instincts to activate when we encounter someone society conditioned us to believe is threatening. Being raised by doting parents may heighten our parental instincts. Trauma can influence our instincts too (and our impulses). For instance, sexual assault can result in future intimacy triggering our survival instincts.

+ Impulses are sudden driving forces within us that seek prompt action. For example, we may feel a powerful urge to overeat, hit someone, or call an ex-lover. Impulses are highly susceptible to conditioning, and our emotional state can drive them (e.g., if I feel guilty, I'm likely to have impulses to make amends). Without training, distinguishing between instinct, impulse, and intuition can be difficult, which is one reason developing discernment is critical. Viewing feelings through the lens of our well-being can help with distinguishing intuition from impulse and instinct. Our Higher Self, for example, isn't encouraging us to eat a cake in one sitting, no matter how strongly we feel impelled to. Also, while it may guide us toward self-care, it won't steer us toward selfishness. Otherwise, impulses often grow in relation to our following them, and the ego regularly uses them. When we disregard impulses, as in meditation, they fade.

Here are some additional factors that can affect how we feel:

+ Astrology: The transiting planets influence our feelings. This is most apparent with the lunar cycle, which psychiatric workers can tell you correlates with a rise in many people's psychiatric symptoms. Sometimes we feel things simply because of astrology, which we can gain insight into through studying transits.

+ Psychic/communal: When we're near others, their emotions and even thoughts can pass through us. We may feel sad simply because someone around us does. When we recognize this in the moment, the emotion can disperse immediately. When we don't, we may start brainstorming reasons why we might feel sad, which then makes us feel sadder.

+ Weather: Weather can influence emotions. Many people are more susceptible to depression when they receive less sunlight during the winter, for example.

I share these lists for two major reasons. The first is that it's critical in metaphysical work to understand that the ego can manipulate intuitive information, instinct, and impulse. We can't trust that something's true simply because we feel it is. Once we've exposed the biases in our emotional system and developed discernment, we can rely on our intuition. Until then, it's easy to be misled if we wholly defer to what we feel. Second, it's critical to understand that feelings aren't some immutable dimension of the human experience. What we feel isn't beyond our or external influence, so taking feelings with a grain of salt is important.

This isn't to suggest that we disregard our feelings and the insights they can provide. We just approach them with discernment, understanding that feelings can be distorted and biased because everything we feel is filtered through our mind, consciously and subconsciously. This is especially relevant when we can identify a clear reason why our feelings might be biased (e.g., "I keep feeling like I can't trust anyone after the third date. Maybe my last two breakups are affecting my feelings"). While a gut instinct can protect us from walking down a dangerous street at night, what feels like a gut instinct can prevent us from applying for our dream job because we're afraid of not getting it (or getting it!). We may feel like quitting something that's good for us largely because our egos are scared of how that thing could change us. In situations like these, the point isn't to ignore what we feel. It's to explore our feelings against the backdrop of our wisdom and then act in our best interest.

Generally speaking, the most salient feelings to focus on for inner alchemy are emotions. As I shared earlier, there are varying opinions about what emotions are and what their biological purpose is. Some theorists believe emotions are part of our survival system, providing guidance (e.g., we feel good when something's good for us and bad when it isn't). As we know from exploring the ego, we can feel repelled by actions that are healthy for us and drawn to ones that aren't, so this theory is limited at best. Also, whether emotions began as a guidance system or not, in contemporary human life, emotional reactions can be complex, diverse, and disconnected from survival. Most of us live in a flood of stimulation, which our emotions are entangled in. We may feel a hodgepodge of emotions in a day that have little or nothing to do with the events of our day-to-day life (e.g., sadness while hearing a mournful song, frustration after reading a political article, suspense while watching a TV show, etc.). Because of how our emotions can factor into our magic, this is worth minding.

Emotions are like a bridge between our mind and body. They can influence how we think and act and compel us with physiological reactions (e.g., tears, surges of warmth, shivers, blushing, etc.). Many animals appear to experience emotions that parallel ours, like anger, sadness, joy, and grief, suggesting that emotion is fundamental to the natural world.

Our emotional state profoundly influences what feels true to us. For example, a thought like "Nothing ever works out for me" might sound absurd when we're happy. But while depressed? It resonates. Not because it's true, but because it gels with how we feel, and feelings, by nature, feel true, which is another reason it's critical not to take them or our emotionally charged thoughts at face value. Since much of mental life is associative, we also have thoughts and thought patterns that tend to reemerge more when we feel down (or up). This is an aspect of a well-researched psychological phenomenon called "mood-dependent memory."

Many CBT practitioners conceptualize emotions as being of two main types (which can greatly facilitate inner alchemy, in my experience): primary and secondary. Primary emotions are what we feel when events occur. They're reflexive, and like physical reflexes, they're fleeting unless the event that evoked them persists. In fact, Jill Bolte Taylor, a prominent neuroanatomist, shared in her book *My Stroke of Insight* that the physiological components of emotions like these run their course in less than ninety seconds.

Primary emotional reactions are often inherent, though they can also be conditioned. Feeling fear at a lion's roar without having previously encountered a lion is a primary emotional reaction, as is feeling happy at our mother's touch as an infant and grief when a loved one dies. An example of a conditioned primary emotional reaction is a sexual assault survivor feeling numb after invited erotic touch rather than aroused. Other examples include feeling sad upon hearing that someone else is happy or jealous when someone gets something we wanted.

In contrast, secondary emotions are how we feel in response to our emotions, or any time we experience emotion as the result of thought. Secondary emotions are largely governed by how we think about whatever evoked a primary emotion in us and our interpretation of that emotion. For instance, if someone's kind to me, after feeling warmth (primary), I might question their sincerity and feel queasy (secondary). If someone's cruel to me and I feel angry (primary), I might reflect on this and feel angrier (secondary, even though it's the same emotion). In most cases, we transition rapidly from primary to secondary emotions.

Our emotionality is powerfully intertwined with our memory, which keeps the past vibrantly alive within us, manifesting in many of the feelings we experience. This can harmfully skew some of our primary emotional reactions, as we explored in the example of the person whose childhood abandonment experiences created subconscious beliefs that kept derailing their relationships. Given the connection between memory and feeling, we can often ferret out the causes behind why we feel significant emotions, which we do with the practice of a learning outlook. When an emotion seems disproportionate or inappropriate in a situation, it's usually about more than the situation at hand (e.g., "Why am I furious about this waiter being a little rude to me?" "I have a long history of feeling disrespected").

Primary emotional reactions are difficult to change, though some, particularly the conditioned ones, shift with alchemical work. Others are simply part of the human experience or too nested within us, the latter of which can also be said of some of the thoughts that appear when we experience primary emotions. For example, if someone yells at me, I might always feel a flash of aversive emotion and have some kind of fearful thought pop into my head. What this emotion becomes is up to me, though, because secondary emotions are guided by our thoughts. For instance, even if I feel jealous after someone wins an award I wanted, by sincerely appreciating their accomplishments, my jealousy can shift to pride for them.

Most of our patterns of thought and secondary emotion were learned or developed. Consistently thinking about familiar circumstances differently can shift our emotional reactions about them or ones like them, sometimes even at the primary level, particularly when this is coupled with ritual, meditation, and affirmation practice. By diligently practicing compassionate thinking, we can reorient ourselves to have secondary emotional reactions that align with our values and compassion, regardless of what the primary emotion involved is. Two of the most disempowering beliefs we can hold are that our feelings are outside of our influence and our now is "just how life is," which can become self-fulfilling prophecies, but not because they're true.

THE HOLY DARK

"Mystery and manifestations spring from the same source.
This source appears as darkness. Darkness within darkness.
The gateway to all understanding."

—LAO TZU

As we explored earlier, emotions are sometimes conceptualized as "energy in mo-tion." They affect our subtle body and psychic emanation's flow, strength, and what frequencies it matches. They also have different rates of vibration, with some emotions being higher frequency and others being lower. This generally corresponds to the spectrum of the major chakras, meaning that feeling empow-ered is higher in vibration than feeling feeble, feeling connected to others is higher than feeling misanthropic, feeling connected to the divine is higher than the inti-macy of casual friendship, feeling humbled by awe is higher than feeling proud, etc. From the perspective of divine unity, all emotions, like all planes of existence, are equally divine. Higher and lower primarily has relevance when considering our subjective experience and alchemical work.

On a strictly metaphysical level, an emotion is positive if it raises our vibra-tion and negative if it lowers our vibration. When we tend to hang out in lower frequencies, we feel lonely, weak, or unhappy. When we rest in higher ones, we feel better. A critical piece to understand here is that whether or not an emotion (or thought) is positive or negative can depend on where we are psychologically. If I feel depressed, a motivating selfish desire is positive. If I feel united with all beings, it's negative.

This is a nuanced subject, and it's frequently misunderstood, resulting in the pathologizing or demonizing of difficult emotions like grief, sadness, anger, and fear, which are fundamental to the human experience. When we condemn, deny, or avoid difficult emotions or experiences under the notion that they're unspiri-tual (e.g., as if we should only feel good), we engage in a harmful behavior called "spiritually bypassing." Spiritual bypassing, in essence, is the rejection of healthy parts of the human experience in the name of spirituality. It has detrimental con-sequences in our psyche and psychic emanation, like most forms of denial and avoidance. Beyond the fact that feeling bad feels bad, one of the main reasons people spiritually bypass hearkens back to the broadcast TV analogy I made early in the book: they worry that experiencing and processing difficult emotions will manifest increased difficulties in their lives. They'd rather stay tuned to the Happiness and Prosperity Channel. This isn't totally off base, especially if we tend to ruminate and stew in difficult emotions without compassion, but it's rooted in a false premise that we can eject our difficult emotions.

Difficult emotions we avoid or suppress don't go away. They get buried within us and can fester until they manifest in illness or other situations that match their frequency (and because of our avoidance and denial, we won't realize that's what's happening). It's far better to admit we're having a difficult emotion and process it healthfully than pretend otherwise because we don't want to lower our vibration. Also, trying to force ourselves to feel positively creates stress in our psyche and subtle body, which can cause problems in both areas.

In this system, the aim with difficult emotions isn't to banish them, but rather to mature, develop wisdom, and release karma by virtue of them. We do tend to increasingly feel better while practicing this system, but that's from living more healthfully, gaining coping skills, developing wisdom, and connecting spiritually, not forcing ourselves to feel good. Otherwise, it's better for spiritual aspirants to be open to feeling any emotion than attached to feeling good. Attachment to feeling good bars our vibration from rising to the higher frequencies, which are beyond the veil of our likes and dislikes. When we're unwilling to process difficult emotions, we get stuck at the level of ego.

Another phenomenon that's accompanied this campaign against healthy difficult emotions is the pathologizing of darkness. In nature, light and dark are balanced. There's day and night, light and shadow, etc. Consequently, darkness is part of the pathway to revelation, and integrating the shadow is necessary in any sincere spiritual journey. All seekers must spend time with the Holy Dark, which takes many forms.

The Holy Dark is the dark of the new moon. It's in the underworld journey, the sign of Scorpio, and the planet Pluto. It's in alchemical transformation, the occult, and witchcraft. An initiation by candlelight occurs in the Holy Dark. Drumming by a bonfire, the depths of a womb, and the wrinkled face of the Crone are all manifestations of it. It's in a leafless grove in the dead of winter. In balanced metaphysical systems, the Holy Dark is represented and revered. In Kabbalah, there's Binah, the dark mother and formative black ocean of Eternity, in complement to Chokmah, the light father and primal force of creation. There's also the abyss of consciousness, dark and unfathomable. In Hinduism, the fierce goddesses Kali and Durga complement goddesses like Lakshmi and Saraswati. Taoism features the interplay between yin and yang, with each containing a seed of the other, each vital. We all have these aspects within us. Without these opposites, there would be no emotional depth to life. Summer and spring lose considerable meaning without fall and winter, as would life without death. We can't know light without knowing dark, and we can't know dark without knowing light.

The Holy Dark is present in experiences like aging, loss, dying, and the dark night of the soul. It reminds us that our bodies are mortal, and that some things that break can't be fixed. The "hard truths" of life dwell in the Holy Dark. It's in the grief of a mother who buries her child, the hunter who kills to survive, and the anguish of a person diagnosed with a terminal illness. Times of reckoning, atonement, and regeneration are home to the Holy Dark. The hospice nurse, undertaker, and trauma-focused psychotherapist all labor within it.

As magical practitioners, many of us are born emissaries of the Holy Dark. This needn't mean we're lopsided toward darkness, but rather that part of our sacred duty is to integrate the shadow within ourselves and model this, overtly or otherwise. We may actually greatly fear the shadow, but our instinctive knowing that the dark deserves to be honored and explored is stronger than that fear. Our shadow work is a necessary element of a healthy society, but when we come from one that fears the shadow and integrating darkness, we get marginalized. The fault of this is with the society, not us. There's nothing unhealthy about a draw to the dark when it's the Holy Dark, and the Holy Dark isn't low vibration. Fear of darkness and aversion to it can lower our vibration, but that's from our interpretation of darkness, not darkness itself.

When we don't accept the dark as natural and holy, it gets shunned. What we shun, we can't integrate into our understanding of self and tend to suppress. Given how substantial the dark is in life, this is like flimsily damming a river, and we end up living in fractured, skewed ways. Because the dark lacks healthy expression yet remains within us, it can manifest pathologically in substance abuse, urges to dominate others, non-genetic mental illness, sexual violence, etc. I'm not suggesting that an unhealthy relationship to darkness and the emotional immaturity inherent in that are the only causes of these issues (and potential others were already shared), but I do think this is often a factor. On the other hand, what we accept as human, we can develop a mature, healthy relationship with.

Honoring the Holy Dark is fundamentally different from championing unhealthy emotional reactions that evidence immaturity or lacking empathy or effective coping skills. Possessiveness, greed, bloodlust, and emotions like them aren't the Holy Dark. It doesn't behoove inner alchemists to feed them, though we do explore them with a learning outlook. When we meet an emotion with compassion and it remains, it belongs where it is. The grief of heartbreak is legitimized by wisdom, as is the anger of a spouse who's betrayed by their partner and the anxiety of a person who's lost their home. The emotional reactions that compassion dismantles generally arise from conditioning, trauma, or immaturity. As we heal, mature, and gain wisdom, they'll become whispers of what they were if we even still have them. Self-hatred, for example, withers as our thinking sincerely shifts from, "I corrupt everything I touch" to "My childhood abuse resulted in toxic behavioral patterns, which I'm doing my best to work on."

Growing up in a society that's disconnected from spirit and nature and emotionally immature, as many of us do to varying degrees, is traumatizing, and it impedes our psychological development. We can see a parallel to this in animals that are raised in unhealthy conditions and exhibit psychological disturbances afterward that almost never occur in the wild. Like those animals, it's not our fault that we have these issues. That said, it is our responsibility to do something about them. Dealing with these issues can be a lengthy, difficult process, but every breakthrough within it gives us greater emotional fluency and peace of mind.

In this system, we learn to accept our emotions and apply compassionate thinking to our emotional reactions, which fosters a healthy and mature emotionality. This never involves blaming or judging ourselves for how we feel, as if we're opting not to flip an internal happiness switch or we shouldn't feel as we do because of how much work we've done on ourselves. We're human beings, and there's only so much we can do from where we are, which may include extremely difficult life circumstances. Our work is to do the best we can, allowing our emotions as we'll learn to do in this chapter.

On Suffering

"The wound is the place where the Light enters you."
—RUMI

To shed light on the Holy Dark's place in the human experience, it's important to explore the subject of suffering. Many spiritual masters teach that suffering is the most significant human experience because of how it can humble us and therefore catalyze spiritual awakening. The more comfortable our status quo is, the harder motivating ourselves to seek beyond it tends to be. When our status quo is shaken or uncomfortable, we can reach the open-mindedness that's often necessary for seeking answers in unconventional territory. For example, after hitting rock bottom and feeling powerless or helpless, taking risks and exploring novel perspectives almost becomes our path of least resistance. Many people experiencing addiction commit to recovery after hitting rock bottom, unable to fully do so beforehand. A suffocating depression humbled me enough to submit to my spiritual teacher in magic school. Barring that, I was too prideful, anti-authority, and in denial of my insecurities to admit I needed help or embrace what help was offered.

Suffering can also foster insights into ourselves that'd be difficult to discover otherwise and provoke us into action around them. For example, a debilitating two-year illness essentially forced me to clarify my priorities because I lacked the energy to sustain unhealthy circumstances. This helped me release some toxic relationship dynamics and prioritize self-care. Chronic illnesses and trauma from abuse have been my greatest antagonists, but also some of my profoundest teachers. I wouldn't wish them upon another, but I also wouldn't trade where I am internally today and I can't imagine getting here without having mined the ore of those experiences. I think the sense that I was fighting for my life is what led me to vigorously pursue my spiritual training, which I believe is the main reason I got the results I did (in terms of what I can control). Suffering can profoundly transform us once we learn to process it without spiritually bypassing. Our experiences of suffering can also help us empathize with others' suffering, inspiring us to aid them.

Opportunities to learn and develop from suffering are examples of the alchemical value of the Holy Dark. That said, suffering can also become something of a lifestyle, which isn't what the Holy Dark is about (e.g., "drama" isn't fundamental to the adult experience). That's a manifestation of factors like egoic ignorance, conditioning, trauma, and immaturity, and while starting there to varying degrees is normal, alchemical work is meant to take us elsewhere. Suffering is generally an extension of pain, and though pain is an inherent reality of life, our thoughts about pain and their ramifications can exacerbate it well beyond its inherent magnitude. We can even induce emotional pain with thought, which is often part of suffering, and ultimately within our power to control. In this system, we offer the secondary emotional reactions that make us suffer to the forge within, and what's inessential will burn away over time. We work to accept and understand pain, which is a sacred, necessary process, and allow it to be what it is. No more, no less.

ALLOWING OUR EMOTIONS

"We cannot change anything unless we accept it."
—CARL JUNG

Now that we have some understanding of how emotion operates, we can learn how to approach it alchemically. The overall process is straightforward: we allow emotions to move through us while thinking compassionately (*allow your emotions* is another tenet of the Little Work). The aim is be able to healthfully experience any emotion.

Emotional suppression is unnatural. Neither young children nor animals suppress their emotions, and they're healthier for it. Though we must learn to process emotions differently than children so we can navigate adversity without falling apart, the solution isn't suppression. How many adults medicate stifled emotions with food, TV, alcohol, or drugs? Or hurt others because they don't know how to have a difficult emotion without it hijacking their behavior? How many make decisions they deeply regret because of emotions they struggle to process? Additionally, emotional suppression has energetic consequences. Many medical intuitives believe stress, unprocessed difficult emotions, and psychological trauma are among the leading causes of illness. When we don't healthfully process difficult emotions, we tend to develop complexes related to them. They become obstructions to well-being in our psyche and subtle body.

Those of us who come to inner alchemy numb to feeling may believe that difficult emotions are scary or dangerous because when we have them, they tend to be overwhelming or volcanic. Most difficult emotions aren't extreme by nature though. Anything that's suppressed is likely to explode upon release, and meeting a difficult primary emotion with distorted or biased thoughts can rapidly escalate it beyond what it need be. Most difficult emotions cool when we consistently engage with them in a healthy manner, enabling them to flow through us. The main exceptions to this are situations involving trauma, deep conditioning, major loss, and mental illnesses.

Here's a formal process for allowing emotion:

First, go somewhere safe and private. Then wholly feel the emotion or emotions. No resistance, denial, avoidance, or judgement. Just feel. Fully accepting emotions makes them more bearable and enables us to process them. Any sense of "I shouldn't feel this" stifles an emotion's flow. However we feel is where we are with this situation, and that's OK. An emotion needn't become anything other than a feeling we had in a moment in time.

When thinking about whatever provoked the emotion or emotions, we aim to keep our thoughts compassionate (i.e., fact-oriented, accurate, and wise). This includes being candid about our involvement in the matter. It's one thing to feel scorned and another to conveniently ignore everything we did that contributed to a situation. While it's critical not to judge ourselves for having distorted or biased thoughts (and some will likely be automatic), we don't validate them either beyond "I can understand why I might think this." All of this takes practice, but it gets much easier (and quicker if compassionate thinking becomes a daily habit).

After we've felt and honored our emotions, we relax and pivot into mindfulness, observing what we feel and think for some time. Then we comfort ourselves with compassionate thoughts. Once we feel more settled, we explore what we felt with a learning outlook. This includes considering the deeper levels of our reaction. For instance, might we feel hostile less because the person's behavior was egregious and more because we feel deeply disrespected by them? With whatever we discover, we offer ourselves compassion.

If the situation in question requires a decision, we postpone making it until we can do so with a clear-minded integration of our feelings and wisdom. For years, I had a rule that I wouldn't act on intense emotions for twenty-four hours unless I had to, which served me well. When we feel rage, anxiety, or upset, making impulsive decisions that relieve some of this emotional pressure can be tempting, but these may be the worst decisions we make, as the tidal force of impulse overpowers our better judgement. This isn't the time to reply to a work email that we feel so insulted by that we could lose our job if we said what we feel. By waiting to respond, we give ourselves space to figure out how to act in our best interest, and our urges to act impulsively while feeling difficult emotions will fade.

The initial period of practicing allowing our emotions can be surprising and uncomfortable. This is where we plumb the depths of the overgrown garden within. Many of us learn things about ourselves we'd rather not as we unmask our psychological defenses. We may feel unsettled if we encounter emotions that contrast with what we think a "good person" is. It's important to remember that many of the more disturbing emotional reactions we experience were conditioned by common external influences, making these reactions normal to have. When we discover these reactions, we explore them with a learning outlook (e.g., by asking, "Why don't I just feel happy when someone I know succeeds?" "Where might these intense habits of judgement come from?"). This exposes the conditioning, bias, immaturity, psychological trauma, etc., in how we feel.

As we answer these questions, we compassionately challenge any beliefs we find that don't serve us. For example, "Part of why I'm jealous of others' success is because I was conditioned to believe my worth is based on accomplishments, which I don't believe anymore." While doing this, we treat ourselves with care and respect. We then close by meditating on our heart, feeling unconditional love for ourselves as best we can. The catharsis of allowing our emotions alongside meeting our thoughts with compassion helps us heal and transform, eventually shifting some of our future emotional reactions.

This process quickens considerably over time. When we generally understand our emotional patterns (which the major events timeline greatly aids with), we can speed through the introspective and compassionate thinking portions of this process. In my experience, we can reach a place where this entire process takes less than twenty seconds, with the emotion flowing out as quickly. This makes it possible to viscerally appreciate how distinct primary and secondary emotions are because we stop having as many secondary emotional reactions or they significantly transform. Without a thought like "She's evil!" when we're hurt, we don't end up in the emotional state that train of thought goes to. Particularly if instead, we think something like "What she said really hurt me, and I don't even value her opinion! Time to work on my self-worth."

When we consistently allow our emotions, fact-check our interpretations, and think compassionately, our emotional lives even out. We become less susceptible to extreme swells of emotion that depend upon parallel extreme thoughts to persist. A fire will die without oxygen, as will secondary emotional reactions we don't sustain or exacerbate with thoughts. Metaphysically, this results in a subtle body that's more stable. Magical and meditative processes that require anchoring attention to one end for long periods of time become more attainable goals.

I know this may sound surreal or unrealistic to some of you. As a former emotional disaster who'd get so possessed by anger and insecurity that I couldn't stop myself from talking, even at the expense of my self-interest, I assure you that this can work. My emotionally charged thoughts were so intense and relentless that I was an insomniac for the better part of seven years. Anxiety about something would storm within me for days, sometimes weeks or even months. Inner alchemy changed that. The blinding rage that would hijack my tongue has become a fleeting surge of energy the vast majority of the time, and when it's more than that, it's nothing like it was. The practices in this book enabled me to make these changes, and I firmly believe they can help others experience similar results.

As we deepen in inner alchemy, whatever emotions we harbor from psychological trauma will surface, and powerful healing from trauma can come from consistent spiritual practice. I once believed it was impossible to reach the degree of recovery that my life is now evidence of, which is part of what inspired this book. That said, if you feel apprehensive about this level of alchemical work, I encourage you to supplement it with psychotherapy.

Here's a summary of the process for allowing our emotions:

1. Go to a safe, private place.
2. Feel your emotions wholly.
3. Strive to keep your thoughts fact-oriented, accurate, and wise.
4. After openly feeling your emotions, relax.
5. Mindfully observe your thoughts and feelings.
6. Compassionately offer yourself comfort and support.
7. Introspect into the emotions at hand with a learning outlook and offer yourself compassion while doing that.
8. Tune in to your heart and connect with love.
9. Begin thinking about any actions to take related to this situation. If possible, postpone any major decisions for at least twenty-four hours.

At any time during this process, we can invoke elemental support—for instance, by drawing the invoking pentagram of fire for strength, the invoking pentagram of water for empathy, or the banishing pentagram of air to expel unruly, unsupportive thoughts.

Here's an example of this process in action:

We have a loud argument with our partner, who then drives away. At first, we're fuming. We feel unheard and resentful. We breathe and allow ourselves to feel like this. We think about how this spells doom for our relationship, and respond to those thoughts by thinking, "Having an argument doesn't mean a relationship is over. This stinks, but let's keep perspective. What I don't know is if I can stay with someone who drives off after an argument rather than working it out." We yell at our partner in our mind, criticizing them for being unreasonable, not being supportive enough, and driving off. Because these thoughts appear to be fact-oriented, we let them play out.

We take some breaths and relax, coming into the present moment. We observe ourselves. It's like there's fire in our bodies, and our thoughts are racing. We simply watch and breathe, reminding ourselves that it's OK to feel like this and normal to feel angry after a loud argument.

Then we look at the situation with a learning outlook. We think through the argument from more of an eagle-eye perspective. We notice that while our partner was being unreasonable, so were we. We expected them to know what we need to feel supported and to argue as we tend to, which may not be what they're comfortable with. We also recognize that underneath our anger, we're more hurt than anything else. Part of us didn't feel seen, as we haven't in the past, and we were so hoping we'd be in this relationship. Part of us is also scared this relationship is ending, like our other relationships have. Additionally, we recognize that the level of anger we displayed was extreme and could be perceived as hostile, which we resolve to apologize for. We start considering that maybe we were more antagonistic in this situation than our partner was.

Next, we visualize the parts of ourselves that feel scared, unseen, and insecure and imagine they're inside our heart, in the orb of golden light we meditate on each day. We offer ourselves comfort, love, and affirmation, recognizing that it's understandable that we reacted to this situation as we did. We think some about what we'd want to do differently in the future. Because of this situation's time constraints, we text our partner, "I'm sorry I was so harsh during our argument. I felt like you weren't hearing me. Can we please talk about this?" When we feel steady and complete with this process, we ground and center ourselves.

Additional Techniques for Dealing with Difficult Emotions

"He who wants a rose must respect the thorn."

—PERSIAN PROVERB

When dealing with difficult emotions, there are other techniques we can use to help comfort ourselves and process them. One involves modulating our self-care. Difficult situations and heavy emotional labor increases our need for self-care, and different self-care activities often fit particular emotional states better than others. For example, if we're in low spirits, we may feel best supported by taking a bath, whereas if we feel overwhelmed, watching a movie, calling a friend, or listening to a guided meditation might feel better than that. If we feel frustrated, a brisk walk might suit us or even doing chores.

For optimal self-care, we can harness this understanding by creating a scale of self-care, which is a list of self-care activities that match up with our emotions. With this list, we can trust that however we feel, there's a supportive action we can take on our behalf (and we already know what one is). The key to this exercise is recognizing that we can support ourselves in almost any emotional state, provided we don't strain from where we are emotionally.

To create a scale of self-care, identify at least three self-care actions you feel you'd be up for while experiencing the emotions listed below (feel free to add emotions to this list). To facilitate this, you can number the activities and then write the numbers next to each emotion the activities apply to, since activities usually fit more than one emotion.

+ Rage
+ Anger
+ Frustration
+ Disappointment
+ Depression
+ Sadness
+ Grief
+ Boredom
+ Fear
+ Worry

+ Anxiety

+ Stress—low level

+ Stress—mid level

+ Stress—high level

+ Giddiness

If we struggle with offering ourselves compassion while processing difficult emotions, another technique we can try is to imagine we're speaking with a loved one going through our identical situation. What would we say to comfort that person? Additionally, given the interrelationship between our levels of being, some people feel substantial improvement in their mood through tidying up their home and taking extra care of their physical appearance. It's like being put together on the outside can help us feel more put together inside.

Otherwise, we can always ask for guidance and help from the unseen—for example, by requesting aid while visualizing ourselves offering the difficult situation or emotion to a higher power. Higher powers are willing and able to help us if we let them, and even if this assistance is purely from our belief in it, when results come, they speak for themselves. Just ask the millions of people in recovery from addiction who swear that a higher power has enabled them to do what they otherwise couldn't for themselves.

ANGER, FEAR, GRIEF, GUILT, AND SHAME

"The cave you fear to enter holds the treasure you seek."
—JOSEPH CAMPBELL

In learning to allow our emotions, anger, fear, grief, guilt, and shame merit individual attention. Anger has a bad reputation in many healing circles, which is understandable given that it can cause extreme stress and throw our psyche and psychic emanation into disarray. By following angry impulses, we can hurt others and ourselves and sabotage things we worked on for a long time. If we write off anger as just destructive though, we miss out on its value, including what it can teach us.

Anger signals an unmet want or need. It alerts us that we had a desire, expectation, or hope that didn't pan out or was even actively challenged (sadness often does too). This might connect with something superficial (e.g., "I wanted to watch that movie tonight") or deep (e.g., "I want to be respected"). Anger highlights that something's important to us. Otherwise, we wouldn't feel so strongly about it being a certain way. As we examine our anger to figure out what desires fuel it, we can determine if we feel like it's appropriate and when it isn't, we can work to release it. For instance, if I'm angry that my lover doesn't want to spend all their time with me, I can recognize the immaturity in that and work to release it with compassionate thinking. Additionally, sometimes people feel generalized anger (e.g., being "angry at the world") as a result of experiencing or witnessing significant pain or injustice or from mental illness. The underlying desire with the former is often for love, respect, or justice, which they or others were denied.

Inner alchemy involves developing ourselves such that we aren't constantly buffeted about by day-to-day frustrations, especially to the point of becoming angry. When we find ourselves feeling highly frustrated over little things we can't change (e.g., "It's too hot in here," "I can't believe they messed up my order," "My cat threw up on my bed," etc.), that's an opportunity to cultivate our ability to tolerate frustration. With acceptance, allowing emotion, mindfulness, and compassionate thinking, most of these frustrations can pass in seconds. Conversely, if we let frustrations like these consistently seize us, it becomes hard to maintain a set psychic emanation. We're also too at the mercy of external conditions to meditate deeply. That said, if we notice ourselves experiencing more of these frustrations than usual, that can indicate that we're depleted or something isn't working in our lives. For the former issue, self-care is in order, and for the latter, we may need to consider making significant changes.

Otherwise, when we deem that anger about something is appropriate, it can spark constructive change. For example, we may feel so stuck in a situation that our discontent erupts in a blaze, calling us to bold transformation, like the mythical phoenix that burns up and is reborn. These surges of fire after periods of stagnation can be healthy, like a cry from our core sense of self, and we can channel this energy to make the shifts our heart yearns for.

Anger can also call us to advocate for ourselves and others. For example, we may find ourselves in situations where people behave disrespectfully or exploitatively, and anger gives us energy to do something about this. If we act on this anger without recognizing the unmet wants or needs in a situation though, we can lack the insight that would enable us to effect helpful change. After exploring our anger and identifying what to specifically advocate for, we're likelier to advocate effectively.

Though anger may feel destructive or violent, it needn't be expressed accordingly. Responding to most, if not all, angry reactions peacefully is possible with a dedicated practice of allowing emotion, mindfulness, and compassionate thinking. Resolving not to lash out while angry can also lead to more effective confrontation, as others are likelier to hear us if they don't feel attacked. If we're unsure of how to proceed in a situation we feel angry about, it can be helpful to consider the outcome we seek and then plan how to reach that outcome through ethical actions. In dialectical behavior therapy, which was designed for people with severe difficulties regulating emotion, this technique is called "doing what's effective."

By exploring anger, we can gain a host of insights regarding our wants and needs, what motivates us, and what others' behavior means to us. This information can then help us find healthy resolution with anger, release beliefs and behaviors that don't serve us, and act in alignment with our values.

Next, we come to fear. Fear is inherent for humans. It's a biological alert that we're facing something that could harm us or others. Anxiety, in most cases, is fear that emerges from worry about a future event, and having some anxiety is normal. For example, there's nothing concerning about feeling anxious before meeting new people or giving a presentation for a large audience. If we have an anxiety disorder, we may feel excessively anxious about situations like those (i.e., to where we can't do them), in circumstances that wouldn't usually provoke anxiety (e.g., "I'm terrified to buy groceries"), or for no apparent reason. Clinical anxiety is one of the most common mental health symptoms today. It frequently features an overestimation of a threat and an underestimation of our ability to cope with it (e.g., "I feel like I'll die if I attend that party"), and it often involves the fight, flight, or freeze response. In my experience, inner alchemy can profoundly mitigate clinical anxiety (and clinical depression). Because of the potential challenges in treating mental illness, however, I encourage anyone with clinical symptoms to seek professional help.

During inner alchemy, we learn to navigate fear and anxiety so we can step outside our comfort zone to pursue our intentions. Without doing this, the ego can use fear or anxiety to anchor us in our status quo when it doesn't want us to do something. We also explore our fears with a learning outlook because that aids us in knowing ourselves deeply, unmasking the ego, and gaining clarity about what drives some of our thoughts and behaviors.

There are many effective methods for dealing with fear and anxiety. First, we can allow them using the process we learned, as with other emotions. This necessarily includes comforting and reassuring ourselves (e.g., "It's normal to fear starting a new relationship," "Feeling like you can't do this doesn't mean you can't," "You've survived other scary things before"). With a learning outlook, we discover what we're specifically afraid of in a situation, and if that connects with something in our history, we address that too. Relaxation and mindfulness can also make a huge difference with fear and anxiety, and I recommend that anyone experiencing consistent anxiety practice both daily until they can readily enter those states. Additionally, fire meditation can help strengthen us to face fear and anxiety, as can daily navel meditation and affirmations like those I shared earlier. I've also known people who experienced significant anxiety relief from Hatha Yoga, acupuncture, and acupressure, including the Emotional Freedom Techniques (EFTs), which involve tapping on acupuncture points.

When navigating a situation that evokes anxiety, some people benefit from considering the worst-case scenario and strategizing how they'd handle it. This helps them realize that even though they don't want this scenario to happen, they could probably manage it, which reduces their anxiety about the situation. For example, let's say we have a dreaded upcoming conversation with our romantic partner. Worst-case scenario? We hear harsh things and break up, which could lead to some awful ramifications, but ones we can weather. I've frequently used this technique, and it's helped me considerably. As long as we believe this is a thought exercise, it won't tune our psychic emanation to manifest in alignment with it.

We can also expose ourselves to things we fear in safe, small doses, which is a technique that comes from exposure therapy. For instance, if I fear approaching strangers but must network in my career, I can challenge myself to attend social events and introduce myself to a set number of people. This may be scary at first, but as I face this fear and catastrophe doesn't strike, my fear will lessen (which is the premise of exposure therapy). Generally speaking, when we avoid things we fear, our anxiety about them strengthens. Conversely, when we face them and discover we can handle them, it weakens. We can also incrementally face our fears.

For example, if I fear singing publically, I can begin by singing with a chorus, then solo for friends, then singing at an open mic night, etc.

Fear and anxiety are inevitable in inner alchemy. They accompany challenging ourselves. By accustoming ourselves to facing fears in a safe manner whenever we notice them, which is a powerful will development exercise to try (and turn into a habit), we can keep fear from derailing our intentions.

Now we come to grief. Grief is deep sorrow that's caused by loss or the threat of loss. It's seen in the animal kingdom and may take years to process. Because it's inherent in the human experience and can be debilitating, addressing it explicitly in this book is important. As we live, we experience loss in a variety of domains: relationships end, people move, we leave jobs, our health deteriorates, and people we care about die. Loss and the unknown are what many of us fear most, and things ending and people dying places our mortality before us, which can be terrifying. Loss often evokes other experiences of loss, which makes sense given their mental associations, so much can surface during grief. Grief can also evoke intense feelings and extreme reactions we don't see in other areas of our emotional lives. As a grief counselor, I learned that the healthiest thing to do with grief in many cases is to not resist it. If extreme emotions come, we can allow them to the degree we feel capable based on our current ability to process difficult emotions healthfully. Not pressuring ourselves, judging ourselves, or pushing our grief into a particular shape is important. All of that can bar grief's healthy, natural expression. That said, pacing ourselves while grieving can be key to staying well.

There's often a tendency during grief to reflect upon what happened, and there are healthy and unhealthy ways to do that. As always, it remains important to anchor our thoughts in facts, accuracy, and wisdom. Otherwise, mulling over a loss to gain wisdom and discern how to act differently in the future is healthy, although not in a way that keeps us from honoring our feelings (e.g., by lunging into learning to avoid our pain, anger, etc.). That said, some people find that listing what did and didn't work in a situation like a relationship or job helps them process their emotions and identify what they won't tolerate or would do differently in the future. Thinking through the broad implications of a loss can be part of healthy grieving too, like acknowledging that a deceased loved one won't be around for future holidays and allowing ourselves to mourn that. Telling our story to others (or ourselves) to help move through our grief is healthy too, if we feel so inspired. On the other hand, unjustified thoughts like "I'll never find love of any kind again" or continuous thoughts of "if only" or "what if" that cause suffering aren't healthy (e.g., "If only I hadn't said that" or "What if I'd arrived sooner?"). Having these types of thoughts is understandable, and some of them may be automatic, but feeding them leads to unnecessary pain and prolongs grief.

Some people become "stuck" in grief, struggling for years with a loss, usually replaying "if only" stories about the situation in their mind. When I encountered this clinically, it was often because clients felt unable to accept the reality of the loss. Ruminating kept the deceased person or ended relationship present in some form, pushing the more untenable feelings of grief to the background.

Many cultures have distinctive rituals or customs for grieving that highlight different ways of expressing it. Reading about some of them may prove validating if you feel like you grieve in a manner that others around you don't, which is common, even within families. Some people emote extensively during grief while others focus more on administrative tasks. There's no one right way to grieve, and some losses are so painful that we may never fully accept them. That's OK. As with everything in inner alchemy, our task is to do our best and try to make peace with whatever that is. If you feel that grief impairs your ability to function, grief counseling or a support group might help.

Though there's no right way to grieve, there are "tasks of grief" that were proposed by psychologist William Worden, which have replaced the famous "stages of grief" in much of grief counseling. These tasks are: accepting the reality of the loss, working through the pain of the grief, adjusting to an environment without our loved one, and emotionally relocating them in our lives in a new way. An example of emotional relocation could be placing pictures of our loved one around our home. These tasks needn't occur separately or sequentially, and how we do them can be individual. They affirm that we honor our pain, what was and is, and continue living.

Sometimes grief lingers because of elements we can regain. There are certain things we never get to experience again, like a day in childhood with friends or our first exhilarating kiss. We can often recover aspects of these experiences though, and these aspects may be a substantial part of why these experiences linger with us. For example, it's not just that we miss our first relationship, but also its passion, which our current relationship lacks. Once we identify a feeling of lack like this, we can strive to address it in our lives today (e.g., by being more romantic in our relationship). This won't necessarily end our grief, but it will likely ease our feeling of lack when remembering those times.

Little can help us move beyond our limited ego's perspective than accepting the reality of loss. This is one of the greatest and most difficult gifts of the Holy Dark. As we honor our grief and persist with our spiritual practices, we increasingly connect with the unchanging divinity within us, which re-contextualizes our experience of grief.

Lastly, we come to shame and guilt. Shame is the feeling that something's fundamentally wrong with us. It frequently derives from harsh or critical treatment from others while growing up. Shame can also emerge from doing, thinking, or saying something we feel bad about to the point of generalizing this to mean we have a character defect. Almost all of my clients with depression have struggled significantly with shame.

In contrast, guilt is feeling badly about doing, saying, or thinking something that doesn't align with our conscience without taking this to mean we have a character defect. If I hurt someone's feelings and feel remorse, that's guilt. Guilt can also arise from not taking action that aligns with our values when it's called for. For example, if our country has a food surplus, we may feel guilty thinking about countries that are experiencing famine. If our country has systems that oppress people and we're in a privileged group, we may feel guilty about these systems' existence even though we didn't create them. This guilt is our conscience prompting us to consider doing something to address these situations, which brings up a critical point about guilt: it can inspire healthy, supportive action. Miring ourselves in guilt or conditioning ourselves to feel it inordinately is unhealthy, but appropriate guilt is important in life. Shame, on the other hand, isn't healthy.

Guilt and shame aren't always as distinct as these definitions suggest. When guilt lingers, it can transmute into shame because feeling bad about something we did, said, or thought for a long time is tough to not start taking personally. For example, if my mother frequently criticizes me for not making my bed, I may initially feel guilty. If I don't change my behavior and hers persists, this guilt can transform into shame as I begin feeling like I'm not making the bed because something's wrong with me. I may develop an abiding feeling that I can't do what I must to live properly, which generalizes into a core belief like "I'm unable to manage my life."

With guilt, it's beneficial to learn from it and modify our future behavior accordingly, where appropriate. With shame, we dismantle it with compassion. As our hearts open from spiritual practice, shame fades from our lives, even if it persists to a degree due to deep trauma or conditioning.

INNER ALCHEMY AND RELATIONSHIPS

"If the traveler cannot find a Master or friend to go with him, let him travel on alone, rather than with a fool for company."

—BUDDHA

There are libraries of books about healthy relationships if you're interested in exploring this topic in depth. Here, I focus on four primary areas that are relevant to inner alchemy: boundaries, toxicity, communication, and healing relationship issues from the past.

A boundary is a limit we establish regarding how we want to engage with someone or something. We can have boundaries with many subjects, from relationships to the amount of time we watch TV. Regarding relationships, we have a finite amount of emotional energy, and relationships can consume much of it and profoundly influence our psyche. Whether or not the popular quote that "you're the average of the five people you spend the most time with" is valid, we're highly influenced by the people around us. Deciding what role we want relationships to play in our lives, and how much time and energy to devote to them, is part of inner alchemy and a personal matter. Aspirants to the Great Work generally pare down their relationship involvement to conserve energy, spend more time in spiritual practice, and hold their psyche and psychic emanation in a particular state.

Regardless of what your intentions are, considering what boundaries support them is important. Boundaries can make the difference between achieving goals or not, and having healthy or unhealthy relationships. They can make the difference between a cocooned, deep practice and one that's scattered, as we explored in the section at the end of chapter four on keeping silence, which is a type of boundary. When we establish boundaries, we create psychic and psychological barriers that strengthen as we uphold them. What particular boundaries to form depends upon what we feel comfortable with and intend for ourselves, except that generally speaking, healthy relationships won't ask us to violate the amount of self-care we need to function healthfully. The major exceptions to this are when we're in a caretaking role or a loved one is in crisis.

When we set boundaries, adhering to them is critical. Not abiding by a boundary communicates to others that it's not firm. This is operant conditioning again. If I tell someone I don't want to communicate via text, but I respond whenever they text me, I've shown them I'm available by text. If I respond days later instead, my boundary will hold. Behavior may be the one universal language throughout the animal kingdom. Relatedly, if you don't want a pet to seek your attention while you're meditating, never acknowledge them during meditation. They'll get the point.

Toxic Relationships
"When people show you who they are, believe them."
—MAYA ANGELOU

Many people believe we forge a psychic connection with everyone we're in relationship with, enabling energy to pass between us. There's potential here for amplification, where we're stronger together, as well as exploitation. Many of us have experienced the former in love and the latter in dysfunctional relationships. Attention directs our energy, and some people may constantly seek and drain ours. While wanting attention from loved ones is normal, problems arise when the energy flow in relationships is consistently lopsided or otherwise dysfunctional. Relationships like these are called "toxic relationships," and it's unhealthy for us, psychologically and metaphysically, to remain in them as they are. There are many types of relationship toxicity, and little can subvert our well-being like a close toxic relationship, which is why toxic relationships must be addressed during inner alchemy. In a venue where we expect to find acceptance, we can find threats to our sense of self. Boundaries are one way of navigating toxic relationships, but sometimes we must end them to stay healthy.

We can usually tell a relationship is toxic (or becoming toxic) if it consistently leaves us with a sense that something's fundamentally off about it. The most common symptom is feeling like we must walk on eggshells around the other person. We may also frequently feel drained, patronized, used, or otherwise disrespected. We might enjoy certain aspects of a toxic relationship, but the toxicity will outweigh that. Though many relationships take work (and all romantic ones likely do), on a fundamental level, they should just work. If we find ourselves boldly modifying our behavior to try to make a relationship function, it's probably toxic (contortion isn't a healthy relationship habit). When dealing with a toxic relationship, it's critical to understand that the behavioral modifications we make in response to the toxicity do not reflect our typical way of being in relationships. For example, setting limits with someone who wants constant attention doesn't mean we're generally an unavailable friend.

Sometimes relationship toxicity is one-sided. For instance, we may have a friend who's consistently bossy, petty, passive-aggressive, condescending, cruel, insensitive, manipulative, disrespectful, self-involved, or constantly trying to one-up us. When navigating a relationship that's one-sidedly toxic, the most important consideration is our well-being and what we need to do to foster it, and we don't owe the other person an explanation for whatever that is. Someone who's been repeatedly harmed isn't responsible for the culprit of that harm's personal growth or peace of mind. That said, if we feel able, we can offer that person feedback, which may be of great benefit to them. Some people are genuinely unaware of their behavior's impact, particularly if they're from a culture that has different behavioral norms than ours. Otherwise, most people know what common courtesy is, and it's more that they lack self-awareness or the ability to regulate their behavior (or they're choosing not to). It's not our responsibility to facilitate a friend or lover becoming a respectful adult, and putting ourselves in that position creates an unhealthy, unbalanced relationship dynamic. Though therapy isn't accessible for everyone, this is one thing it's for.

To be clear, these issues aren't the types of difficulties that occur in most romantic relationships, which naturally surface people's insecurities and rough edges. This isn't about expecting others to have perfect interpersonal skills either. Social maturation occurs in relationship, and sometimes we skin our knees during it. People may also go through rough patches where what they're dealing with makes them hard to be around, like a friend being crabby while working sixty hours a week. None of that is toxicity. Toxic issues are like "He tries to control me," "She acts like I'm incompetent," or "He can't argue without intimidating me." If we have toxic behaviors, they'll become apparent through consistently reviewing our actions with a learning outlook.

A critical part of navigating toxic relationships is understanding that while relationships can be toxic, there's no such thing as a toxic person or energy vampire, as if these are inherent identities. Instead, there are people who behave toxically or syphon energy because of their dysfunction, which usually results from how they grew up. Maybe harsh language was normal in their family and people bossed each other around. Maybe they were neglected and so attention-starved that they'll latch onto whoever gives them some. Maybe their community taught them to try to be better than everyone else, including their friends. Maybe they were abused and their subsequent suffering manifests through toxic behaviors, or they're acting out an intergenerational cycle of violence. Compassion calls us to understand this, avoid demonizing the other person, and free ourselves from resentment toward them as best we can. That said, that's also where this calling ends. Empathizing with people we had or have toxic relationships with doesn't mean we must keep them in our lives or be their doormats or punching bags, and reinitiating a relationship that was once toxic is never a requirement of healing. Compassion helps us discern what we can handle in toxic relationships and protect ourselves accordingly.

Relationship toxicity can also develop when people grow apart but don't allow themselves to organically shift to a new relationship dynamic. Clinging to relationship dynamics that don't fit us can cause stress, bitterness, and resentment. As we clarify our values, we develop a strong sense of what behaviors contrast with them. Any relationship that features even one of these contrasting behaviors will become toxic for us, albeit to varying degrees (like how any action we take that opposes our values would). We may find ourselves in situations where what once worked for us doesn't anymore, which can happen during inner alchemy since we change deeply. For example, maybe we used to revel in gossiping, which now feels unhealthy and uninteresting to us. In situations like this, we must choose to either stop these problematic behaviors or persist with them while aware of their toxicity, which will harm us.

How to address relationship toxicity is a personal matter. The salient point for inner alchemy is if we don't address it, it can impair our well-being, magic, and alchemical process.

THE MAGIC OF MINDING OUR BUSINESS

"Were I to solve problems for others they would remain stagnant;
they would never grow. It would be a great injustice to them."

—PEACE PILGRIM

One toxic behavior we may fall into with the best of intentions is giving inappropriate unsolicited advice. As we start experiencing amazing results from inner alchemy, wanting to share it with others is natural, especially when we see them suffering in ways we no longer do (or do far less). It's also natural after experiencing our inherent divinity to want everyone to experience this too. There are several problems with this though. One we explored in the section on keeping silence is that people interpret from their level of perception and can't understand experiences they haven't had, so proselytizing about inner alchemy sets us up to be misunderstood. Another problem is that in most cases, telling other adults what to do is disrespectful. We each have a right to rule our lives. The primary circumstances in which it's appropriate to challenge this sovereignty that seem justified to me are if someone's in our care, incapacitated, or a threat to themselves or others. Otherwise, giving unsolicited advice can seem extraordinarily judgemental, regardless of our intentions. It can appear like we're implying that someone can't navigate life or solve certain problems on their own, which may feel condescending, invalidating, belittling, etc., especially if what they sought in sharing something with us was emotional support or validation. This may turn them off to inner alchemy, which could actually help them, and cause them to resent or otherwise dislike us.

A third problem, which is critical to understand for inner alchemy, is that we don't know other people's karma, which means we don't know what's best for them. The job we think they should quit? The relationship we think they should leave? We don't know the metaphysical significance of these circumstances in their life, and determining what's best for someone is hard enough on a purely psychological level. To actually know what's best for another, we need to know them deeply: their history, potential, family, culture, strengths, weaknesses, interests, etc. Even when we know someone well and feel like we have "everything" in common, we lack much of this information, and we're always far more different from others at the thought-dependent level than like them. What commonly happens is we project our experiences and notions onto others, seeing them through our filters without realizing it, which leads us to feel like we know them better than we do. I'm not suggesting we can't have many similarities with others and know them deeply, but the mind also unconsciously tries to reduce what it's exposed to into what it understands.

When it comes to what's best for someone else, we simply don't know. This doesn't mean we're clueless. People often have noticeable behavioral patterns and we needn't know them profoundly to recognize these. It may be self-evident that someone struggles with decision-making, for example, though this still doesn't mean we know what's best for them. The right partner for someone? The most satisfying career? We can only speculate about matters like these, and in most cases, speculating is already going too far unless the other person asked for our help. The relationship we think they should leave might be helping them evolve in ways we're unaware of. Just because leaving a situation that seems similar was good for us and helped us grow doesn't mean that's what they should do. If we incorporate the lens of astrology, we can appreciate that they may be working on developing in highly different ways in this lifetime than we are. The fruit of our experience may not be what their process is growing. Logic and reason being on our side doesn't make us right either, and neither does having seen them make many mistakes like this before. We simply don't know what's best for them, which is liberating because when we don't know what's best for others, we needn't assume the responsibility of guiding them accordingly. We can mind our own business.

None of this means we can't or shouldn't help others, and if the issue is more basic, like "Everyone deserves food," we're not imposing ourselves by advocating for a comfortable standard of living for all. That said, it does mean helping others with as little paternalism as possible. Additionally, if others seek our advice or expertise, we can certainly give it. No one is an expert in everything, and an outside perspective may also provide insights that are harder to have when someone's overwhelmed or too close to a situation. Passing on knowledge and wisdom is also a sacred part of life when it's done respectfully, and when someone goes through something similar to what we have, our experience may help them. But when we provide this aid, it's because they asked for it and with the understanding that our perspective isn't necessarily what they should do because we don't know what that is. At the very least, if we strongly feel like our advice could help someone, we can ask if they want it and release any attachment we have about offering it.

If we find ourselves frequently thinking about what others should do or giving unsolicited advice, it's worth investigating that impulse. It's rarely as simple as "I just want to help." For example, it can be a defense in that by fixating on other people's problems, we avoid our own. It can also reflect an unhealthy desire to control others or be needed or valued, codependency, a superiority complex, a savior complex, etc. It can simply be conditioning too. I come from a culture where unsolicited advice is normal even though, as far as I can tell, almost none of us like receiving it.

One of the greatest wastes of psychic energy is excessive involvement in other people's business. In terms of intentional action, if we can't come up with a good reason to be in someone's business (and mostly, the good ones are: they requested our help, we're justifiably worried about them, or we're being supportive), it's best to stay in our own. When we let go of other people's business, a massive amount of energy becomes available to us, which we can then use for other things. Our mind also becomes clearer, enabling us to focus on our intentions more and keep our psychic emanation more concentrated.

I can barely describe the tremendous psychological and metaphysical unburdening that occurred once I understood that I don't know what's best for others and started minding my own business. Consider for a moment how often you think about what others should do, even quick flashes of judging someone for doing something. Imagine how much freer you'd feel if this habit was gone, not to mention how much more open time you'd have and how much less stress you'd feel. You can be free like this. Just affirm, "I don't know what's best for others" whenever you catch yourself judging people and watch this habit wither away. To be clear, I'm not referring here to actions people take that could harm others. There's a difference between community and personal business. For example, if I see someone championing a bigoted belief that could lead to harm for others, that's not the time for "to each their own."

Otherwise, everyone has their own karmic journey. We develop at our own pace in our own way, and we can't learn other people's lessons for them. We can't upload our wisdom into them either, and they can only hear us from where they are. As we inevitably discover in inner alchemy, personal development is difficult. The ego constantly tries to anchor us in our status quo, and without pushing ourselves elsewhere, it'll succeed. Most sustainable transformations require an internal drive to change.

As we start minding our business, questioning our assumptions, and releasing our habits of judging others and considering what they should be doing, we become more present in our relationships. We become able to actually listen to people, rather than predominantly hear our interpretations clothed in their voices. We can see them far more for who they are than we could have before. Sensitive people will perceive that we aren't judging them. They'll feel that we aren't trying to force them into a mold or push an agenda onto them, which can greatly improve our relationships.

I-STATEMENTS

"In all sincere speech there is power."

—GEORGE HENRY LEWES

As we explored before, our word choices have powerful psychological and metaphysical implications, which holds for communication in relationships too. The primary aim with communication in this system is to communicate with intentionality and compassion. This isn't always easy when we're upset, and that's where specialized tools like I-statements can help. I-statements are statements composed of a fact-oriented recollection of an event and a description of how it impacted us. They use "I" as the subject instead of "you." For example, "When people treat me how you did, I feel angry." By design, I-statements help us offer others non-judgemental feedback, which can lessen the likelihood of them receiving it defensively. The above example, for instance, stands in stark contrast to a statement like, "You made me so angry by acting like a jerk."

I-statements are a way of reclaiming our agency over our emotions. In the second statement above, we're the object of the statement and at the mercy of the other person accordingly. In the first, we're the subject, which shifts the locus of power. Though we feel angry when people treat us as that person did, we could take this reaction to the forge within and work on it if we want to. If not, we've alerted the other as to how not to engage with us in the future if they want to avoid angering us.

Another example of I-statements is saying, "When people are late and don't call, I feel disrespected," instead of "Do you know how rude and disrespectful you are for not calling?" The latter might provoke defensiveness or guilt in the other that overshadows our point, while the former factually describes their behavior and expresses our reaction without judging them.

There's little to argue with in an I-statement. Our feeling was whatever it was, even if we were being unreasonable, and the facts of the situation are objective, whereas "You acted like a jerk" is an opinion. For inner alchemy, it's beneficial to use I-statements not only in communication, but also in our thinking when we experience antagonism. This helps us root in our personal power and recognize where we do and don't have agency in antagonistic situations.

Exercise

Describe three of your recent emotional experiences with another person using I-statements.

MAKING PEACE WITH THE PAST

"To err is human, to forgive, divine."
—ALEXANDER POPE

One of the most difficult parts of inner alchemy can be making peace with past experiences that haunt us years later. As we develop in our ability to allow emotion and be compassionate, we're less likely to end up in new situations like these, but we may still have nagging thoughts about ones from the past. In terms of the alchemical process, making peace with the past helps us weed our mind, clear our psychic emanation, develop wisdom, and release karma. We aim to open our present as wide as possible through removing any obstructions from the past.

There are many ways to address something we feel unresolved about. We can always try our standard practices of allowing emotion, a learning outlook, and compassionate thinking. When the subject is a relationship issue, the most direct approach is to contact the other person and respectfully discuss what happened. If this is impractical, could harm us or them for readily foreseeable reasons, or is otherwise unadvisable, there are other options too. One is to process our emotions through writing out everything we want to communicate to them (we can also imagine ourselves saying it to them). We can then ritualistically burn this document or keep it to reread if these feelings return (or both if we photograph it). Expressing our perspective may help us feel like we got these issues off our chest even if the other person never hears it. After doing that, we can compassionately address any insights we gained during this process. Maybe we feel like we failed in the relationship or didn't have the courage to show up as we'd prefer. Maybe we're furious because we feel like we should've stood up for ourselves more. Admitting this can be powerful and cathartic, and this knowledge can help us behave differently in the future.

When we struggle to find closure because of unanswered questions from the past that haunt us, we can explore them with a learning outlook: What do these questions signify to us? What answers might we hope to receive? When we understand why these questions are important to us, we can pursue our own satisfying answers, which can include imagining the worst ones we could hear. "I didn't love you." OK. "I thought you were a terrible person." OK. "I never wanted to be a parent." OK. When we own the facts of our lives, connect with our cores, and look at ourselves candidly, as we must during inner alchemy, there stop being bombs others can drop that threaten our sense of integrity or self. This doesn't mean we don't regret things we've done, but it does mean that in most cases, compassion can help us forgive ourselves and others and move on. Otherwise, we can also ask a higher power for help in finding closure and wait for guidance to come.

Another way to facilitate finding closure is to challenge our general beliefs about closure. For example, many people believe a closure conversation is required for moving on from a relationship and give their emotional power away accordingly. The belief that we must be heard and understood, as well as hear and understand, to make peace with a relationship ending is untrue. This may be a deep human want, not to mention a respectful component of a healthy relationship's end, but that doesn't make this a need. Also, though these conversations can be profoundly healing when they go well, I've worked with people who had the closure conversations they sought without getting the resolution they craved. If we're too caught in our story to hear someone else's truth, what they say isn't going to bring us closure, and if we're unwilling to move on at a deeper level, talking to them likely won't change that. There's also value in accepting that not all questions can be answered in life. By learning from what lingers with us and sitting with the discomfort of unanswered questions, we can still gain wisdom and find a deeper peace.

Sometimes longing for closure is a way of denying grief through not accepting the loss (e.g., "I can't move on until I know this," "I must say this to her," etc.). When this is the case, working the tasks of grief intentionally can prove helpful—for example, by writing out what the relationship meant to us and why we're pained to let it go. Exploring this pain is healthier than anchoring the relationship in our consciousness over a faulty premise that getting one or two answers from the other person will suddenly ferry us on.

A nagging desire for closure may also come from some notion of "I want to know more about what I did so I can improve my behavior." We can specifically request this information, and if the relationship break was messy, we can also let the other person know this is all we're after so we don't open a wound without containment (e.g., "I'm sorry to bother you. I just want to know what I did. I won't even reply if you don't want me to"). That said, relationship problems aren't rocket science. We can examine our behavior too. Were we selfish? Manipulative? Aloof? Condescending? Argumentative? And if the person says that actually, they were going through something that shifted how they felt about the relationship, are we prepared to believe them? Sometimes people grow apart (and when one person undertakes inner alchemy, that can happen more one-sidedly than usual).

If a situation lingers with us because we hurt others, we can also try to make amends. Maybe we behaved toxically and having grown during inner alchemy, we see that now and want to apologize. Though some may recoil upon hearing from us, most will not be hurt further by a no strings "I'm sorry" message. Then we can move forward knowing we acknowledged our wrongdoing and tried to make up for it.

Another way to facilitate releasing past experiences and relationships is to sever our psychic ties to them. For example, by centering and visualizing a cord of energy connecting us to the other person that we then cut, absorbing our part of it into ourselves and sealing the space in our aura that it occupied with golden light. We can also imagine our memories of this person (or other past experiences) and ground the energy out of them through visualizing grounding cords connecting the memories to the earth. We can imagine these memories burning up or being absorbed in the earth too, or we can write about the situation on a piece of paper (or otherwise represent it) and then burn the paper. This may help us vent emotions about the situation. If we feel like someone has some of our energy, we can imagine this energy returning to us and being absorbed into our aura, with anything we perceive as theirs being grounded out. These symbolic acts send a powerful message of release to our subconscious mind, and in all of them, we can involve assistance from higher beings if that resonates with us (e.g., by imagining that burning the paper offers the matter to the divine, by working with guides on the healing work, etc.).

One way to keep from ending up in positions like this again is to take care to act as healthfully as possible in our relationships, to apologize when we hurt others, and to make peace with what happens as best we can. Admitting when we were wrong about something and apologizing for it, where appropriate, is highly important for inner alchemy. Doing this helps us release karma, and doing otherwise reinforces ego.

Beyond the techniques we covered earlier, making peace with what happens often involves what's colloquially known as avoiding "crying over spilled milk." Many situations don't come with do-overs, and while learning from our experiences and grieving is important, there is a point when it's unhealthy and unproductive to keep fixating on something, especially if we aren't thinking compassionately. For example, what likely results from wishing we'd acted differently ten years ago for the hundredth time? As we develop control over our mind, we become able to choose which trains of thought we board. If we don't like where one's headed (e.g., to the bottom of an ocean of spilled milk we've visited before), we can opt not to take it, which isn't denial or avoidance. It's an intentional action that comes from a desire not to suffer needlessly and squander time and energy.

Exercise

If you're struggling with any relationships or experiences from the past, pick one this week and apply a technique listed above to it.

Effectively Utilizing Intuition

"One should always beware of 'remembering'
that one was Cleopatra or Shakespeare."
—ALEISTER CROWLEY

The last tenet of the Little Work is to *follow the guiding light within*. We have access to profound intuitive guidance, which we can trust in once we develop discernment. Unfortunately, most of us come to inner alchemy unaware of how the ego can sabotage us and with this guidance tangled in a mixture of unhealthy conditioning and psychological trauma. Clearing the window of our mind enough to receive guidance from within without misinterpreting it can be an involved process. That said, there are many things we can do to expedite it.

One is to start distinguishing intuition from instinct and impulse, as well as other factors that influence feelings, like the weather, astrology, anxiety, etc., as we explored earlier. We can also examine our feelings with discernment rather than assume they're flawless guidance. Once we've learned to expose the ego, we can clearly see how it affects our feelings.

Additionally, it's critical to differentiate between the information we receive from our intuition and our interpretation of it, which is another area where the ego gets involved. For example, we may rightly intuit that our partner's upset, but assuming that means they're holding a grudge from a fight we had weeks ago? That's dubious. When we feel emotionally attached to a situation or outcome, receiving information about it clearly can be tough. Striving not to read more into something than is justified by the facts can help with this, as can staying mindful of what the information actually was versus how it shifted once our mind started processing it.

A pitfall with interpreting psychic information is that there's a high potential for melodrama. As we explored earlier, something can feel true for many reasons other than that it is, and an intuitive feeling of truth doesn't mean our interpretation of something is accurate. For instance, we might experience déjà vu upon seeing a piece of Celtic artwork, which could mean we were a Druid in a past life. We may quickly lunge from this impression though to an interpretation like, "I was Merlin!" On the heels of our intuitive surge, this may feel true, but that doesn't mean it is. We must be equally wary of situations like "I feel crappy. It must be a psychic attack!" when the junk food we recently ate or the disturbing memories we sifted through last night are likelier culprits. It's easy when developing psychic abilities to see and hear what we want to (or don't want to!).

In Hermeticism, it's said that the astral realm seeks to deceive. We look across a dark room and feel panic upon seeing a snake, only to turn the lights on and reveal a belt. We visualize an animal before us and it feels real, particularly as we develop our imagination through consistent ritual practice. Is it? In a way. When working with astral senses, we're called to a higher level of discernment than we apply in day-to-day thinking. Visions can come to us purely out of egoic fear or desire. In general, it behooves us to be tentative with interpretation and ask for concrete signs favoring certain interpretations if we feel unclear. The ego is too wily, and higher powers are as capable of giving us clear signs as sending intuitive messages.

When we have a question about how to proceed in life, we can turn to the guidance from within by simply asking our question and waiting for an answer to come. My experience is that this is highly effective once we develop discernment, particularly as we deepen in our spiritual practices. Also, by the Law of Correspondence, there are signs around us related to our lives that we can learn to interpret. One way of proactively working with this is through divination systems like tarot and runes. These systems also help us simultaneously develop our intuition and discernment with it. My experience is that the best way to learn a divination system is constant practice, including divining for others, though I recommend keeping questions from others light until we feel confident in our skills. We tend to have an easier time being objective with others, where we're less apt to be attached to certain interpretations. This helps with learning how to receive information with minimal distortion, as well as recognizing what psychic information feels like.

One of my first jobs was as a phone psychic. I performed between ten and twenty tarot readings a day in that job and discovered that psychic abilities are like muscles we can strengthen and develop in particular ways. By consistently seeking certain types of information, I started receiving it, like tuning myself to a radio signal, and this connection became stronger and clearer with practice. I grew up having psychic experiences, but by the time I left that job, I was amazed at what was coming to me. Importantly, I also learned later that these "psychic muscles" can atrophy if we don't continue using them, though we can strengthen them again.

A helpful aspect of developing intuition via divination systems is that while these systems are open to interpretation (and effective interpretation is part of being a proficient diviner), their elements also have designated meanings, even if there is some flexibility within these meanings. The Death card from tarot, for example, doesn't mean "Resist change at all costs." Meanings can be like divination training wheels that enable us to gradually shift from reasoned interpretations to intuiting more. My experience with interpreting and receiving psychic information is that it's best not to force it. Forcing can lead to bias and distortion. Instead, we can become as still as possible, enter the semi-trance state we utilize during ritual, and allow impressions and insights to come, which usually takes practice and gets far easier over time.

The elements that appear during divination can also help us see our biases, as we emotionally react to elements or favor interpretations. Tarot is well-suited for this because many cards feature images that can have uncomfortable meanings. Relatedly, a side benefit of regularly reading tarot for ourselves is that this can help us sit with fear in small doses, since a reading could imply something that scares us. To that end, tarot's holistic presentation of the human experience, from elation to despair, is like a built-in deterrent to spiritual bypassing. Alternatively, utilizing pure intuition without discernment can become a self-indulgent, ego-affirming free-for-all (e.g., "The sun angels told me I'll never feel grief again").

Divination is also a means of gaining insight into our karmic and alchemical process, as well as any resistance we have to developing ourselves, since we can do readings specifically about these things. It can alert us to factors we don't perceive with our rational mind regarding these and other issues. We can use divination for insight and guidance regarding issues from the past that we struggle with too. Divination also encourages us to stay in a reflective learning mode, and to view life archetypally.

The bottom line here is to cultivate discernment and detachment from results to minimize biased interpretation of psychic information. As we become adept at spotting conditioning, trauma, and our ego, we'll be more able to effectively receive intuitive guidance. The point isn't to second-guess ourselves forever, but to polish the windows of our mind enough to see through them clearly.

Exercise

Select a system of divination and begin practicing it. Before divining, I recommend casting a banishing earth pentagram over any physical implements being used to clear the ego from the process as much as possible, followed by connecting with spirit. Try to do a reading for yourself at least weekly.

When reading for ourselves, speaking our interpretation aloud as if we were reading for another person can be beneficial. This forces us to explain our interpretation, which we might skimp on otherwise (e.g., "The last card looks affirmative, so the universe votes 'yes!'"). This can also help us cultivate detachment and new insights may dawn on us while we're talking through our interpretations.

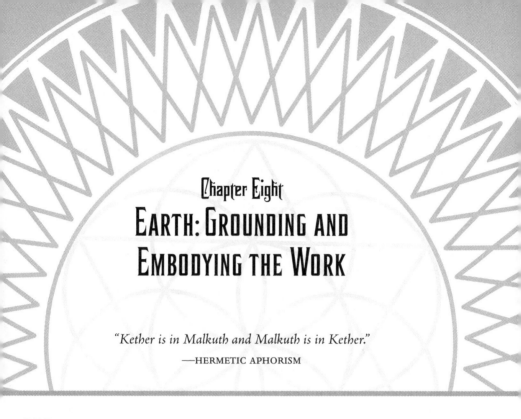

Chapter Eight
Earth: Grounding and Embodying the Work

"Kether is in Malkuth and Malkuth is in Kether."
—HERMETIC APHORISM

With emotional fluency, a discerning mind, and a developed will, we can actualize bold intentions on the earth, provided we equilibrate the earth element. When we lack equilibration with earth, we struggle with the physical plane.

The magical tool of earth is the pentacle, a flat disc that contains a pentagram and signifies everything a pentagram does (in the Golden Dawn, a hexagram was used). To earn the pentacle, we cultivate ourselves in key ways, taking what we've learned thus far and applying it. One way is becoming as physically healthy as we can in a manner that itself is healthy. This involves developing awareness of and comfort within our bodies, eating healthy food, and exercising. The aim of these efforts is to feel physically well. This has nothing to do with meeting conventional beauty standards. Alongside this, we strive to see and experience our bodies as divine.

Another task for earning the pentacle is developing finesse on the physical plane. This involves learning to manage money and handle our responsibilities in areas like work and home with an increasingly reduced amount of energy, while also harnessing our experiences in these areas for inner alchemy. Regarding money and work, our aim with them in this system is to reach a place where they facilitate our alchemical process, and what this means can vary between people.

Fundamentally though, a wealthy CEO who's frequently stressed about money and work hasn't met this objective. Meanwhile, someone who lives comfortably with a modest job and income has, as has someone who feels invigorated by a sometimes stressful job, provided they can drop external concerns when it's time to meditate. Once we achieve physical plane fluency, our mindset and energy stops being at the mercy of external factors like these.

An additional aspect of earning the pentacle is aligning our physical space with our intentions as best we can. Sacred space stops being an isolated part of our home and grows until the entire place becomes a sanctuary. This needn't mean we decorate our home like an altar, but rather that we bring the intention of sanctity to it, which includes how we care for it. The general aim is to enter our home and feel like we're in an oasis. Consensus realities can be whatever they are, but when we come home, we're in a reality that reflects our intentions. If we feel uncomfortable within our living space, we're not there yet.

In essence, equilibrating earth enables us to lead the metaphysical lives we feel called to while functioning highly on the physical plane. We increasingly perceive the divine everywhere, and the self-control and stability we gain from inner alchemy enables us to feel that ocean of ecstasy while thriving in the world.

Many people have extraordinary spiritual experiences or epiphanies without practicing inner alchemy. The difference is without work like this (and it needn't be this system) holding on to those experiences and integrating them into our day-to-day lives is difficult. Equilibrating the elements makes that stop being an issue for us. This is like the difference between glimpsing the bottom of a ravine while bungee jumping versus hiking into it.

Body Awareness and Sanctity

"The world is holy. Nature is holy. The body is holy. Sexuality is holy.
The imagination is holy. Divinity is immanent in nature;
it is within you as well as without."
—MARGOT ADLER

On average, people today are more disconnected from their bodies than ever in human history. Constantly using computers, smartphones, etc., coaxes us out of our bodies and into our heads. Americans watch an average of approximately thirty-six hours of television a week,[9] and while younger generations may watch less TV, many of them are glued to their phones. This throws off our alignment of being such that many of us are consistently uncentered, numb to our bodies, and overactive in the air element.

Centering in our bodies and maintaining an awareness of our bodily sensations is essential for inner alchemy. Like any level of our being, if our body is misaligned with our intentions, it can work against their manifestation. Avoidable health issues like postural misalignment and repetitive stress injuries can cause discomfort, pain, stress, and a lower mood, which affects our subtle body accordingly and makes meditation more difficult. Hatha Yoga teaches that our energy flows differently when we have a healthy posture, resulting in us feeling more alert, vital, and present. An erect spine is said to aid in clearing and quieting the mind, while slouching can induce sluggishness. Consequently, one dimension of body awareness is striving for a healthy posture.

Another aspect of body awareness is listening to our bodies' ongoing communication with us. We all experience this communication in feeling tired when we need to sleep. As we attune to our bodies, we receive subtler signals than this that we can act on. For example, we may notice we're becoming ill days sooner than we would've before, which facilitates us taking preventative measures.

Many of us also store suppressed emotion in our bodies, which often manifests in physical problems (e.g., tightness in our shoulders, clenching in our abdomen, etc.). Activities like self-massage and Hatha Yoga can help us address these emotional issues from the physical level. There are even Yoga poses that specifically help relieve anxiety, promote confidence, and open the heart.

In addition to body awareness, it's beneficial for our well-being and inner alchemy to cultivate the attitude that our bodies are divine. Many of us were taught to see our bodies as unspiritual, stifle our sexuality, ignore bodily signals to rest, and believe our bodies are ugly or unworthy of love when they don't fit a beauty standard. How good will our relationships with our bodies be if we hate them, criticize them, or treat them poorly? And how much better if we see them as holy? Many of us experience tension in our body or detachment from it related to

---

9. Koblin, John. "How Much Do We Love TV? Let Us Count the Ways." *The New York Times*, June, 2016. https://www.nytimes.com/2016/07/01/business/media/nielsen-survey -media-viewing.html.

issues like these, as well as if we have trauma that inclined us toward self-hatred or feeling unsafe in our bodies.

In this system, we strive to perceive the divine in all things, including our bodies. We learn to treat it as a temple and seek the divine within it as best we can, whether we're performing ritual, meditating, eating, having sex, etc. Regarding sex, sexual energy is one of the most powerful forms of energy available to us. Sex can literally create new life, and sexual energy can greatly amplify our magical and meditative practices. As we learn to direct subtle energy and get a feel for ritual, we can integrate sex with our alchemical process, whether alone or with others. We return here to the diverging trajectories of the Devil and the Magician and High Priestess. Sex can be used to reinforce our ego, and it can also open us to higher consciousness and foster inner alchemy. There are many books on sacred sexuality and sex magic, which I encourage you to research more if you're interested.

Otherwise, staying present with our bodies during ritual, meditation, and relaxation exercises, alongside cultivating the belief that our bodies are divine, usually builds sufficient body awareness and sanctity for inner alchemy. We aim to be able to hold our awareness in our bodies and comfortably feel throughout them, eventually perceiving the divine there. This may take extra time and effort for those of us who feel uncomfortable in our bodies due to factors like chronic illness, chronic pain, abuse, and body negativity. In these cases, "My body is divine" can be a fruitful affirmation to use (or aspire to if it feels insincere), alongside consistent mindfulness practice. As with other alchemical processes, we do the best we can in this area while working to accept whatever that is.

Exercise

While bathing this week, pay attention to your bodily sensations. Wash yourself in a loving manner. Try to sense the divinity within yourself as you do this. If possible, make this a daily practice.

EXERCISE

"It is through alignment of the body
that I discovered the alignment of my mind, self, and intelligence."
—B. K. S. IYENGAR

Becoming physically healthy as best we can is fundamental to equilibrating earth in terms of embodiment and finesse on the physical plane. This includes regularly exercising, and exercise has long been associated with a myriad of health benefits (e.g., sleep improvement, reduced blood pressure, and cardiovascular health). Contemporary research demonstrates that in many cases, exercise can work as well as antidepressants for mild to moderate depression.[10] For those of us with chronic health conditions, the objective with exercise in this system is to do our best without pressuring ourselves to do more.

Many people find that starting small with exercise helps them launch a sustainable routine. It's better to pick an easier routine we can maintain and build from than a harder one we abandon after a short time. To create an exercise regimen, we can begin by brainstorming exercise ideas that feel possible at our fitness level (e.g., jogging, aerobics, dance, kickboxing, Hatha Yoga, strength training, or walking). There are many free workout videos available online if we're unsure of where to start, across a variety of fitness levels. After we establish a habit of exercising, we can raise our workout difficulty. A healthy goal is at least thirty minutes of aerobic activity five days a week, with some form of strength training for each major muscle group two days per week.[11]

Hatha Yoga is a potent form of exercise that can combine strength training and aerobic fitness. It has specific metaphysical benefits too: the poses were designed to bring the body and mind into an aligned state that facilitates meditation. Hatha Yoga also helps us connect with our bodies and learn to relax and breathe healthfully. Many people experience mood improvements from regular Hatha Yoga practice. As I mentioned earlier, intensive daily Hatha Yoga practice cured my seven-year stretch of insomnia. There's a full spectrum of difficulty within Hatha Yoga, ranging from gentle to vigorous cardiovascular practice, and there are many free Hatha Yoga videos online we can try. That said, correct posture is important in Hatha Yoga, so if you can attend a class, that's a better way to start.

---

10. "Exercise is an all-natural treatment to fight depression." *Harvard Health Letter*. April, 2018. https://www.health.harvard.edu/mind-and-mood/exercise-is-an-all-natural-treatment-to -fight-depression.

11. Labskowski, Edward R. "How much should the average adult exercise every day?" Mayoclinic. org. August, 2016. https://www.mayoclinic.org/healthy-lifestyle/fitness/expert-answers /exercise/faq-20057916.

In addition to set periods of exercise, taking breaks during the day to connect with our bodies and stretch or move around after we've been sitting is important. Sitting for many hours a day without breaks increases our risk of metabolic problems, even when we exercise regularly.[12]

DIET

"When one's food is pure, one's being becomes pure."
—CHANDOGYA UPANISHAD

Note: although I'm a certified holistic health practitioner, I'm not a doctor or nutritionist. The following information isn't offered as medical or nutritional advice.

Food has a profound effect on our physical health and how we feel, which becomes increasingly apparent as we attune to our bodies. Many doctors believe healthy eating is the most important thing we can do for our health. In terms of inner alchemy, certain foods increase our well-being, thus facilitating our overall alignment, while others result in mental and physical stress and misalignment. In Ayurveda, there are three types of foods: foods that increase sluggishness, foods that agitate or excite, and foods that spiritually uplift and promote balance and well-being. What these are partly depends on our individual constitution, which an Ayurvedic doctor can determine. Additionally, fresh foods are believed to have more vital energy than foods that aren't fresh. Yogis following an Ayurvedic diet predominantly eat foods that balance them. This helps keep their minds and bodies in states that support deep meditation. In this system, dietary considerations depend upon our intentions. As long as we're physically healthy, we can eat more diversely than a Yogi and practice effective inner alchemy, in alignment with the tenet of seeking moderation, even with moderation. That said, if we decide to undertake a metaphysical retreat, following a diet conducive to that is important.

Another way of conceptualizing food is that foods harm, heal, or are somewhat neutral, which can depend some upon our individual reaction to them. Harmful foods tax our bodies' systems and can be outright toxic. They work against our bodies' inclination toward well-being and evoke stress. White sugar is an example of this. Conversely, healthy foods aid our bodies' systems and pro-

---

12. Labskowski, Edward R. "How much should the average adult exercise every day?" Mayoclinic. org. August, 2016. https://www.mayoclinic.org/healthy-lifestyle/fitness/expert-answers /exercise/faq-20057916.

mote well-being. For example, leafy green vegetables are loaded with nutrients that facilitate organ and brain function (although not everyone digests them well). Neutral foods tend not to have a prominent effect on our health. Iceberg lettuce is an example of this. It has little nutritional value, yet it's also a vegetable that most people easily digest.

One of this book's themes is that our society can condition us into unhealthy habits. Few contemporary societies have failed us more than in the area of diet, where before the recent healthier food boom, food quality had plummeted to scary, unchallenged lows in many parts of the world. Food-related health conditions, like pediatric type 2 diabetes, continue to plague people in unprecedented ways. Growing up with unhealthy food has warped many of our taste preferences in favor of excessive salt, sugar, or dairy. When we try to eat healthier, more natural foods may taste bland to us, which can make healthy dietary changes harder to sustain (though these taste preferences will shift over time). Food is also a primary comfort for many of us, which is often a deep habit begun in infancy, and our preferred comfort foods may be unhealthy. Consequently, stopping eating unhealthy foods can be difficult. This is particularly true if food is one of our main sources of pleasure and we don't have other well-developed ways of coping with difficult emotions. Our aim here isn't to eliminate comfort or pleasure eating, but to move toward healthier foods and portion sizes.

Establishing the habit of eating healthy food can be a long journey. In addition to our food habits from growing up to reckon with, many of us are surrounded by influences encouraging us to eat junk food. That said, every bit of healthy eating makes a difference, and this can be an area where we focus on progress over perfection. We can begin small too, with will development exercises like: eat a piece of fruit daily, a serving of vegetables, etc. Many people find more success in developing healthy eating habits by gradually adding healthy foods into their diet rather than cutting unhealthy ones out immediately. The latter can lead to strong feelings of deprivation that recoil us to our dietary ground zero. That said, this is one domain of inner alchemy where many of us must push ourselves to do something because we know it's healthy for us even though we don't want to, albeit gently. As we develop body awareness, our bodies will signal what foods do and don't work for us. While striving to heed this inner guidance, it's critical to be compassionate with ourselves about where we are with our eating habits.

External factors have made the journey to eating healthfully an uphill climb for many of us, and that's no fault of ours.

Beyond what we eat, it's also important to consider how. Many of us eat too quickly, which stresses our bodies and encourages overeating. Practicing becoming present while eating helps us stay aligned and supportive of inner alchemy as we engage with food. We can encourage being present by praying before eating, savoring our food's taste, not engaging in other activities while eating, and breathing intentionally or putting our fork down between bites. The alchemical aim with eating is for it to become a conscious, healthy, and intentional experience.

Exercises

1. Research healthy eating systems and think about what healthy eating approaches could work for you.

2. If you eat quickly, try to eat at half your normal speed. How is eating different when you do this?

ENERGY MANAGEMENT

"All we have to decide is what to do with the time that is given us."

—J. R. R. TOLKIEN

Most forms of energy are finite, and part of intentional action is recognizing this and managing our energy intentionally. In this section, we explore tools that can help us use less of our time and energy while still achieving high quality outcomes. The less time and energy we expend in day-to-day tasks, the more we have for other things. With the additional energy generated by ritual and meditation, we can reach a place where we expend little energy managing our day-to-day responsibilities relative to what we have.

How we choose to use these tools and our increased capacity is an individual matter. Some people may want to launch businesses and aggressively schedule their time. Others may prefer that their lives feature art, relationships, and many days with few to-do items. The Little Work approach isn't about assuming a particular form. It's about becoming able to use our time and energy intentionally, to feel like they aren't slipping away from us or overspent in day-to-day tasks. When people get a handle on these tools, they can complete tasks with greater ease, which often results in significant stress reduction.

One of these tools involves declaring how we intend to harness our energy by writing out our intentions for each day, which is conventionally called a "to-do list." A to-do list is a list of tasks we intend to perform. To-do lists have many benefits. As with will development exercises, one of the best ways to cultivate the habit of acting with intent is setting intentions and acting on them, which we do with to-do lists. Though writing to-do lists isn't a formal ritual practice (although we can make it one), it's a way of directing energy, aligning our being around intentions, and manifesting in the world with intent. To-do lists give us experience feeling what aligned, directed energy is like, which builds our ability to align and direct energy.

When we cross items off a to-do list, our sense of self-efficacy increases. Even if we include activities we already complete each day, there's usually a good-feeling sense of "I accomplished something" as we cross them off. Actions like preparing meals begin feeling like evidence that we're capable adults. Creating a daily to-do list, even if it mostly contains items like this or there are many days where the only item is "be spontaneous," automatically orients us toward acting with intent and increases our ability to live consciously. As we feel more able to manage our affairs, our psychic emanation strengthens too. Consequently, it's important not to fill daily to-do lists with items we think we won't get to. If we do, the impression can be more of "I'm sort of capable" or "I never make enough progress," which isn't the desired result.

To aid with this, we can prioritize lists based on when items need to be accomplished or create multiple lists. This can also help us feel less overwhelmed or stressed about what we need to do, and more able to visualize the flow of how we'll do it. I learned to prioritize my to-do lists with the letters A, B, C, and D. A items must be done today, B items in the next two or three days, C items by the end of the week, and D items at another time. Within these categories, we can prioritize items again by making the top task A1, the second A2, and so on. With this approach, we seldom have to wonder what would feel like a beneficial next step to take in our day. This approach also helps us integrate our goals into our day-to-day lives as they fit in one of these categories.

Using daily to-do lists helps us assess our capacity because we gain a sense of how much we can do in a day. To-do lists also train us to be aware of our energy because making them necessarily involves asking ourselves what we think we can do today, this week, etc. They also help us set realistic goals because we develop a clearer idea of what carrying our goals out will entail. Relatedly, when we create to-do lists regularly, we become more aware of what we tend to follow through on or not, and how. There may be certain tasks we complete with ease and others we consistently avoid, which is fruitful to explore with a learning outlook.

Another huge benefit of to-do lists is that they free up whatever mental energy and space we would've devoted to retaining and managing their content. Rather than wonder what we have to do, we know that information is safely stored. Gone are the days of thinking, "I have to do this, and that, and what was that other thing?" Now, we can use this energy and space for other purposes, including simply enjoying the day. We become freer to concentrate on the present moment and attune to the divinity within as superfluous thoughts about to-do items recede. Without juggling so much in our mind, we're also abler to concentrate our energy one-pointedly. In terms of inner alchemy, we pare down our conscious mind's content to de-clutter our psychic emanation and get stiller in meditation.

In today's world, there are many options for making to-do lists, including phone and computer apps and specialized journals. We're each free to explore what works for us. I generally use a combination of online and paper to-do lists. I experience a strong benefit from writing my daily to-do list out, and I feel greater satisfaction from crossing something off a list than deleting something on my computer. In terms of inner alchemy, the salient point is to find whatever to-do list system best yields the impacts listed in this section.

Another tool we can use to aid in energy management is a calendar (and there are many options for these today as well). Calendars can help us reduce our stress by releasing any worry we have about forgetting important events. They also give us a feel for how busy we are, which aids us in deciding if we want to take on more in a given moment. Generally speaking, calendars help us be more intentional with our time. They also make us more able to align the future around our intentions, which aids in our ability to do this metaphysically.

Most people don't experience time as linearly as a clock would suggest. As the saying goes, a minute with our hand in a fire feels like a lifetime, whereas an hour staring into the eyes of a new lover can feel like minutes. I find that when I pay attention to time, whether by creating a schedule or regularly checking a clock, it slips away from me less than it does otherwise, and I usually get more done.

Some of these tools might feel restrictive at first, especially if you currently leave your free time open. The point isn't to restrict though; it's to be intentional with resources. Energy management skills enable us to live with a foot firmly planted in mysticism while thriving in the external world.

Here are some additional energy management techniques:

- Handle a piece of paper once (or a couple times). If we have an action item like a bill to pay, we pay it the same day if we can. Getting in the habit of completing tasks as soon as possible leads to fewer loose ends. Loose ends take up space in our mind and can clutter our psychic emanation, even if we forget about them. Conversely, tying up loose ends helps us stay clear, focused on the present moment, and aligned with our intentions.

- If we can't tie up a loose end or release something from our mental or physical space, we can put it in a designated place. Organizing things saves us the energy of having to remember where they are, which also keeps things neater in our mind. This is a "How you do anything is how you do everything" issue. The less of an imposition something is in our lives, the less it affects our psyche and subtle body. For this system, the minimum with this is knowing where important items are, which can be done simply based on our needs. For years, I kept my highly important items (e.g., leases, passport, taxes, etc.) in a box, which was mostly it in terms of formal organization. By having that box, I expended almost no energy managing these items.

- Save repeated lists. Rather than write a new grocery list weekly or a packing list whenever we travel, we can store one of each. Adding or removing items from a preexisting list takes less time and energy than creating a new one.

- To remember to bring something somewhere, we can put our keys on top of it.

- In general, reflect upon how to use less energy to reach the same end when engaged in tasks.

- If we're unsure of what to do, we can always ask, "What's the best use of my energy right now?"

Exercises

1. For the next week, write a to-do list daily. It can be simple or complex. For added metaphysical benefit, write an affirmation, inspirational quote,

or spiritual statement atop it. If you're working with a sigil, try drawing it on the to-do list.

2. For the next week, document how you spent your time on a blank calendar, tracking significant events (e.g., grocery shopping, watched TV for two hours, etc.). What does this show you? Also, find a calendar system you resonate with and begin writing events in it to the degree that you feel comfortable.

HOME AS OASIS AND SANCTUARY

"The ache for home lives in all of us.
The safe place where we can go as we are and not be questioned."
—MAYA ANGELOU

Our home is usually the physical space we have the most control over, and it's another level of being for us to align, which can profoundly impact our psyche and subtle body. In this system, the primary aim here is to appreciate how our home affects us and integrate it with inner alchemy by decorating and caring for it in a manner that supports our intentions. There's a Chinese spiritual art and science called "Feng Shui" that rests upon the notion that how we decorate spaces affects their energy, as well as how we feel within them. Feng Shui is an elaborate system, but fundamentally, it validates the concept that how we arrange and decorate a space can promote our well-being and support or hinder certain intentions. For example, my psychotherapy office featured earth tones and warm lighting because this evokes feelings of being nurtured in many people, which therefore supported my intentions of creating a healing environment. We can decorate spaces to support many other intentions too, like creativity, serenity, or inspiration. Think about your living space for a moment. How does it feel? Is it supportive or unsupportive of your intentions?

Spaces can also be used to foster particular thought-dependent realities, and one of the easiest ways to support our intentions is to surround ourselves with what we want to become—for example, by decorating our home with sacred symbols and objects that help us tune to the divine and reinforce beliefs we want to cultivate internally. When we live in consensus realities that don't mirror what we believe in (or even invalidate it), making our home reflect our desired reality is profoundly beneficial. This gives us an oasis in which to feel nourished, nurtured, and affirmed in our beliefs, values, and sense of purpose. Without doing this, we're likely to unconsciously digest more of those consensus realities than we'd prefer, affecting our psyche and psychic emanation accordingly.

Beyond how we decorate our home, there's also the matter of how much stuff we have and how we keep it. Our possessions carry a psychological and psychic heft, with everything we own taking up some of our energy (and more of it when items are in disarray). The aim in this system with possessions is to have an amount of them and organizational approach such that our home feels aligned and comfortable to us. If we have so many possessions that we feel overwhelmed or burdened by them, we may benefit from downsizing. With every item we own, it's worth considering what value it holds for us and if keeping it serves our well-being.

Regarding cleanliness and tidiness, these are largely matters of personal preference. That said, I think it's safe to say that a sink that's consistently full of dishes, laundry that sits for weeks, and a bathroom that hasn't been cleaned in months are unsupportive of inner alchemy. They don't help us stay aligned. Will development exercises can aid us in establishing habits of cleanliness and tidiness if we lack them—for example, by creating exercises like "put things away after using them." If we struggle with doing the dishes and laundry, we can temporarily pare down what we use in order to develop new cleaning habits. For example, we can pack up much of our clothing and dishware, leaving just enough for two loads of laundry and two meals. This forces us to do these chores. During magic school, I did this with my dishes and it's how I created the habit of washing dishes daily.

There's a tremendous difference between the psychological and metaphysical impact of a home that's tidy, intentionally arranged, and decorated with items that affirm us versus one that's not. To an extent, our home and mind are interconnected. If we want to hold our mind a certain way, keeping our home accordingly can facilitate that.

Exercises

1. Contemplate how you want your home to be. If cost were no object, how would you decorate it? How would you like to maintain it?
2. Implement one cleaning strategy this week if cleanliness or tidiness isn't your strong suit.

MANAGING MONEY

"Having lots of money while not having inner peace
is like dying of thirst while bathing in the ocean."
—PARAMAHAMSA YOGANANDA

In today's world, financial stress is a tremendous psychological burden for many people, and it's common to hate money. Consider for a moment the type of relationship you have with things you hate. Where do hateful thoughts and feelings tend to lead? How inspired will we be to manage money well if it repulses us? What does hating money likely do metaphysically? We may as well build a fence around our bank account that keeps it from expanding beyond the limit of our disdain.

Money is a tangible form of energy. It's a means to an end, and it's part of life in most of the world. Wishing this isn't so to where we have an antagonistic relationship with money can subvert our ability to manage it effectively and torpedo any magic we have related to financial prosperity. We don't have to love or like money though, and we can strive to change wealth's place in our society while establishing a comfortable relationship with money. All we need to do for inner alchemy is bring our thinking about money to a neutral enough place to establish financial prosperity. We can do this by jettisoning thoughts about money that are inaccurate and detrimental to our financial well-being and affirming others that support it. Beyond the thoughts shared above, we might try on ones like:

Money isn't inherently good or bad.
Money and greed are separate issues.
There's nothing unspiritual about money.
Happiness doesn't come from money.
There are ways I can increase my income if I want to.
I only need enough money to be comfortable, and I can find avenues to that.
If I want more later, I'll think about that then.
As my relationship with money becomes comfortable,
I'll have more energy to spend in other areas of my life.
I'm not a sellout if I earn enough money to be financially comfortable.

In the last ten years, researchers have conducted compelling studies on wealth and subjective appraisal of life satisfaction. They've consistently found that once we make enough money to afford a comfortable standard of living and not stress about money, there's little added psychological benefit to being wealthier.[13] Per the data, the adage is true: money can't buy happiness, but until we hit our figure where we feel financially comfortable, financial stress can negatively impact our well-being.

To determine this figure, we can consider questions like: What kind of life-style do I want? Home? Entertainment or travel opportunities? How much money would I need to earn per year to afford all of that? Questions like these help us figure out what financial goals to set for ourselves. As usual, the aim in this system is to be aware and intentional, with the intentions themselves being a personal matter, provided they support inner alchemy.

In addition to figuring out how much money we want and tidying up our thinking about money, developing money management skills is important if we lack them. Many people don't grow up with strong financial modeling and aren't taught money management in school, much less about matters like investing and asset development. Many could be in a better place financially even with their current income if they learned money management skills. We can light a thousand financial prosperity candles, but if we're unable to manage money, this is like pouring liquid into a broken vessel. Fortunately, we can learn these skills. Developing habits as adults that we didn't grow up with can be difficult, particularly with topics we struggle with emotionally, but with the self-discipline developed in this system, we can do it.

A first step in learning to manage money is becoming aware of our current spending habits. Finances are another dimension of the energy monitoring we undertake in this system. Many people experience stress around money when they spend it inattentively, often due to inadvertent overspending. One way to become aware of our spending habits is to write down everything we buy each day for a month. The results of this practice can be surprising and illuminating.

Another step in learning financial management is to create a budget, which is a document that lists our standard monthly expenses and subtracts them from our income. Budgets show us how much money we have available for pleasurable activities, which enables us to plan accordingly. When we budget, we're more likely to think something like "If I want to go to that concert, I should cook more

---

13. Ducharme, Jamie. "This Is the Amount of Money You Need to Be Happy, According to Research." Money.com, February 14, 2018. https://money.com/ideal-income-study/.

of my meals this month." Budgets should also include an allotment for savings, even if we can only save a small amount each month or are living paycheck to paycheck. In the latter case, this is to create a psychic and psychological space for savings to grow in, and it's OK to write "$0" in the savings line of our budget at first. As with the sacred space in our home, by establishing a foothold for savings in our consciousness, we will begin to manifest opportunities to save.

One of the surest ways to alleviate financial stress is learning to live comfortably within our means. This is actually a general aim of energy management in this system, whether it's physical energy, mental energy, etc.: assess our capacity and then strive to function within that. From a place of strength and stability where we are, we can then build if we want to. This can be difficult to reach though because in many nations today, a comfortable standard of living isn't guaranteed in exchange for working hard. Employee benefits have continually declined over the last forty years, and the reality of being able to afford a home and comfortably support a family on a single income has dwindled. Because debt is often tied to education, many of us enter the professional world weighed down before we've even reached cognitive adulthood. What this system prompts us to do in situations like this is be practical. Revolution may come tomorrow, and we can work to bring it if we want, but it's not here now. So what must we do to afford the standard of living we want in the meantime? Are we willing and able to do that or not? If not, how can we make peace with less in a society that constantly pushes us to buy more?

If we desire things we can't currently afford, we have two choices: earn more or spend less, assuming that spending less will enable us to afford these things. If we're unwilling or unable to do what it takes to earn more and spending less won't work for us either, a more fruitful use of our energy can be to release some of our wants. As we become spiritually full and dismantle conditioned consensus reality desires within ourselves, we can thrive with little money because we look for satisfaction less and less in what it can buy. Recall for a moment Peace Pilgrim, who had almost no material possessions and was arguably one of the happiest people who ever lived. There are also creative solutions we can undertake to minimize expenditures like buying a house with friends, and fortunately, libraries remain free and the internet provides virtually endless entertainment options.

The more conscious and intentional we are with money, the less likely we are to be blindsided by financial problems. This financial awareness enables sound planning, which can set the stage for a sustainable financial future. Otherwise, it's also important for inner alchemy to recognize that we needn't compete in society's money game. We can free ourselves from conditioned wants and, in doing so, win in a manner that no one in the game can even imagine.

Exercises

1. For the next month, write down your daily expenses. Afterward, reflect on what you spent.
2. With that information, create a budget for the month ahead. Many budget templates are available free online.

THE LITTLE WORK IN THE PROFESSIONAL WORLD

"Every act we do in our daily routine can be sacramental to us if we make it so, and our daily toil become an exercise for the soul's growth."
—DION FORTUNE

Many of us spend more of our waking hours at work than anywhere else, and work is one of the primary venues in which we pour our energy. Even if we loathe our job, we return week after week because otherwise, we won't be able to afford even a minimally comfortable standard of living for ourselves. Unless we leave our society or become an ascetic, working to afford a standard of living is how things are for us.

With so much of our time and energy being spent at work, if we don't make work an extension of inner alchemy, it'll be difficult to perform inner alchemy deeply. A primary aim of this system is to integrate every aspect of life with our spiritual path, with each domain feeding our alchemical process. This is possible in all life domains through training ourselves to think and act in ways that align them with our path. Given the amount of time we spend at work, little can feed our alchemical process more than utilizing work for it.

There are two primary ways I know to align our professional world like this. The first is to have a career that explicitly involves metaphysics. The second is to bring the spirit of inner alchemy to our work itself, whatever it is. Regarding the former, this is a matter of personal preference. Many of us would love having an occult job, while others wouldn't, and this isn't a requirement for inner alchemy.

If we do yearn for this, we can use magic and the skills we've developed to make it happen (e.g., self-discipline, goal-setting, to-do lists, etc.).

For example, let's say we want to be a professional psychic who also sells charged candles. Two early steps to make this happen can be creating a vision for the business and researching the practicalities of launching it, thinking through matters like how much we want to earn a year, how much business we'd need to do that, etc. We can also look to others in our field who are successful and try to ascertain what's worked for them, perhaps even contacting them with questions. Many people will gladly help up-and-coming folks who approach them respectfully. Once we've gathered enough information, we can create a business plan where we strategize how to make this career objective real with SMART goals. Magic can be involved throughout this process, but especially then. We can place the business plan on our altar and cast a prosperity spell to support its actualization, as well as design a logo that becomes a sigil for the business's success. Building this career can also include incremental steps, like performing psychic readings and selling our candles at weekend farmer's markets while still working a nine-to-five job.

That said, we may want a metaphysical career that doesn't require this much ambition, and there are options for that too, like working at a metaphysical store. We can also develop a trade that metaphysically overlaps with our metaphysical practice. Many magical practitioners become massage therapists and energy healers, which allows them to work within paradigms that overlap with occultism. Some even become doctors of traditional Chinese medicine or Ayurveda. A trade like massage can be useful if we want to launch a full-scale occult business because it provides income without the constraints of a nine-to-five job.

There are wide divergences regarding how important career is to people. For some of us, employment is mostly how we pay the bills, and there's nothing wrong with that. As we reviewed earlier, the main objective with career in this system is to earn enough money for us in a manner that aligns with our values and doesn't detract from our spiritual practices. That said, if we have gifts that could be of service to others, it'd likely feel good to us (and others) to find work that utilizes them. We can also pursue what we know brings us joy, like art, working with animals or young children, etc.

Depending on where we live and our education or skill level, we may not be able to find a job that aligns with our values. For example, the opportunities available to us may mostly be with businesses that exploit their workers. In these cases, we can still practice inner alchemy in whatever job we get with the techniques we'll explore in this section. Over time, we can combine spellwork with the self-discipline and goal-setting skills we've developed to find other opportunities, which may involve attending college or trade school. In whatever job we have, the deeper alchemical work is in how we do it, not what we're doing.

Here are some time-tested steps and techniques for using work to feed an inner alchemy process:

An early step for aligning work with inner alchemy is to tidy up our thinking about work in general. As with money, if we hate or resent work, we'll experience psychological and metaphysical consequences from that. Because of how much time we spend at work, little can torpedo our overall life satisfaction like hating our job. If we resent having to work in general, which is understandable since there's no inherent reality to working aside from meeting basic needs, we'll experience considerable professional discomfort and stress. Instead, we can cultivate thoughts about how work can support inner alchemy, how aligned action is its own reward, how we can serve others through work, etc.

Another step is to sanctify our work as best we can, anchoring our mind in spirit throughout each workday. The most potent method I know for this is Karma Yoga, the Yoga of action. Karma Yoga involves training ourselves to perform actions attentively, selflessly, and without attachment to outcomes. It is the primary focus of the *Bhagavad Gita*, which we explored some in the section on magical ethics, and I highly recommend reading the *Bhagavad Gita* if you want to dive deeper into it. Karma Yoga is often called "selfless service," and the term selfless is meant literally: we aim to release all thoughts of self and become fully present with our action, thus approaching the unity sought in each type of Yoga. Many metaphysical training programs I've encountered, Eastern and Western, have featured Karma Yoga, and for good reason. Karma Yoga can profoundly transform us, and we can practice it in a variety of circumstances.

In Karma Yoga, we devote ourselves completely to what we're doing. If we notice ourselves thinking about rewards or outcomes (or liking or disliking what we're doing), we refocus on the task at hand and the present moment. If I'm performing Karma Yoga at work, this means I'm not thinking about the money I'm earning, getting a promotion, how frustrated I feel about performing a task, etc. I'm fully present with each action, only considering the future to the extent I must to complete a task or manage my workday timewise. In Karma Yoga, we align our levels of being around the action itself, like during ritual. This yields a harmonious state of consciousness that's strikingly similar to one that's sought in popular psychology, called "flow."

Another way to practice Karma Yoga is to dedicate each of our actions to our concept of the divine. For example, a devotee of the Divine Mother could begin their workday with a prayer that their actions serve her and that they perceive her in everyone. Then they strive to remember her in each moment, offering any thoughts of outcome or self to her. Singing devotional songs, chanting, and reciting prayers internally (or externally if we're alone) can facilitate this. In this approach, each action essentially becomes part of a large ritual. To the extent that we can pull this off (which increases with practice), it has tremendous metaphysical and psychological ramifications. It also supports the famous objectives in the Great Work to "Invoke often" and "Inflame thyself with prayer." There are ways to do this without a formed divine conceptualization too. That just takes some creativity. Karma Yoga erases the division between our spiritual practices and the rest of our lives, such that eventually, living becomes a ceaseless act of worship, which nears us to the Great Work.

Being unattached to work outcomes may seem like it would reduce productivity or weaken results, but this isn't so. In Karma Yoga, we perform every action to the best of our ability (becoming able to do so on command is an aim of the practice). We just do this without the burden of attachment to outcomes or fixating on how much we like or dislike what we're doing. Considerable recent research affirms that this kind of attitude can yield better performance outcomes.[14] Stress, worry, and other issues that can accompany fixating on outcomes can be distracting and otherwise foster reduced attentiveness. This is part of why mindfulness practice, which greatly parallels Karma Yoga, has become popular in the corporate world. That said, practicing Karma Yoga or mindfulness with the aim of increasing our productivity isn't in the true spirit of Karma Yoga or mindfulness. At the same time, even when performing these practices in their intended spirit, it's hard to ignore their benefits.

---

14. Kersemaekers, Wendy, and Silke Rupprecht, Marc Wittman, Chris Tamdjidi, Pia Falke, Rogier Donders, Anne Speckens, Niko Kohls. "A Workplace Mindfulness Intervention May Be Associated with Improved Psychological Well-Being and Productivity. A Preliminary Field Study in a Company Setting." *Frontiers in Psychology*, Volume 9 (2018).

I've approached my work with a Karma Yoga mindset for almost fifteen years, and I've consequently experienced improved professional results and diminished stress. When others enter crisis mode or panic, a Karma Yoga mindset of acceptance and alertness helps me stay grounded, focused, and efficient, and when the workday is over, work stays at work. Karma Yoga practice also helps me feel less bothered by work I don't feel like doing. Tasks that once seemed burdensome or like wastes of time have become opportunities to deepen my spiritual practice.

As we dutifully practice Karma Yoga (and like all practice, this is a "progress, not perfection" situation), our ability to detach and concentrate strengthens. The moments when we find ourselves distracted and redirect our focus increase our willpower and ability to focus, which then strengthens our ritual and meditation practice. Conversely, the energy, focus, and willpower we generate from ritual, meditation, and will development exercises enable us to practice Karma Yoga more attentively. We create a feedback loop where our focus and attentiveness in each area of life increases our overall ability to focus and be attentive, and it's wonderful to feel the benefits of hard work during a meditation session. Once we get a taste for that, practicing Karma Yoga becomes far easier.

Additionally, the ability fostered in Karma Yoga practice to let go of personal concerns and attachment to outcomes while rooting in the present moment extends to other areas of life. Karma Yoga practice has made me far less attached to events unfolding as I'd hoped and more likely to shrug off disappointments (or to not create attachments to outcomes to begin with). Serenity arises as we release stressful thoughts and center in the present moment, which Karma Yoga practice teaches us how to do. This stabilizes our mind and subtle body, priming our psychic emanation for whatever intentions we launch. Karma Yoga practice has made me look forward to the harmony I know I can feel in tasks I can meditatively complete, like folding laundry, washing dishes, and tidying up.

When practicing Karma Yoga, bear in mind the following:

+ Remain present within your body.
+ Do your best to fully attend to the tasks you perform.
+ When you find yourself distracted, refocus on your breath and the action at hand.

+ If you have a devotional practice, try beginning each Karma Yoga session by praying that your actions be an offering to the divine and refocus on the divine when you find yourself distracted.

Writing this list on an index card or phone can prove helpful so it can readily be reviewed before practicing.

Another layer of sanctity we can bring to work involves staying aware of our heart and spirit throughout the day. We can cultivate this habit by training ourselves to frequently think affirmations like "We're all divine beings" and "Every act is an opportunity for alignment." We can also strive to feel others' divinity (and our own) through tuning in to their energy. To aid in this, we can begin each workday with a ritual or prayer that affirms these intentions. We can also integrate the sacred with work by placing workplace-appropriate sacred objects in our workspace. If we have an office, we can perform rituals in it when convenient to help us stay anchored in our intentions and aligned.

Beyond integrating the sacred into our workday, we can also use our job as a personal growth laboratory, where we experiment with developing skills and qualities within ourselves that benefit inner alchemy. In addition to Karma Yoga, we can perform will development exercises like:

+ Strategize how to perform each task efficiently. See how quickly you can complete your tasks without sacrificing quality.
+ Consider your system of organization and what could improve it.
+ Reflect on how aligned you feel at work. What could make you feel more aligned?
+ Draw a sacred symbol or sigil on each piece of paper you work with (that only you handle).
+ Set an intention for the flow of the workday and try to hold to this regardless of what happens.
+ Consider how your work actions align with your authenticity, or how to align them with it.
+ Prioritize tying up looses ends in work projects.
+ Be concise in your speech.
+ Be friendly and accommodating (in a healthy manner) with every person you work with.

+ Greet everyone you see with a warm smile.

+ Try to complete tasks before they're due.

+ Arrive early for the workday and meetings.

In addition to these, we can also practice holding attitudes. When we don't proactively assume an attitude, we're more likely to react to what happens around us. When we assume one, we can often hold it where it is (or not shift as far from it), especially with practice. For example, if I'm going into a performance review and set my attitude to "I will listen compassionately," I'm less likely to react defensively. This also holds for other qualities we try to develop, which includes the qualities that generally compose the conventional notion of a good employee, like: active listening, attentiveness/detail-orientation, assertiveness (in a respectful manner), centeredness, speaking concisely, being collaborative, compassion, dependability, discipline/diligence, enthusiasm, flexibility, focus, pragmatism, upbeat attitude/fostering an enjoyable workplace, and self-motivation. We develop these in this system because they serve the dual purpose of improving our work performance and fostering inner alchemy.

As we practice these qualities, we allow our emotions even when we don't act in alignment with them (e.g., being friendly with a customer when we feel like being rude). While doing this, we contextualize our behavior with our alchemical intentions. The internal impact of "I must pretend to be nice because I'm at work" is vastly different from "I'm cultivating the freedom to be unconditionally kind." There may be some "Fake it until you make it" in this at first, but the ultimate goal is to find a compelling motivation for everything we do at work (as best we can). This helps us feel authentic and like our time is being well spent.

A powerful way of combining this personal growth laboratory work with our sense of the sacred is to integrate tarot with developing the qualities we seek. These qualities all align with the Major Arcana cards, as does the Little Work system because its tenets each match a Major card. Depending on how deeply we want to cultivate these qualities, we can draw a card daily or as we feel compelled, though anything beyond weekly could dilute the practice. If we don't resonate with tarot, we can write the qualities listed above on slips of paper and use those instead.

Incorporating tarot with work aids us in keeping archetypal consciousness and magic in our mind throughout the day. The cards can hold meaning for other areas of our lives too, turning this practice into both professional development and divination. We can also draw cards outside of work to just focus on the tenets of the Little Work. Although I provide interpretations below, feel free to use your own. With each card, I included the Golden Dawn astrological attributions. These can be used for self-development at work too. For example, we could decide to focus on our nurturing side after drawing the Chariot, which corresponds with Cancer.

THE FOOL—0

Air, Uranus
Enthusiasm
Intentionality

Intention is magical.

Intent initiates the Fool's journey. What brought you to this job? What do you intend for it? Practice being intentional throughout the day. Consider that each day is part of a journey. Strive to approach situations like a beginner, releasing judgements and biases.

THE MAGICIAN—1

Mercury
Assertiveness
Intentionality
Strategic Thinking

What thought created, thought can change.

How can you align your job-related thoughts with your greater intentions? What opportunities exist for you to be creative at work? The Magician calls us to harness our thoughts and actions, as well as manifest our visions. Strive to use your creativity and will at work.

The High Priestess—2

The Moon

Active Listening

Awareness

Centeredness

As above, so below. As below, so above.

Align your work with your spirit. Tap into your intuition and psychic senses at work. Become as centered as you can each day.

The Empress—3

Venus

Collaboration

Compassion

Supportive Attitude

There is no such thing as the mundane.

Seek the divine in all things and each moment. Be compassionate with your coworkers. Look for ways to feel abundant and productive. Feel the power you gain from being centered and compassionate.

THE EMPEROR—4

Aries

Assertiveness

Strategic Thinking

Everything is energy.

What areas of your job do you have control or influence over? Own your personal power at work. Develop your leadership and/or assertiveness skills.

THE HIEROPHANT—5

Taurus

Dependability

Discipline

Master the basics.

What systems are in place where you work? Study the structures that exist in your job and understand the rationale behind them. Practice deferring to your boss's judgement and following the rules. Contemplate the value in doing so. Is there any structure you feel it would be beneficial to add or change with regard to how you work? Try being structured each day.

THE LOVERS.

The Lovers—6

Gemini

Active Listening

Collaboration

Welcome the support of others.

Can you collaborate more effectively with your co-workers and/or better support or be supported by them? Look for ways to collaborate, support others, and receive assistance.

THE CHARIOT.

The Chariot—7

Cancer

Focus

Goal-Orientation

Surround yourself with what you want to become.

Where are you going in your job? Your career? Where do you want to go? Take the wheel in each moment of your workday. Mind the greater journey of your career alongside the microcosmic level each day. Review your work goals or create some.

STRENGTH—8

Leo

Discipline

Focus

Try your best.

How hard and well are you working? Where could you do more or try harder, in a healthy manner? Challenge yourself to work harder than normal.

THE HERMIT—9

Virgo

Awareness

Detail-Orientation

Intentionality

Live consciously.

How efficiently are you working? How intentional and aligned are you being? How can you increase your awareness at work? What do you notice as you pay extra attention?

The Wheel of Fortune—10

Jupiter

Acceptance

Pragmatism

Embrace your karma.

Practice accepting where you are and what happens in the moment as best you can. Look for opportunities in what occurs. What wisdom can you develop from being with what is at work like this?

Justice—11

Libra

Accountability

Centeredness

Thoughtful Speech

Monitor your energy.

Practice monitoring and balancing your energy, particularly in how you approach tasks and interactions with others. Also, consider how fair you're being with others and yourself. Strive to have a fair perspective with anything that comes up at work.

The Hanged Man—12

Water, Neptune
Dependability
Flexibility

Let go of what you believe you are.

Are there beliefs that hold you back at work? How might things change if you let them go? The Hanged Man can call us to sacrifice our individual wants for the greater good. If you have downtime, ask your supervisor for additional work.

Death—13

Scorpio
Acceptance
Flexibility

Accept change and where you are.

What transitions are called for at work? How could you benefit from doing things differently? Are there behaviors or beliefs it would be helpful to release? Also, have you considered how you want to end this job when the time comes?

Temperance—14

Sagittarius

Balance

Focus

Seek moderation, even with moderation.

How disciplined are you at work? Where could you be more temperate? Temperance calls us to use our energy intentionally and with minimum excess. Consider ways to be efficient. Also, reflect on the balance between your work and personal life. If it's unbalanced, are there ways of changing this or taking care of yourself more?

The Devil—15

Capricorn

Pragmatism

Keep an eye on the ego.

How is your ego showing up at work? Do you feel resistance to working more attentively? Upon reflection, do you notice any work-related unconscious self-sabotage? If you find some, plan what to do about it.

THE TOWER—16

Mars
Acceptance
Flexibility

Release your attachment to control.

Can you better accept what comes at work? How are you in a crisis? If there are any metaphorical fires at work this week, help with them as best you can. Strive to gain wisdom from that experience.

THE STAR—17

Aquarius
Centeredness
Self-motivation

Follow the guiding light within.

Have you received any intuitive guidance about this job and how you're showing up in it? Tune in to your guidance daily and follow where it leads.

The Moon—18

Pisces

Active Listening

Compassion

Allow your emotions.

How do you feel about your job? What do you tend to feel throughout the day? How can you harness your emotions at work? The Moon also calls us to integrate our imagination with our work. What dreams do you have and how can they fit with where you are in your job or career?

The Sun—19

The Sun

Enthusiasm

Self-Motivation

Supportive Attitude

Center in your authenticity.

How authentic do you feel at work? If the answer is "Not very," how can you change that? The Sun also "looks on the bright side" of things. How can you frame your work mentally in a good-feeling manner? Strive for optimism, though not in an insincere-feeling way. Also, consider your ambitions in this job. What do you want for yourself here?

Judgement—20

Fire, Pluto
Accountability
Awareness
Thoughtful Speech

Apply discernment to each thought and feeling.

What kind of judgement do you exhibit at work? Be discerning with your thoughts. Consider how to align them with your broader intentions for yourself. Judgement also involves awakening to higher states of consciousness. How can your work support your alchemical process? Your increased awareness?

The World—21

Saturn
Compassion
Goal-Setting
Pragmatism

View everything with compassion.

What's the big picture of your job? Are there areas where you aren't seeing it enough? How do your job and career goals align with how you're showing up each day? How can you be compassionate with yourself about where you are in your professional journey? Consciously align your job with the big picture of your alchemical process, striving to feel unity with the whole of your work.

The Minor Arcana can be used in conjunction with these cards for more specific intentionality. For example, drawing Death and the Knight of Wands could indicate a challenge to vigorously move into change with determination.

Developing these new work habits can be a lengthy process, and that's OK. Even a bit of effort toward them can improve how we feel and perform at work. Also, most people don't undergo the type of training we do in this system. As we become self-disciplined, conscientious, attentive, discerning, compassionate, efficient, accepting, unattached to outcomes, and flexible, we'll start outperforming others, which can lead to advancements in our career. We'll look like we're pouring ample energy into our work, and at first we are, but ultimately, we're just being aligned, efficient, and intentional. Internally, working like this increases our energy level and capacity.

Before leaving the topic of work, it's important to address toxic work environments. The acceptance-based orientation in this system isn't intended to be used as justification for tolerating workplace toxicity (e.g., exploitive conditions, toxic leadership, etc.). The first step in acceptance is being candid about where we are and what's happening. As we practice identifying ego, we'll recognize the difference between a job that's helpfully pushing us outside our comfort zone and one that's toxic. When a job is toxic, we must leave it. Some of us may have to stay in toxic jobs for a while though, in which case we do our best to perform the Little Work in them while creating an exit strategy. We can also increase our self-care and claim whatever power we have to improve the situation, including advocating for ourselves and using magic.

CONNECTING WITH NATURE

"When we lose touch with our blessed planet, we lose touch with divinity."
—SCOTT CUNNINGHAM

One way of equilibrating earth while increasing our overall alignment of being is to spend time connecting with nature. All beings emit emanations that we can perceive once we're able to sense subtle energy. Feeling these emanations provides us with a way of learning from and engaging with the life that surrounds us. For example, trees (and other plants) offer ceaseless, clear demonstrations of how to live authentically, be present, stay aligned, connect spiritually, and allow the natural vitality within to flow. If we sit in a grove, quiet our mind, and open ourselves to feeling and receiving, they'll guide us to our center and point us toward the divinity within. This is like replicating a note we hear someone else singing, and the natural world is always singing.

Nature is our home. It exists in inherent reality, immune to the effects of thought-dependent realities when left be. They simply don't exist there. By visiting nature with an open mind and heart, we can increasingly see through thought-dependent conditioning. Nature can help us come home within ourselves, reorienting us to our aspects of self that are more fundamental than our thoughts.

As I write of nature's gifts, I'm not idealizing or romanticizing nature. Violence, fear for survival, and wild destruction are inherent parts of the natural world. My point is that nature is beyond the mind. It's aligned in a way that the bulk of us aren't.

Most of us suffer from thought-dependent issues that needn't exist. Even if we lack the power to change the consensus reality structures that sustain these issues (like our society's economy), we can still connect with the parts of ourselves that are always beyond them. Thought-dependent realities feel less real when we consistently experience more inherent levels of reality, whether that's via ritual, meditation, visiting nature, or another method. It's like thought-dependent realities are two-dimensional and inherent reality is three-dimensional. The more we experience three-dimensionality, the less we feel bound by what happens at the two-dimensional level. Three-dimensionality also provides us with powerful insights into the two-dimensional level that we couldn't have had before.[15] This is a quantum leap of consciousness, and it's part of completing the Great Work.

In India, there's a well-known story about a zoo visitor who sees a large elephant tied to a brittle fence. Confused, the visitor asks, "Why is this elephant tied to this? It could free itself at any time." The zookeeper replies that the elephant was tied to the fence throughout its youth, which conditioned it to believe it can't break free. It doesn't even think of testing the rope anymore. It simply accepts this bondage as real.

This is what thought-dependent reality limitations are like. Those that aren't rooted in inherent reality have no power over us beyond what we give them unless there are external structures that support them. At any time, we can tug on the rope and free ourselves. The problem is that most of us have no idea how to do this, and hearing about it leads to us thinking about it, which acquaints us with the concept of the experience, not the experience itself. It's like trying to

15. As explored in terms of physics by Carl Sagan in *Cosmos* and consciousness in the film *What the Bleep Do We Know?* Both of these were inspired by *Flatland*, a story by Edwin Abbott.

understand three dimensions from the vantage point of two. That's the position I was in before I joined my magic school. My intellect told me the rope wasn't real, but I felt choked by it nonetheless. With practices like ritual, meditation, mindfulness, and tuning in to nature, we start moving into three-dimensionality. We begin to perceive how brittle the fence is and break the thought-dependent bonds that restrict so much of our now.

As we break these bonds, our relationship to suffering changes. One way of navigating suffering is to compassionately comfort ourselves as we've explored thus far, which is effective, but not revolutionary. A deeper freedom and transformation related to suffering comes from experiencing that many of these issues don't exist beyond the level of thought. We can enter a reality where they cease to be, a reality that feels far realer than they do in comparison, like people do when contrasted with paper dolls. When we intellectually understand this and try to avoid suffering accordingly, we spiritually bypass because we're still operating at the level of thought. When three-dimensionality is our lived experience, there's no denial or avoidance involved. We step off the page and these issues can't follow. This is like turning off a television show we'd lost ourselves in and reorienting to the world around us.

Experiencing this deeper part of ourselves in an abiding manner fundamentally changes us. Thought-dependent realities can never feel as compelling to us as they did before. Even as we struggle with conditioning and psychological trauma that's etched in our brains, it's a different process once we know these issues aren't as real as we believed. Dreams are experienced differently when we know we're dreaming and have woken up before.

Exercise

Go to a setting that's full of trees (and ideally, free from human structures beyond things like trails). Center and open yourself. Spend a minimum of thirty minutes silently experiencing this area. Pay close attention to what you feel.

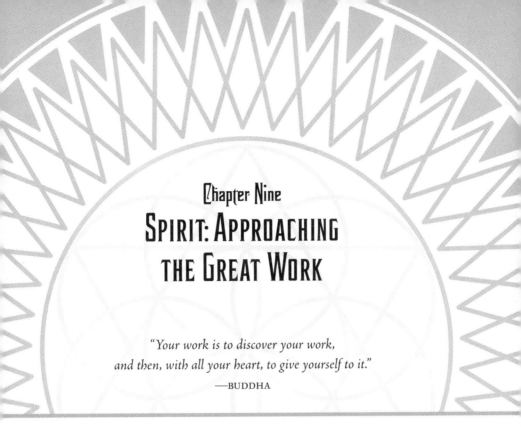

Chapter Nine
SPIRIT: APPROACHING THE GREAT WORK

"Your work is to discover your work,
and then, with all your heart, to give yourself to it."
—BUDDHA

Air, fire, water, earth. Mind, will, feeling, and form. Over the course of this book, we've explored how to practice inner alchemy in each of these areas and align them with our intentions. What you do from here is your decision, and with the self-development that accompanies inner alchemy, you're primed to succeed in whatever you choose. In forging ahead, we reach the crowning point of the pentagram: spirit. As we explored earlier, spirit isn't really an element, and there's no tool of spirit for us to earn. In equilibrating the elements within ourselves, we open the way to spirit, where we can find guidance toward the most purposeful, satisfying life we can lead. The path to spirit is simple, though not easy: turn toward it. Over and over. Feel your power, feel your heart, and feel the divine. Let yourself be guided.

Everything is divine. The Great Work is the complete realization of this, and in today's world, that path is open to everyone. We needn't reach that summit to lead a fulfilling life or connect with the divine though. With the tools provided in this book, we can fundamentally shift our current reality and find a sense of satisfaction or peace in most moments. Our lives can become largely straightforward: something delightful happens and we enjoy it. Something difficult happens and we deal with it. No drama. We nurture our spiritual connection each day and live from our sense of purpose. We learn from our experiences and treat everyone with compassion. All of this raises our vibration, and everyone who raises their vibration benefits the world, whether they pursue the Great Work or not, provided they don't offset this with spiritual bypassing.

As our magic crescendos and we feel the power of creating with little to no doubt, we can also move deeper. In the assurance that we can manifest almost anything that doesn't defy natural law, life can begin to feel somewhat like a lucid dream. Exciting, perhaps even astonishing, but we're still asleep, and we sense that. This ignites the fire for the Great Work in those of us who hunger for more, if it wasn't lit already. We rocket inward, striving to cleanse ourselves and raise our resting awareness as high up the energetic spectrum as we can. We use the discipline and habits we've created to sustain our external world such that we can hold our energy to this one point. Then we wait.

In 2007, I left my magic school. Leaving meant being shunned by the community, and many people believed catastrophe would befall anyone who left (in fairness, I never heard the teacher say that). Part of me was terrified. I'd effectively withdrawn from society to concentrate entirely on magical study, and while reeling from the culture shock of reentering society and fearing I'd made the worst mistake of my life, I plunged into months of deep practice. Eventually, I went through a dark night of the soul experience. As I persevered with my spiritual practices despite sitting at rock bottom, a day came when my being filled with light during meditation, and I surrendered to it. My self-concepts appeared like glass pieces behind me and as I chose to move toward this light, many of them shattered. It was like the thoughts I had that burst like soap bubbles during meditation, which happened frequently by that point, except with parts of my identity. The experience was exhilarating.

While walking the next morning, I tuned in to a grove of trees, and my mind went completely still. For the next five days or so, I had almost no thoughts, and I experienced the indescribable serenity of internal quiet. Thought-dependent reality vanished, alongside the suffering endemic to it. I lived in the bliss and ecstasy that's beyond names and concepts. Then I got really sick (I don't think anything surfaces karma like stillness), fell asleep, and woke up thinking and identifying with my thoughts, though never again to the degree of before those days in silence. It became evident that I still had an ego, behavioral patterns, and deep trauma etched in my brain, but I was permanently and fundamentally changed, and the shattered pieces of thought-dependent "me" never reconstituted. I persisted with my practice as I'd learned to do throughout magic school, trusting that I'd reenter that silent state, and a few weeks later, I did. Soon I became able to enter it at will, and I found an underlying peace that hasn't left me for even a day in over ten years that's made every difficult situation in my life bearable.

Earlier, I wrote that the most accessible way of releasing karma is through developing wisdom. Once we reach stillness, stillness itself will burn the seeds of our karma if we simply offer what arises within us into it. High Magic, inner alchemy, meditation, and Yoga brought me to this stillness, and entering stillness is not the end, but the beginning of deeper practice involving subtler and subtler aspects of ego. They can for you too if that's what you want, provided you do the work, grace is with you, and you surrender when the moment comes.

To Serve the World

"I slept and dreamt that life was joy. I awoke and saw that life was service.
I acted and behold, service was joy."
—RABINDRANATH TAGORE

In Lurianic Kabbalah, there's a concept that all things hold a divine spark within them and our sacred duty is to liberate these sparks, which we do through awakening spiritually and serving others. This process is called "tikkun olam" in Hebrew, which means "repairing the world." Performing inner alchemy accomplishes this within ourselves, and as our heart opens and the spark is freed, our eyes can turn to aiding others in this process. One of the greatest secrets to life satisfaction is that service brings joy. While we must take care to serve others in a manner that's respectful, there's nothing like service, and there are many ways to serve.

Generally speaking, we can serve by being kind and compassionate, and if we see a piece of trash, literally or figuratively, we can pick it up. We can also challenge the oppressive and unjust conditions that exist around us. Seeing through thought-dependent realities and perceiving the energetic dimensions of existence provides us with insights that most people don't have. Not because they can't have them, but because they haven't done work likes this. The greatest revolution comes not in untying the elephant from the fence but in the elephant realizing it's not actually restrained. This is what the Little Work helps us experience within ourselves, and once we experience this, we can aid others in doing the same. We can tug at the threads of the unhealthy status quo beliefs in consensus realities that we're part of, which can ultimately unravel them. History is full of examples of this. The idea of women voting was once absurd. Then some radicals challenged that consensus reality belief, and in most of the world now, the notion of women being unable to vote is absurd.

Claiming the ability to set thought-dependent realities aside gives us the power of true revolution. We become able to approach two-dimensional problems from a three-dimensional perspective and find answers that don't inadvertently perpetuate old problems in new ways. Many societal problems are easily answered when we step into inherent reality. People are hungry? Feed them. People are sick? Treat them. It's a consensus reality myth that an acceptable quality of life for many must come at the expense of the suffering of others. Even a cursory glance at how much food and medicine is thrown away each year, and how many homes are unoccupied, shows that we can be doing far better than we are. Not to mention what we can accomplish with technology to help end poverty.

Another way we can serve is through modeling. Humans are affected by the examples of others, and many of the dysfunctional patterns in our lives result from the modeling we grew up with. Throughout life, seeing others do things can make doing them feel more possible for us. For instance, if we see our family members go to college, it'll feel easier to us to go too. If we have a friend who heals from psychological trauma to a great degree and establishes healthy self-esteem, it can feel more possible for us to do the same. Even though we keep silence regarding much of our alchemical work, we can tell people we meditate and are on a path of self-development. Seeing the results inner alchemy has in our lives might inspire them to work on themselves. Moreover, when we model responding to life with compassion, it helps others do the same.

Otherwise, our alchemical work itself is service. Everyone who awakens to the fact that they're not their thoughts and feelings, heals from psychological trauma, removes conditioning from their minds, or opens their hearts offers service to the world. Every person who discovers what their deepest self calls out for does too. This isn't the only service we offer in a world where millions don't have their basic needs met, but this inner work is critical toward establishing a just future. We're all cells in the body of humanity, which itself is a cell in a larger body, and so on from the lowest below to the highest above. The spiritual practices we perform and the alchemical transformations we experience help raise the collective vibration of our species. Everyone becomes freer in the long run when we undertake this work, and the Mysteries aren't consigned to remote temples anymore. We can start now, wherever we are.

We're each part of a story that's bigger than ourselves—but a story that we can influence, especially at the local and community levels. We can gain wisdom from our suffering such that we become compassionate rather than closed, and we can bring the light of our hearts into everything we do, thus creating a different story. We have magic, and we can weave that into this story too and use it to help repair the human world. We're also each born with gifts. I believe they're meant to be shared. Though we can't do everything to ease others' suffering, we can usually do something. There are also many ways to serve while still pursuing individual goals. We simply must be daring enough to ask ourselves, "How can I serve?" and humble enough to accept the answer.

What we do in this moment has profound implications for the future, and creating a brighter one can be so simple. One of the greatest myths is that it's hard to know how to lead a contented life. It's actually quite straightforward, and the heart will take us there every time: Love. Serve. Explore your sense of purpose until you find a way to offer your gifts to others. Let the practice of compassion bring you peace.

If we can love and serve others and ourselves against the backdrop of inner alchemy and the discernment it's instilled in us, the doors of the Great Work will open for us. We can have the spiritual experiences we yearn for, and the wild moments that make our hearts sing, while leaving the world better off for those who come after us. Through acts of love and service, we continue aligning our levels of being and allowing our vibration to rise. Then one day we experience it: the bliss of the present moment and the undimming effulgence of a wide-open heart. There's nothing like it, and it never gets old. If someone asks us how we got there, we can say, "There is this thing called 'the Little Work.' It's a path as old as time, and it's available to anyone who dares to take it on. How much do you want to be free?"

The Tenets of the Little Work

There is no such thing as the mundane.
Everything is energy.
As above, so below. As below, so above.
Intention is magical.
What thought created, thought can change.
Try your best.
Master the basics.
Live consciously.
Monitor your energy.
Seek moderation, even with moderation.
Surround yourself with what you want to become.
Welcome the support of others.
Allow your emotions.
Apply discernment to each thought and feeling.
View everything with compassion.
Keep an eye on the ego.
Accept change and where you are.
Embrace your karma.
Release your attachment to control.
Let go of what you believe you are.
Center in your authenticity.
Follow the guiding light within.

Bibliography

Occultism

Bardon, Franz. *Initiation into Hermetics.* Salt Lake City, UT: Merkur Publishing, Inc., 2014.

Buckland, Raymond. *Buckland's Complete Book of Witchcraft.* St. Paul, MN: Llewellyn Publications, 2002.

Butler, W. E. *Apprenticed to Magic.* Loughborough, England: Thoth Publications, 2003.

Cabot, Laurie, and Tom Cowan. *Power of the Witch: The Earth, the Moon, and the Magical Path to Enlightenment.* New York: Bantam Doubleday Dell Publishing Group, Inc., 1990.

Christopher, Lyam Thomas. *Kabbalah, Magic, and the Great Work of Self-Transformation.* Woodbury, MN: Llewellyn Publications, 2006.

Cicero, Chic, and Sandra Tabatha Cicero. *The New Golden Dawn Ritual Tarot: Keys to the Rituals, Symbolism, Magic and Divination.* St. Paul, MN: Llewellyn Publications, 1996.

———. *Self-Initiation in the Golden Dawn Tradition: A Complete Curriculum of Study for Both the Solitary Magician and the Working Magical Group.* St. Paul, MN: Llewellyn Publications, 1998.

Coyle, T. Thorn. *Kissing the Limitless: Deep Magic and the Great Work of Transforming Yourself and the World.* San Francisco, CA: Red Wheel/Weiser, LLC, 2009.

Crowley, Aleister. *777 and Other Qabalistic Writings of Aleister Crowley.* York Beach, ME: Red Wheel/Weiser, LLC, 1973.

———. *Eight Lectures on Yoga*. Tempe, AZ: New Falcon Publications, 1992.

———. *Magick: Liber ABA, Book 4*. York Beach, ME: Samuel Weiser, Inc., 1994.

———. *Magick Without Tears*. Tempe, AZ: New Falcon Publications, 1991.

———. *The Book of Thoth*. York Beach, ME: Weiser Books, 2000.

Cunningham, Scott. *Cunningham's Encyclopedia of Crystal, Gem, and Metal Magic*. St. Paul, MN: Llewellyn Publications, 1988.

———. *Cunningham's Encyclopedia of Magical Herbs*. St. Paul, MN: Llewellyn Publications, 1985.

———. *Living Wicca: A Further Guide for the Solitary Practitioner*. St. Paul, MN: Llewellyn Publications, 1993.

———. *Wicca: A Guide for the Solitary Practitioner*. St. Paul, MN: Llewellyn Publications, 1988.

DuQuette, Lon Milo. *The Chicken Qabalah of Rabbi Lamed Ben Clifford: A Dilettante's Guide to What You Do and Do Not Need to Know to Become a Qabalist*. York Beach, ME: Weiser Books, 2001.

Fortune, Dion. *Applied Magic*. York Beach, ME: Samuel Weiser, Inc., 2000.

———. *Aspects of Occultism*. Wellingborough, Northamptonshire: The Aquarian Press, 1973.

———. *Esoteric Orders and Their Work*. York Beach, ME: Samuel Weiser, Inc., 2000.

———. *The Magical Battle of Britain*. Bradford on Avon, Wiltshire: Golden Gates Press, 1993.

———. *The Mystical Qabalah*. San Francisco, CA: Red Wheel/Weiser, LLC, 2000.

———. *Practical Occultism in Daily Life*. Wellingborough, Northamptonshire: The Aquarian Press, 1985.

———. *The Training and Work of an Initiate*. York Beach, ME: Samuel Weiser, Inc., 2000.

Kraig, Donald Michael. *Modern Magick: Twelve Lessons in the High Magickal Arts*. Woodbury, MN: Llewellyn Publications, 2010.

Marlbrough, Ray. *Charms, Spells, and Formulas*. St. Paul, MN: Llewellyn Publications, 1994.

Penczak, Christopher. *The Temple of High Witchcraft: Ceremonies, Spheres, and the Witches' Qabalah*. Woodbury, MN: Llewellyn Publications, 2007.

Regardie, Israel. *A Garden of Pomegranates: An Outline of the Qabalah*. St. Paul, MN: Llewellyn Publications, 1985.

———. *The Golden Dawn: The Original Account of the Teachings, Rites, and Ceremonies of the Hermetic Order, Seventh Edition*. Woodbury, MN: Llewellyn Publications, 2015.

———. *The One Year Manual: Twelve Steps to Spiritual Enlightenment*. York Beach, ME: Samuel Weiser, Inc., 1981.

———. *The Tree of Life*. York Beach, ME: Samuel Weiser, Inc., 1972.

Regardie, Israel, Chic Cicero, and Sandra Tabatha Cicero. *The Middle Pillar: The Balance Between Mind and Magic*. St. Paul, MN: Llewellyn Publications, 1998.

Salaman, Clement, Dorine van Oyen, William D. Wharton, and Jean-Pierre Mahe. *The Way of Hermes: New Translations of the Corpus Hermeticum and The Definitions of Hermes Trismegistus to Asclepius*. Rochester, VT: Inner Traditions, 2004.

Starhawk. *Dreaming the Dark: Magic, Sex, and Politics*. Boston, MA: Beacon Press, 1997.

———. *The Spiral Dance: A Rebirth of the Ancient Religion of the Great Goddess, 20th Anniversary Edition*. New York: HarperCollins Publishers Inc., 1999.

The Three Initiates. *The Kybalion*. Chicago, IL: The Yogi Publication Society, 1908.

Wang, Robert. *The Qabalistic Tarot: A Textbook of Mystical Philosophy*. York Beach, ME: Samuel Weiser, Inc., 1983.

Yoga and Miscellaneous Mysticism

Amritanandamayi, Mata, and Swami Amritaswarupananda Puri. *The Eternal Truth*. Kerala, India: Mata Amritanandamayi Center, 2007.

Bharati, Swami Jnaneshvara. *Living the Yoga Sutras*. Fort Walton Beach, FL: Abhyasa Ashram, 2011.

Byrom, Thomas (trans.). *Dhammapada: The Sayings of the Buddha*. Boston, MA: Shambhala Publications, Inc., 1976.

Dass, Ram. *Be Love Now: The Path of the Heart.* New York: HarperCollins, 2010.

Maharaj, Nisargadatta. *I Am That.* Durham, NC: The Acorn Press, 1973.

Maharshi, Ramana. *The Spiritual Teaching of Ramana Maharshi.* Boston, MA: Shambhala Publications, Inc., 1998.

Mitchell, Stephen (trans.). *The Bhagavad Gita.* New York: Three Rivers Press, 2000.

———. *Tao Te Ching.* New York: Harper & Row, 1988.

Myss, Caroline. *Anatomy of the Spirit: The Seven Stages of Power and Healing.* New York: Penguin Random House, LLC, 1996.

Pilgrim, Peace. *Her Life and Work in Her Own Words.* Sante Fe, NM: Ocean Tree Books, 1982.

Subramuniyaswami, Satguru Sivaya. *Dancing with Siva.* Kauai, HI: Himalayan Academy Publications, 1997.

———. *Living with Siva.* Kauai, HI: Himalayan Academy Publications, 2001.

———. *Merging with Siva.* Kauai, HI: Himalayan Academy Publications, 2003.

Tolle, Eckhart. *The Power of Now: A Guide to Spiritual Enlightenment.* Novato, CA: New World Library, 1999.

Trungpa, Chögyam. *Meditation in Action.* Boston, MA: Shambhala Publications, Inc., 1991.

Vivekananda, Swami. *Jnana-Yoga.* New York: Ramakrishna-Vivekananda Center, 1955.

———. *Karma-Yoga and Bhakti-Yoga.* New York: Ramakrishna-Vivekananda Center, 1955.

———. *Raja-Yoga.* New York: Ramakrishna-Vivekananda Center, 1956.

PSYCHOLOGY, SELF-HELP, AND SOCIAL WORK

Beck, Judith. *Cognitive Behavior Therapy: Basics and Beyond, Second Edition.* New York: Guilford Press, 2011.

Bourne, Edmund J. *The Anxiety and Phobia Workbook, Fifth Edition.* Oakland, CA: New Harbinger Publications, Inc., 2010.

Branch, Rhena, and Rob Wilson. *Cognitive Behavioural Therapy Workbook for Dummies, Second Edition.* West Sussex, England: For Dummies, 2012.

Brown, Brené. "Listening to Shame." Filmed in Long Beach, CA. TED video, 20:32. https://www.ted.com/talks/brene_brown_listening_to_shame/.

———. "The Power of Vulnerability." Filmed in Houston, TX. TED video, 20:13. https://www.ted.com/talks/brene_brown_on_vulnerability/.

Carson, Rick. *Taming Your Gremlin: A Surprisingly Simple Method for Getting Out of Your Own Way, Revised Edition.* New York: Quill, 2003.

Crane, Rebecca. *Mindfulness-Based Cognitive Therapy.* New York: Routledge, 2009.

Doidge, Norman. *The Brain That Changes Itself.* New York: Penguin Books, 2007.

Hayes, Steven C., and Spencer Smith. *Get Out of Your Mind and Into Your lives: The New Acceptance and Commitment Therapy.* Oakland, CA: New Harbinger Publications, Inc., 2005.

Hays, Pamela A., and Gayle Y. Iwamasa. *Culturally Responsive Cognitive-Behavioral Therapy: Assessment, Practice, and Supervision.* Washington, DC: American Psychological Association, 2006.

Hepworth, Dean, Ronald Rooney, Glenda Dewberry Rooney, Kimberly Strom-Gottfried, and JoAnn Larsen. *Direct Social Work Practice: Theory and Skills, Eighth Edition.* Belmont, CA: Brooks/Cole, 2010.

Herbert, James D., and Evan M. Forman. *Acceptance and Mindfulness in Cognitive Behavior Therapy: Understanding and Applying the New Therapies.* Hoboken, New Jersey: John Wiley & Sons, Inc., 2011.

Johnson, Sharon. *Therapist's Guide to Clinical Intervention, Second Edition.* San Diego, CA: Elsevier, Inc., 2004.

Jongsma Jr., Arthur E., and Mark Peterson. *The Complete Adult Psychotherapy Treatment Planner, Fifth Edition.* Hoboken, New Jersey: John Wiley & Sons, Inc., 2014.

Kimsey-House, Henry, Karen Kimsey-House, Phillip Sandahl, and Laura Whitworth. *Co-Active Coaching: Changing Business, Transforming Lives.* Boston, MA: Nicholas Brealey Publishing, 2011.

Koenig, Karen. *The Food and Feelings Workbook: A Full Course Meal on Emotional Health.* Carlsbad, CA: Gürze Books, 2007.

McKay, Matthew, Jeffrey Wood, and Jeffrey Brantley. *The Dialectical Behavior Therapy Skills Workbook: Practical DBT Exercises for Learning Mindfulness, Interpersonal Effectiveness, Emotion Regulation, and Distress Tolerance*. Oakland, CA: New Harbinger Publications, Inc., 2007.

Ronen, Tammie, and Arthur Freeman. *Cognitive Behavior Therapy in Clinical Social Work Practice*. New York: Springer Publishing Company, LLC, 2007.

INDEX